HOW POLARIZATION BEGETS POLARIZATION

HOW POLARIZATION BEGETS POLARIZATION

IDEOLOGICAL EXTREMISM IN THE US CONGRESS

SAMUEL MERRILL III, BERNARD GROFMAN, AND THOMAS L. BRUNELL

OXFORD
UNIVERSITY PRESS

Oxford University Press is a department of the University of Oxford. It furthers the University's objective of excellence in research, scholarship, and education by publishing worldwide. Oxford is a registered trade mark of Oxford University Press in the UK and certain other countries.

Published in the United States of America by Oxford University Press
198 Madison Avenue, New York, NY 10016, United States of America.

© Oxford University Press 2024

All rights reserved. No part of this publication may be reproduced, stored in a retrieval system, or transmitted, in any form or by any means, without the prior permission in writing of Oxford University Press, or as expressly permitted by law, by license, or under terms agreed with the appropriate reproduction rights organization. Inquiries concerning reproduction outside the scope of the above should be sent to the Rights Department, Oxford University Press, at the address above.

You must not circulate this work in any other form
and you must impose this same condition on any acquirer.

Library of Congress Cataloging-in-Publication Data
Names: Merrill, Samuel, 1939– author. | Grofman, Bernard, author. |
Brunell, Thomas L. (Thomas Lloyd), 1968– author.
Title: How polarization begets polarization : ideological extremism in the
U.S. Congress / Samuel Merrill III, Bernard Grofman, Thomas L. Brunell.
Other titles: Ideological extremism in the United States Congress
Description: New York, NY : Oxford University Press, [2024] |
Includes bibliographical references and index.
Identifiers: LCCN 2023017662 (print) | LCCN 2023017663 (ebook) |
ISBN 9780197745236 (PB) | ISBN 9780197745229 (HB) |
ISBN 9780197745250 (epub) | ISBN 9780197745243 (ebook) |
ISBN 9780197745267 (ebook other)
Subjects: LCSH: United States. Congress. |
Polarization (Social sciences)—Political aspects—United States. |
Political parties—United States. | Right and left (Political science)—United States. |
Radicalism—United States—21st century. |
Opposition (Political science)—United States. |
United States—Politics and government—21st century.
Classification: LCC JK1726 .M475 2024 (print) | LCC JK1726 (ebook) |
DDC 306.2/60973—dc23/eng/20230609
LC record available at https://lccn.loc.gov/2023017662
LC ebook record available at https://lccn.loc.gov/2023017663

DOI: 10.1093/oso/9780197745229.001.0001

Contents

Acknowledgments	vii

PART I: WHERE DID POLARIZATION COME FROM AND WHY IS IT GETTING WORSE?

1. Making Sense of Polarization	3
2. How Does Party Discipline Generate Polarization?	20
3. Why, Even in Highly Competitive Districts, Are Candidate Positions So Different?	41
4. Heterogeneity across Districts and within-District Partisan Gap and Proclivity	59

PART II: CONSEQUENCES OF POLARIZATION

5. How Do Party Loyalty and Activists Encourage Mobilizing the Base?	75
6. Consequences of Polarized Politics	95
7. Discussion and Conclusions	117

Appendix to Chapter 1: Literature Review on Causes of Polarization	127
Appendix to Chapter 2: The Party-Constraint Model	131
Appendix to Chapter 3: Relation between Candidate and District Ideology: Statistical and Theoretical Analyses	141
Appendix to Chapter 4: Components of Legislative Polarization	149
Appendix to Chapter 5: Derivations for the Appeal-to-the-Base Model	155
Appendix to Chapter 6: Derivations Relating to Chamber and Party Medians	161
Bibliography	167
Index	181

Acknowledgments

Academic research, unlike Athena, does not spring whole from the brow of Zeus; rather, it builds on the work of many scholars. In particular, our own research draws on the considerable body of research we have done jointly or with other authors over the past 20 years. Sam Merrill would like to especially thank Jim Adams for helpful comments and for collaboration on two of the papers we outline in this book—one empirical and one theoretical— that deal with the within-district divergence of party candidates, especially in competitive districts. Tom Brunell and Bernie Grofman would both like to thank Bill Koetzle, with whom they jointly worked for a number of years before he left academia for the rewards of being a lobbyist. Bernie would also like to extend thanks to his long-term collaborator Guillermo Owen and his more recent coauthor Stan Winer for collaborative work directly related to party competition. In addition to thanks to these previous collaborators, from whom we have learned much (but who cannot be held responsible for the flaws in the present work), and to the many scholars whose work we cite in this volume, we would particularly like to acknowledge the seminal work of Keith Poole and Howard Rosenthal, without which this volume would have been impossible.

Tom Brunell would also like to thank Clark Bensen for insightful conversations and oodles of data over the past 20 years. He would also like to thank Jason Sears for his help. Tom dedicates this book to Sandy Bracy, Max Brunell, Nate Brunell, and Chip Brunell. Bernie Grofman would like to acknowledge support from the Jack W. Peltason Chair of the University of California, Irvine, and the incredible patience of his wife Sue for enduring his disappearance behind a computer screen for most of the day, seven days a week. Sam Merrill would like to thank Andrew Merrill for his invaluable help with computer advice.

All three authors thank David McBride at Oxford University Press and two anonymous reviewers for persevering with us as we sought to follow their suggestions to make the text more friendly to a wider audience.

Bernie Grofman would like to dedicate this work to the late Nelson Polsby. One of the greatest Congressional scholars of the 20th century, and not

viii ACKNOWLEDGMENTS

known for his modesty, Nelson once told Bernie that he himself had forgotten more about Congress than Bernie would ever know. Now, a quarter century later, it is hard to disagree with him. Nonetheless, were he alive, perhaps he would find that the models in this book could tell him at least a few things about Congress that he hadn't already known.

This book continues the attempt to integrate ideas from different research streams into a single model that was the intention of two of our previous books: *A Unified Theory of Voting* (Merrill and Grofman) and *A Unified Theory of Party Competition* (Adams, Merrill, and Grofman). The first merged ideas about optimal party ideological location, derived from Downsian proximity models of voting, with work on directional models of voting; the second blended ideas from neo-Downsian spatial models of party competition with social-psychology perspectives on party identification. The present volume integrates work on candidate competition at the constituency level with work on polarization between parties in Congress. Taken collectively, these books are intended to provide their readers with essential insights into voter choice, party and candidate competition, and voting patterns within a legislature.

PART I

WHERE DID POLARIZATION COME FROM AND WHY IS IT GETTING WORSE?

1

Making Sense of Polarization

1.1. Introduction

That the contemporary state of polarization in American politics is viewed as a matter of grave concern cannot be in doubt. There are scores of academic articles and hundreds of journalistic essays condemning polarization,[1] and there are now multiple books on the topic.[2] According to the Stanford law professor and political scientist Nathaniel Persily in the introduction to *Solutions to Political Polarization in America* (2015b), "Political polarization dominates discussions of contemporary American politics," and there is "widespread agreement that the dysfunction in the political system can be attributed to political polarization."

But political polarization has not always been characteristic of American politics. A famous Report from a committee of the American Political Science Association in 1950 called for a more responsible two-party system. As summarized by Arthur Schlesinger, Jr., in his review of the Report in the *ANNALS of the American Academy of Political and Social Science* (1951, 222), "The committee's objective is to transform the present sprawling and illogical system into a centralized and logical system which will define alternative policies with clarity and will guarantee their execution through improved means of party discipline." One could say that this ambition has now been fulfilled, but it is also well known that getting what one wishes for can be dangerous, as Schlesinger also stated eloquently in the same review.

We now have widely separated and internally homogeneous political camps, each responsible to its respective "base," but unfortunately our politics is beset with gridlock, obstruction, and the inability to compromise to get things done. In this book we highlight polarization in Congress and focus

[1] A very small sampling would include Abramowitz and Saunders (2008), Theriault (2008), Abramowitz (2010), Iyengar and Westwood (2015), Klein and Chang (2015), Thomsen (2017), Krasa and Polborn (2018), Zingher (2018), McCarty (2019), and Bartels (2020).
[2] See, e.g., Hopkins and Sides (2015), Persily (2015b), Rosenfeld (2017), McCarty (2019), Klein (2020), and Zingher (2022).

How Polarization Begets Polarization. Samuel Merrill III, Bernard Grofman, and Thomas L. Brunell,
Oxford University Press. © Oxford University Press 2024. DOI: 10.1093/oso/9780197745229.003.0001

4 WHERE DID POLARIZATION COME FROM?

primarily on the first of three aspects of polarization identified by Persily (2015b, 4); namely, "ideological convergence within parties and divergence between parties," which he calls *hyperpartisanship*. But we recognize that polarization can be viewed as a multi-stranded concept, and that sometimes it is hard to distinguish the presence of polarization from its consequences.

1.2. Measuring Polarization in the US Congress

We begin with a definition:

> *Legislative polarization* is the ideological gap between Democratic and Republican ideologies, which is quantified as the difference between the mean ideological positions of the Democratic and Republican delegations in Congress, and in particular within the US House, along with the intraparty variations within each of the delegations.

To be specific, our primary measure of the degree of legislative polarization in the US Congress is the difference—assessed in terms of roll-call voting patterns—between the mean policy/ideological positions of the Republican and Democratic delegations in a one-dimensional spatial model. In this book we focus primarily on the US House of Representatives. The spatial model of which we speak places parties, candidates, and voters on a line, with points to the left representing liberal positions on policy issues or a liberal ideology and points to the right reflecting conservative positions and ideology. A one-dimensional representation of US party competition is an oversimplification, but social and economic dimensions of evaluation by legislators have become more correlated over time, with a single dimension explaining most of the variance in roll-call voting.

To determine the mean positions of the party delegations in the House, we employ the DW-NOMINATE scores, developed by Poole and Rosenthal (1997), which place legislators on a liberal-to-conservative scale from −1.0 on the left to +1.0 on the right. The legislator scores are based on their roll-call votes, using an algorithm that provides comparability between the scores of members of Congress serving in different eras (see, e.g., McCarty, 2019, for an overview of this procedure). The first dimension of the DW-NOMINATE scores reflects primarily economic issues and is conventionally used to represent a liberal-to-conservative continuum.

Figure 1.1A plots the means of the (first dimension of) DW-NOMINATE scores of the party delegations in the US House from 1856 to 2020.[3] These party means were at their most disparate about 1900 and again after 2000, whereas they were least separated from one another shortly after the Civil War and particularly for a period around 1940–1970. It is thus clear from the historical record that, in the US House, the degree of legislative polarization has ebbed and flowed over the past century and a half of the modern two-party era. In particular, we note the apparent cyclic nature of the pattern of ideological change in the House throughout this period.

Figure 1.1B shows that, furthermore, for both parties our secondary measure of legislative polarization—intraparty variation—was relatively small (i.e., variation within each party was lower) at approximately the times that partisan separation was greatest (during the late 19th century and, for the Democratic Party, at the beginning of the 21st century). Intraparty variance was high when partisan separation was low (for a short period around 1860 and again from about 1950 to 1980). Figure 1.1C places in sharp focus the inverse relationship between party separation and intraparty variation by plotting the separation between the parties and the pooled intraparty standard deviation on the same graph. The negative correlation between partisan separation and pooled standard deviation is highly significant, as are the negative correlations between partisan separation and the separate standard deviations for Democrats and Republicans, respectively.[4]

Thus, typically, when Congress, and the House in particular, is highly polarized, variance *within* each party is low—that is, party delegations are relatively homogeneous. Despite the noise in the data, high separation between narrow distributions of partisans is characteristic of strong polarization; reduced separation and broad (often overlapping) distributions are characteristic of low polarization. Hence, a theoretical model of polarization should predict an inverse relationship between party separation and intraparty variance over the long term (as we will see from our model in Chapter 2). In the next section we introduce that model.

However, for purposes of conceptual clarity we wish to distinguish polarization within Congress from ideological differentiation between the

---

[3] The data for Figure 1.1 are obtained from the website: https://voteview.com/data (accessed Feb. 20, 2022).

[4] The correlation between the difference in means and the pooled standard deviation (over both parties) is −0.72. For Democrats, the correlation between the difference in party means and intraparty standard deviation is −0.77; for Republicans, this correlation is −0.51. All three correlations are significant at the 0.001 level.

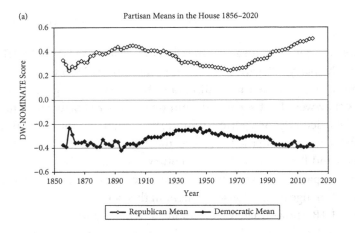

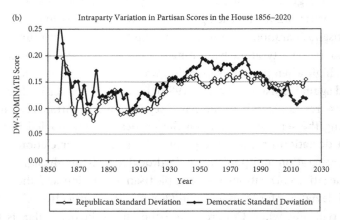

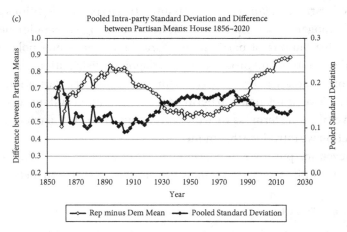

Figure 1.1. Partisan Means and Variance in the US House

Notes: The first dimension of the DW-NOMINATE scores is used throughout in Figure 1.1. The horizontal axes in Figure 1.1 and similar figures throughout the book are indexed by the election year of each Congress; for example, the 117th Congress, labeled 2020, served from 2021 through 2022. House members whose parties were coded from 100 to 199 were classified as Democrats, those coded between 200 and 299 as Republicans.

candidates of opposing parties at the district level. Party strategies for electing the US House must accommodate races in numerous Congressional districts, each with its own political makeup and district-specific ideology. National party constraints motivated by national policy-seeking goals, when imposed on the campaign positions of local district candidates, may conflict with the interests of party candidates who feel the need to temper the national party position by shifting to be more representative of the district. In later chapters we will consider the trade-offs of candidates and parties in judging how to balance between appealing to their base and seeking to win the support of the typical voter in the district.

1.3. Explaining the Growth of Polarization in Congress

How did we get to where we are now? Various explanations have been offered for increasing polarization that are specific to the past 50 years (following a decline in polarization in the previous half century). In the Appendix to this chapter, we discuss research concerning several suggested contributing factors—including income inequality, immigration, racial and ethnic divisions, and party leadership structure—that may have influenced the rise and fall of polarization and, in particular, triggered polarization trends during the past half century. Moreover, the growth of talk radio and politicized cable news channels—accompanied by declining audiences for the major TV networks—and the rise of tweets and other social media have led to a "siloization" of political communication that reinforces polarization to a remarkable degree. In sum, in seeking to explain polarization, we are blessed with a superabundance of forces and events to credit or blame.

While there is a debate about how much of the polarization we see is only at the elite and activist level, and a related debate about the extent to which voter polarization lags or mirrors elite polarization, what can be said with confidence is that, over the past half century, activists, party officials, and other power brokers have intentionally moved American politics toward what once were called "ideologically responsible parties." Rosenfeld (2017) notes that in the decades following the 1950 APSA Report, activists and politicians in the middle ranks of American politics, who had reason to think that forging disciplined, programmatically distinct parties would solve endemic problems in American politics, intentionally began the movement toward responsible parties. He recounts how, by effectively drawing new

8 WHERE DID POLARIZATION COME FROM?

party lines across a wide array of issues, these activists helped to catalyze a partisan resurgence, first among Democrats, then later among Republicans. Slowly, these newly responsible parties became identified with opposing issue bundles and became dominated not by non-ideological bosses but by issue-oriented interest groups that imposed their own exacting discipline, and more and more polarization.

Furthermore, during the second half of the 20th century, party control was influenced by the replacement of many office-oriented professional political leaders by amateur activists and moneyed interests operating on their own (Rosenfeld, 2017). Both of these groups frequently had a deep commitment to policy change and relatively extreme views. For example, Morris Fiorina et al. (2005) quotes Aaron Wildavsky (1965) about "[purists'] emphasis on internal criteria for decision, on what they believe 'deep down inside'; their rejection of compromise; their lack of orientation toward winning; their stress on the style and purity of decision—integrity, consistency, adherence to internal norms." In addition, think tanks and partisan media outlets, particularly on the right, have been heavily funded with private money, with the aim of influencing party policy for the long term (Mayer, 2016; Fagan, 2022). Thus, movement toward ideologically distinct parties can be intentional, fostered by activists with strong policy views who at times wish to implement extreme policies or by ideologically motivated media for whom controversy increases audiences and who find it profitable to demonize the other side.

In this book, however, we focus on less well understood processes that reinforce polarization but that operate in a "behind-the-scenes" fashion, and to which even the involved actors may be oblivious. Specifically, we focus on linkages between the level of party discipline on Congressional candidates, forces that affect voter party loyalties, the influence of activists within each party, the differences between the candidates of the two parties at the constituency level, and polarization in legislative voting patterns. While a huge amount has been written about polarization both at the mass and the elite level, we believe that our approach, in which we view polarization as a complex system with many moving parts, provides original insights involving extensive modifications of the classic Downsian model of party competition (which we discuss later). In particular, we focus on the reciprocal relationship between the level of polarization in Congress and the nature of political competition in US House elections at the district level.

But we also show why hyper-polarization can be expected to facilitate the development of extreme partisan loyalty, and vice versa. Perhaps the epitome of this development occurred in the presidential elections of 2016 and 2020. Ezra Klein, in his book *Why We're Polarized* (2020), asserts: "The fact that voters ultimately treated Trump as if he were just another Republican speaks to the enormous weight party polarization now exerts on our politics—a weight so heavy that it can take an election as bizarre as 2016 and jam the result into the same grooves as Romney's contest with Obama or Bush's race against Kerry." Compounding party loyalty is *negative partisanship*—that is, disliking and even detesting the other party, its office holders, and indeed its supporters. When voters are loyal to their party and strongly dislike the other party, extremist candidates can more easily be elected.

Alienation from mainstream ideology and increased activism by ordinary voters and wealthy individuals on the extremes bring about greater reliance on the respective blocs or bases that form in part from these previously alienated voters. The more the two parties separate, furthermore, the more the activists of the out-party react to the extremism of the in-party, and the less willing these opposition activists become to offer moderate candidates. The out-party mean becomes more extreme, while the in-party, relying on its safe majorities, dares to implement extreme policies. Out-party activists demand ideological purity as a litmus test for its candidates so as to combat the "evil" in-party. In turn, the in-party activists—because they are already winning—see little reason to forsake ideological purity and seek to expel moderates from their own ranks.[5]

Also, as Fiorina et al. (2005, 5) argue, even if voters have not become more polarized in terms of developing more extreme views, "partisans have become better sorted into the parties." Such sorting has occurred in part because of activists' insistence on issues, on party responsibility, and on ideological purism, so that catchall parties cease to be viable. Associated with the growing strength of ideological activists are other developments that often lead to more divergent party nominees, such as more open, primary-driven, candidate-centric presidential and Congressional nominating processes, accentuated by the reforms in party primaries initiated by the McGovern-Fraser Commission following the 1968 elections.

As the parties move further apart, policy polarization at the elite level reinforces tendencies for the electorate to polarize, as sorting mechanisms

---

[5] This certainly is one element of party politics in the era of Trump, but we had already seen this tendency with Tea Party primary competition against those Republicans seen as not conservative enough.

10 WHERE DID POLARIZATION COME FROM?

shift voters into the party to which they are ideologically closest.[6] In particular, voters whose policy attitudes on given issues are not that well anchored tend to adopt views on those issues that are consistent with the reference groups and the information sources to which they are most attuned, including leaders in the party with which they identify. This leads to increased correlation among voters across multiple issue dimensions (Abramowitz and Saunders, 2008, Abramowitz, 2010, 2015) such that not just party leaders and ideologues but ordinary voters develop stronger partisan identities, since there are no longer crosscutting cleavages that foster split-ticket voting (cf. Glazer and Grofman, 1989). Such developments feed on each other, generating self-reinforcing positive feedback.

In the model of party competition and its consequences that we offer, as party delegations in Congress polarize along ideological lines, national party discipline and expectations, as well as the power of activists, applied at the district level, force candidates further and further away from the preferences of the median or typical voter in their constituencies. Change in the ideological location of each party's Congressional delegation is generated by, and then reinforces, differentiation in the ideological locations of the candidates of the two major parties in each constituency.

We make no claim that the electoral and structural factors on which we focus in this book are the only forces that impel polarization or that exacerbate its consequences. The alignment of partisan affiliation with personal identity—along racial, ethnic, class, religious, or educational lines—has served to buttress party allegiance against the influence of policy arguments and indeed against information and facts themselves.[7] Significant as these factors are, their analysis is not the focus of this book.[8] We focus instead on institutional factors that underlie the rise of polarization but may be less visible—factors that are tied to the existence of single-seat political competition under plurality—which we believe will give a fuller understanding of the rise of polarization, its perpetuation, and perhaps its eventual reversal. Our

---

[6] Still, whatever the level of polarization in the electorate, there is no dispute that it is not as severe as polarization among party officeholders (cf. the recent "culture wars" debate about whether it is voters or just party elites that are polarized).

[7] Unfortunately, at both the elite and mass level, partisan polarization arises not just about ideology per se but also about "beliefs" concerning facts that should be indisputable (see, e.g., Barker and Marietta, 2020), most prominently the baseless claim that Biden's election to the presidency in 2020 was the result of election fraud. We do not deal directly with this "joker in the deck," but rather limit ourselves to ideological nonconvergence, although the two are clearly highly correlated.

[8] See, e.g., Glazer, Grofman, and Owen (1998) for a discussion of the role of race in realignment.

MAKING SENSE OF POLARIZATION 11

approach allows us to address the puzzle of why we get a pattern of *steadily increasing* polarization. By proposing a clear institutional mechanism that fosters party separation and legislative polarization, this approach provides clues as to how the increasing polarization trend might be reversed, clues that augment previous recommendations such as those of McCarty, Poole, and Rosenthal (2006) or Putnam and Garrett (2020).

1.4. How Does Polarization in Congress Relate to Candidate Polarization at the District Level?

At the heart of this book is a dynamic model that links polarization in the US Congress to the nature of electoral competition at the district level. Our argument is based on the proposition that the positions candidates of a given party can offer the voters in their constituencies are constrained by the national expectations of their party, as well as by the ideology of the constituency. When this constraint is relatively weak, as it was in the middle of the past century, Republican candidates, for example, can be competitive in relatively liberal districts, balancing and hence moderating their overall Congressional delegation; similarly, Democrats can be competitive in relatively conservative districts. Relatively loose constraints during the middle-century era allowed quite conservative Democrats to continue to win Congressional elections, many in the South, despite a national party position that was distant from voter preferences in those districts. Similarly, relaxed constraints by the Republican Party once permitted the repeated election of relatively liberal Republicans such as Jacob Javits in the Senate and Silvio Conte in the House.

Consequently, when restraint is lax, as was typical during the middle of the 20th century, the ideologies of the party delegations overlap and the gap between the means of party delegations is relatively small—that is, polarization is averted. But, when the constraint is tight, as it is now, then the gap between parties widens. In fact, today, when the allowable tolerance for deviance from the party position has narrowed, even a previously popular and respected party leader such as Liz Cheney can be removed from her party leadership position and rejected in her constituency for being out of step with the party.[9]

---

[9] "GOP Ousts Cheney from Her Leadership Position over Her Criticism of Trump," NPR, May 12, 2021; "Wyoming GOP Votes to Stop Recognizing Cheney as a Republican," NPR, Nov. 15, 2021.

12 WHERE DID POLARIZATION COME FROM?

The strength of party constraints also affects intraparty variation, with tighter constraints corresponding to ideologically concentrated party delegations. Hence, polarization at the Congressional level is characterized by concentrated and ideologically widely separated party delegations, whereas during unpolarized periods party delegations are each broadly distributed and overlap.

In turn, when Congressional delegations are highly polarized, each projects a focused national image that is sharply distinct from that of the opposing party. This sets the stage for each of the two parties to espouse extreme views and be relatively intolerant of deviations from the party position. We concur with Persily (2015b, 4) when he observes, "In today's Congress, it would appear that not only are the parties far apart on the issues but also that the ideological distance is matched by a widespread intensity of belief on a host of issues that might not have been seen as so fundamental and defining in previous eras."

Thus, ideological polarization at the national party level typically leads to substantial ideological differentiation between candidates at the district level, which influences which party's candidate is most likely to win in any given constituency. Success in the districts, which is also affected by the ideological distribution of voters in the respective constituencies, in turn shapes the polarization between the parties in the next Congress. Insofar as the national ideological position of the party reflects that of the party's Congressional members, divergence of those members implies that the anchors for the national party constraints likewise diverge. These anchors then drag the policy platforms of each party's winners yet further away from the preferences of swing voters within their districts. These forces generate a dynamic interaction, or positive feedback loop, between district and Congressional politics. Thus, over time—until checked or reversed—*polarization begets polarization.*

Either one or both parties may be induced to take extreme stands by, for example, efforts of policy activists or power brokers to generate a more "responsible" party, that is, a party which is accountable to the policies of its strongest supporters. As extreme activists become more important in influencing the direction of the parties, the party bases become more polarized. As we will show in Chapter 5, if, for any reason, the latter conditions develop beyond a threshold specified by the analysis, optimal party strategies begin rapidly diverging from centrist toward more extreme ideological positions, with these positions representing the parties' own bases rather than the overall electorate. Or to put it more succinctly, *once a polarization threshold is crossed, office-seeking parties and candidates find it advantageous to put more emphasis on mobilizing their base rather than appealing to the middle.*

In sum, over time we experience legislative polarization reflected in seemingly unbridgeable policy disagreements between the two parties, as well as votes on policy issues and confirmations that are sharply and often entirely along party lines. The electoral dynamic we model triggers a self-reinforcing pattern of polarization—a repeating cycle or feedback loop with increasing divergence—until altered by the political environment, either gradually or in one tectonic shift. Such a shift might be induced by the introduction of a crosscutting new issue dimension, or by politics reaching extremes that generate a revolt by more moderate voters. More gradual causes could include changes in the demographic composition of a district's electorate. We will return to the possibilities for reversal of polarization in our final chapter. However, our focus in this book will be on the institutional mechanisms that have created the current dynamic of non-decreasing polarization in Congress, specifically the US House of Representatives, together with the consequences of that development.[10]

1.5. Downsian Theory and Its Extensions

Decades ago, Anthony Downs (1957) and others extended to two-party competition between political parties the idea of two economic entities seeking a middle ground in competing with one another. In the case of political parties, as above, we assume that parties and voters locate along a one-dimensional policy continuum (a spatial model), and that—other things being equal—each voter supports the party whose announced policy is closest to his/her own position. Thus, a party that is motivated to seek office by winning an election has reason to move to the center, specifically to the location of the median voter (the middle voter in the spatial model). A candidate adopting any other position can theoretically be beaten by an opponent who approaches even closer to the median. This result is known as the *median voter theorem*, or *Downsian convergence*, as both parties would converge to the median. In general, forces that tend to draw parties toward centrist positions are referred to as *Downsian pressures*.

---

[10] The same methodology would apply to the US Senate and any democratically elected two-party legislature where competition can largely be understood as taking place in a single dimension.

14 WHERE DID POLARIZATION COME FROM?

Divergence, not convergence, of the two major American parties is, however, characteristic of American politics, although the degree of that divergence varies significantly over time. If parties focus on the policy that they can enact if elected, and if many voters vote according to party loyalty (based, e.g., on retrospective assessments of past policy performance or personal or family history), parties may choose positions that diverge from the median. To assuage activists, moderate candidates may espouse more extreme policies. This effect was seen in the presidential election of 2020, in which the Democratic Party and its moderate nominee, Joe Biden, were motivated to appeal on policy grounds to the supporters of the more left-wing Bernie Sanders, and progressives continued to influence Biden's policy proposals after his election. Many of our arguments based on a spatial model will show that polarization motivates parties to move not only beyond Downsian expectations but to even more divergent ideological positions. The explanatory models we provide predict such divergent party positions. These models take into account party discipline, multiple constituencies that differ in their ideological makeup, party loyalty, the demands of activists, abstention due to alienation, and the loss of moderates in the electorate.

In summary, one purpose of this book is to unify and link two topics previously largely discussed in separate literatures: namely, party competition at the district level, and polarization in Congress. A second goal is to provide a more unified perspective that links, on the one hand, legislative polarization and ideological differentiation of candidates by party, with, on the other, topics well outside the standard Downsian canon, such as party loyalty and the influence of activists (see especially Chapter 5). In our concluding chapter we touch on the paramount question of how polarization might be reversed, drawing on the institutional features of US elections we will emphasize throughout the book.

Other scholars have focused, as we do, on structural factors. For example, Frances Lee (2016) shows that incentives for polarized competition can arise from an expected pattern of closely divided politics over a long time period where it is possible for either party to gain unified control of the levers of power (a governmental trifecta: control of both legislative branches and the executive).[11] Put simply, closely matched competition fuels polarization. The

---

[11] Lee (2016, 2) sums up her argument in the statements, "Intense party competition for institutional control focuses members of Congress on the quest for partisan political advantage," and "The primary way that parties make an electoral case for themselves vis-à-vis their opposition is by magnifying their differences."

21st century has been a time period of intense and close party competition at all levels, of a vehemence not seen since the post–Civil War decades. This close competition makes both divided government and Electoral College reversals of the popular-vote outcome more likely. Thus, we believe Lee is correct in her claim that high levels of competition exacerbate polarization.

1.6. Outline of the Remainder of the Book

In Chapter 2 we analyze the model introduced above that stems from constraints that limit local candidates' freedom to deviate from the national party image and expectations. We dub this the *party-constraint model*. Inflexibility of the restraint in that model is linked to the present partisan polarization in Congress, specifically the divergence in party means and the enhanced homogeneity of the respective party delegations.

Implications of the party-constraint model for the nature of party competition at the constituency level are addressed in Chapter 3. Given variation in the national distribution of median voters over districts, the national party constraints may not allow a candidate of one or both parties in many constituencies to take a position near the median voter. Thus, the party-constraint model allows us to address the puzzle of why even in competitive seats—contra the simple Downsian model—the candidates of opposite parties often both remain ideologically remote from the median voter. Indeed, we confirm this expectation by showing empirically that, in fact, party positions may come no nearer convergence in competitive districts than in non-competitive ones. We then show that, even without party-constraint effects, party loyalty and the threat of abstention can account for a high level of non-convergent candidate behavior even in highly competitive seats. We thus present the basic empirical evidence that winning candidates of both parties diverge from the district median voter's ideology, as well as theoretical explanations of this phenomenon.

We further examine what happens when candidates of one party win victory in districts previously held by another party. Here, we see that, contrary to the standard Downsian model, when there is partisan replacement, there occurs what Bafumi and Herron (2010) refer to as a "leapfrog" effect, with dramatic changes in voting behavior brought about by a new member of Congress from a district previously represented by a member of the opposite party. We also discuss a phenomenon that we refer to as *Polsby's Paradox*,

16 WHERE DID POLARIZATION COME FROM?

after the late Nelson Polsby: that is, when more Democrats are elected, the floor median shifts to the *left*, but the Democratic Party median shifts to the *right*, and vice versa when more Republicans are elected. However, the rightward shift of the Democratic Party median following Democratic gains turns out to be much stronger than any leftward shift of the Republican median following Republican gains.

Chapter 4 links candidate divergence to other important features of US electoral politics, accounting for why and by how much party candidates can be expected to diverge. In addition to partisan divergence within the district, we evaluate two other components: heterogeneity over districts—that is, variance among district ideologies—and partisan proclivity—that is, the tendency of certain districts to choose a given party's candidate even when both nominees are ideologically equidistant from the median voter. We provide empirical estimates of the relative contribution of each of these three factors to legislative polarization. This analysis reveals that the lion's share of House polarization arises from in-district partisan divergence—that is, ideological separation between the two major party candidates in the same district.

Chapters 5 and 6 shift from the causes of polarization to investigate the behavioral and policy implications of polarized politics.

First, in Chapter 5, we show that legislative polarization enhances party loyalty for those voters who consistently identify with a party, especially for activists. As polarization increases, activists come to detest the other party *(negative affective polarization)* and do so more intensely than do moderate party supporters. These effects lead parties to focus on mobilizing their base rather than appealing to moderates. This chapter represents a substantial reshaping of the classic Downsian model by incorporating elements from other research traditions.

We demonstrate that even without the influence of activists—given party loyalty, the threat of abstention due to alienation, and polarization between the party bases—parties are motivated, past a level of polarization that we label the Downsian threshold, to diverge from the median voter. Past twice that threshold, they are motivated to place themselves closer to the center of the party distribution than to the center of the overall distribution. Under strong polarization, this effect advantages parties that focus on appeal to their respective bases rather than to centrists or moderates. Pressures from activists, often with relatively extreme views, amplify this effect.

In Chapter 6, we investigate consequences of polarized parties for electoral competition and voter choice, on the one hand, and for Congressional

MAKING SENSE OF POLARIZATION   17

decision making, on the other. Considered here are the consequences of nationalized forces of polarization for the decrease in the number of competitive districts, the regional support base of the two parties, the likelihood of split-ticket voting, and whether Congress may be polarized without concomitant polarization by voters. In the presence of polarization, we examine the likelihood of gridlock[12] under divided government and of violent policy oscillation between periods of unified government that alternate between dominance by one or the other of two highly polarized and competitive parties.

We introduce in Chapter 6 the concept of Conditional Party Government (Aldrich and Rohde, 2000), which highlights the trade-off between party-centric control, in which the *median of the majority party* is paramount, and legislator-centric government, under which the *chamber median* is indicative of legislative outcomes. As the House polarizes, it becomes less likely that bills that could pass with bipartisan support will be brought to the floor. The modern version of this is the "Hastert rule," named for former Speaker Dennis Hastert, under which bills that lack support of a "majority of the majority" are not brought to the floor for a vote.[13] Similarly, as the chasm between the parties becomes wider, party discipline becomes easier and more routine, since the preferences of the two sides lack much common ground. Moreover, in a world of high polarization and policy-oriented politics, a "trifecta party," with control of both chambers and the presidency, is more likely to seek to end super-majoritarian requirements that constrain its ability to make appointments or set policies. Thus, party polarization means not only that each party looks more and more ideologically distinct from the other and more internally homogeneous, but also that centrist policies become less and less likely to be chosen and policy changes when a new party takes power become potentially more disruptive.

In Chapter 6 we also demonstrate the power of ideologically concentrated minority parties, whose median can be closer to the chamber median than that of the majority party, providing leverage to the concentrated minority party. Furthermore, we relate constrained ideological choices available to voters to the ongoing debate about whether or not polarization

---

[12] Gridlock is described by Persily (2015b, 4) as "the inability of the system to perform basic policy-making functions due to obstructionist tactics."

[13] Several recent House speakers have made comments indicating that their main goal is to please their co-partisans and not help pass legislation for which the other party would get much or all of the credit (en.wikipedia.org/wiki/Hastert_Rule).

18 WHERE DID POLARIZATION COME FROM?

in Congress is entirely elite-driven and the reasons why we can elect legislators who are more ideologically extreme than the voters whom they represent.

In Chapter 7, we offer a brief summary of our main findings and reflect on whether a strong party system with two clearly ideologically distinct and responsible parties, as called for by the 1950 Report of the American Political Science Association, was a wise choice of goals. Finally, we consider what might reverse the trends of the past 50 years toward increasing polarization, which our modeling has sought to help explain. In particular, we discuss three potential developments that might reverse polarization: (1) sustained moderation by a party repeatedly out of power, followed by a moderate response by the other party, (2) changes in redistricting mechanisms, and (3) introduction of a crosscutting new issue or ideological dimension, most likely by a new party or an underdog party seeking majority status. We also note that, if it were possible to reduce legislative polarization in Congress, that success would be a trigger for reversing other aspects of polarization.

We believe that one of our main contributions will be to link national-level polarization and the degree of district-level divergence between the campaign positioning of candidates of opposite parties. We see the party-constraint model, developed in Chapter 2, as a key institutional mechanism, possibly *the* key mechanism, whereby polarization is not only maintained but reinforced. Moreover, polarization leads to and is amplified by higher levels of partisan loyalty and greater importance of party policy activists. But we do not see our work as in any way in contradiction to that of scholars who have identified specific changes in the political landscape—such as a rise in economic inequality, a growth in immigration, growth in the size of the African-American electorate, or a more vigorous role for the federal government in eradicating the lingering stigmata of racial exclusion—as setting the United States on a path toward a more ideologically differentiated party system. We have emphasized the continued relevance of such factors, as well as the more recent growth in the importance of the cultural dimension of US political competition.

The patterns in the data we highlight have been pointed out by many others. What we offer that is distinctive are our explanations for those patterns, explanations that allow us to understand as inextricably intertwined the growing differentiation between candidates of opposite parties at the

MAKING SENSE OF POLARIZATION   19

constituency level, increased ideological heterogeneity among districts, the strengthening of party loyalties and the importance within parties of activist views, and the polarization in Congress as a whole and in national party positions. We model expected changes in polarization over time in a way that generates the clear expectation that *polarization begets polarization.*

2

How Does Party Discipline Generate Polarization?

2.1. The Constraint of Party Discipline

Although there have been only limited changes in electoral rules over the course of more than 150 years of two-party competition, we have seen in Chapter 1 that levels of polarization in the US House have nonetheless varied dramatically over that same time period. Virtually all the work that seeks to provide a dynamic perspective on polarization in Congress looks at macro-level factors such as changes in immigration levels or economic inequality (see, e.g., McCarty, Poole, and Rosenthal, 2006; Fiorina and Abrams, 2009). By contrast, our approach looks at electoral and institutional mechanisms that develop a momentum of their own.

Polarization has been compared to an avalanche. We can debate how it started, and whether there was some special event that may have triggered it, following a long slow buildup of pressure (generated by, e.g., high levels of immigration or rising levels of economic inequality). Regardless, once the avalanche has started, it builds up more mass and momentum as it goes, until it becomes almost impossible to stop. Similarly, once polarization is underway, those who benefit need do little to keep it rolling, while those who are unhappy about it lack the means to stop it.

But why does polarization become self-reinforcing? We offer a mechanism that is based on an interplay between national party expectations and constituency-level electoral dynamics. Party discipline designed to achieve results favored by most party members has become one of the hallmarks of polarized parties. We consider the question of how partisan polarization evolves over time and why we might expect polarization to breed more polarization. In particular, we look at the within-party ideological distributions in the House and how they may be expected to change over time. We show that the ideological differentiation between the two party delegations both shapes and is shaped by the nature of platform differences between the two

How Polarization Begets Polarization. Samuel Merrill III, Bernard Grofman, and Thomas L. Brunell,
Oxford University Press. © Oxford University Press 2024. DOI: 10.1093/oso/9780197745229.003.0002

parties' candidates at the district level in a feedback loop. A number of factors are key to understanding this feedback loop, most particularly the ideological distribution of partisanship over Congressional districts and the degree to which "party discipline" exerts a constraining effect on how far from the national party position any candidate of a given party is "allowed" to diverge. As in Chapter 1, we take as our proxy for polarization the difference between the national parties' positions, where the national position of each party is proxied by the mean ideological location of the party delegation in the US House. In turn, each member location is measured as the first-dimension DW-NOMINATE score. (See Chapter 1 for references, and see additional discussion in Chapter 6.)

When we speak of "party discipline," we use that term more broadly than simply pressure to vote a certain way on specific legislative roll calls, although that is one of its aspects. Rather, the concept also encompasses pressures to offer a campaign platform and to campaign in ways consistent with the party's official and implied positions.[1] This pressure is sometimes applied overtly by Congressional leadership, typically by the threat to withhold campaign funds or desired committee assignments or party positions. As we saw in 2021 with Liz Cheney's removal from a Republican leadership position, the penalty for departures from ideological purity can be severe.[2]

We noted in Chapter 1 that a now seven-decades-old Report of the American Political Science Association advocated improved party discipline and a more responsible party system. During the ensuing years, party leaders and activists deliberately enhanced party discipline around policy goals in an effort to develop national parties responsible to those goals.

In *Party Discipline in the U.S. House of Representatives* (2015), Kathryn Pearson recounts the evolution of party discipline in the House: how it is exerted and enforced, and how the level of discipline has changed over recent decades and varied by party. Discipline is exercised by rewarding members for party loyalty (based in part on their voting record, partisan rhetoric, and fundraising for party objectives) and punishing them for violation of that loyalty. Leadership rewards loyal members by permitting a member's legislation to come to the floor for a vote, providing campaign resources,

---

[1] Cf. McCarty, Poole, and Rosenthal (2001): "Party discipline, we conclude, is manifest in the location of the legislator's ideal point in the standard spatial model. It is not a strategic variable manipulated by party whips from one roll call to another but a part of a legislator's overall environment that forms her induced preferences."

[2] See references in Chapter 1.

22 WHERE DID POLARIZATION COME FROM?

and offering desirable committee assignments or chairs. Party discipline within Congress depends on the willingness of members to cede power to their leaders, and this willingness depends in turn on the homogeneity of members' preferences within the party caucus and the distance between the preferences of the two parties. We will return to the consequences of internally homogeneous but highly separated party delegations in Chapter 6.

In 1910, a group of progressive Republican and minority Democrats stripped the Speaker of much of his power, power that would only begin to be restored in the 1970s. Under the leadership and eventual Speakership of Jim Wright, it was the Democratic majority that first became highly disciplined. The Republicans then responded with increased partisanship, which was raised to a new level in 1995 with Speaker Newt Gingrich, who employed confrontational partisan tactics intended to make the opposition look bad.

Discipline and polarization developed hand in hand. Specific instruments of discipline emerged from enhanced leadership control (especially after members of the Rules Committee came to be appointed by the Speaker and minority leader), and procedural votes gained greater significance as a badge of loyalty. Pearson (2015, 55) quotes Speaker Gingrich: "Procedural votes are infinitely more important because they are about control of the House. [Voting no] is an absolute violation of party loyalty." Pearson highlights what has become an opening for party delegations to cast votes that are more extreme than the voting public. Since procedural votes about rules are out of the public eye, representatives can vote for the party line, even against the interest of their constituents, with impunity. Pearson quotes an unnamed former Democratic whip: "I let members vote against the bill but not the rule. The rule is not an issue in members' districts."

Furthermore, we view party discipline as going beyond pressures exerted by Congressional colleagues and party leaders. Discipline is also enforced by activists and campaign funders, as well as interest groups and media associated with the party. Furthermore, party primaries themselves permit the exertion of party discipline by the primary voters within the district, insofar as their views mirror national ideology and national-level policy concerns.

Although the imposition of party discipline is a deliberate and continuing process, disciplined adherence to policy bundles develops a life of its own once it becomes part of the political culture. Our purpose here is to show how the interactions of national party discipline at the Congressional level, along with the extension of that discipline to electoral competition within

2.2. Explaining Party Positioning at the Constituency Level

In seeking to impose ideological constraints on their elected officials, parties may have conflicting incentives, particularly involving office-seeking versus policy-seeking goals. There have been numerous models of ideological differentiation in two-party contests, beginning with Downs's seminal model (1957), which was generally interpreted as predicting middle-of-the-road politics in any constituency (see section 1.5 in Chapter 1). Later models challenged the assumption that politicians cared only about reelection and not about policy (Wittman, 1973, 1977, 1983). Winer, Kenny, and Grofman (2014) define models in terms of where they fit on a continuum that has two opposite poles. At the office-seeking extreme, each candidate, in an effort to win office, and regardless of party, might offer a platform that is identical to the preferences of the median voter in the district where he or she is competing. At the partisan policy-seeking extreme, each party's candidates might offer a platform keyed to the party's national issue positions that is invariant with respect to district. Furthermore, as Winer et al., 2014, suggest, a national party may withhold support from wayward candidates to keep the party true to its ideals, to establish a more cohesive message, or to enhance partisan effectiveness in Congress by limiting disagreement.

The empirical reality is apt to lie somewhere in-between. National parties are typically motivated by both office-seeking and policy-seeking objectives (Wittman, 1973; Adams, Merrill, and Grofman, 2005). Typically a national party is motivated both to advance a legislative agenda, which requires building up seat majorities, and to establish and protect its political brand, and its members may well have policy positions they wish to advance that differ from those favored by the other party. Hence, optimal issue positions resulting from two-party competition are likely to be intermediate between the national party position and the preference of the median voter in the constituency.

In effect, party leaders may trade off the ability to be competitive in many districts for greater ideological purity that may allocate more weight to the median views inside the party, since it is easier to enforce within-party unity when the party's Congressional members are ideologically homogeneous.

A vexing challenge can occur even when one party controls both chambers and the presidency. This situation faced President Biden in 2021–22, while his party held a razor-thin majority in the House and a tie in the Senate potentially broken by the vice president, but with nontrivial ideological diversity in his party's Congressional delegation. In that situation, as in 2021 with respect to major social policy and infrastructure bills, a small but sufficiently cohesive and determined ideological bloc from within the president's own party—either on the moderate or the progressive flank—can hold the president's policies hostage if the other party is sufficiently disciplined that its members are unwilling to support presidential initiatives lest they boost his party's reelection chances. Similarly, life can be very difficult for a Congressional leader when his or her party holds only a narrow majority in a chamber, as House Speaker Kevin McCarthy has experienced in the 118th Congress. As in McCarthy's frantic campaign to be Speaker, extreme members of a potential leader's own party can exact concessions or block legislation that they deem insufficiently extreme by withholding votes, knowing that, because of polarization, the deficit cannot easily be made up with votes from the opposite party. The chaotic Speaker's election of 2023 also reveals the dangers of one-sided party discipline that opens the door to extremist members (such as those whose efforts McCarthy had at times previously tried to dampen). Ironically, might it be possible that the 2023 rebellion in the Republican Party open the way toward more-balanced party discipline and eventually less polarization?

We might expect that pragmatic party leaders would favor moderate House candidates, in the hope of winning general elections, but a body of evidence is accumulating that local political party leaders now prefer more extremist candidates. This may be occurring for two reasons. First, policy goals have become more important and are now outweighing office-seeking goals. But second, the belief that office-seeking and policy-seeking goals are in conflict is eroding. As we will show in Chapter 5, in a polarized world, mobilizing supporters by taking more extreme policy positions may actually enhance electability. Skocpol and Hertel-Fernandez (2016) find that local party leaders—especially Republicans—are influenced by the claims of activist organizations that only ideologically purist positions can motivate the party's base and thus make electoral victories more likely. Similarly, Broockman et al. (2021) provide experimental evidence that contemporary party leaders strongly prefer extremists over moderates, by about 2 to 1 for Democrats and about 10 to 1 for Republicans. These researchers also find that current party leaders—Republicans in particular—expect extremists to be more likely to win general elections. Furthermore, Amitai (2023)—in a cross-national study—finds empirical evidence that countries with greater activist influence over candidate selection have a higher level of party polarization.

Candidates may also see themselves as forced to take more extreme positions because of a potential big stick facing incumbent legislators— namely, being confronted with a primary challenger financed by party activists. Increasingly, party activists from both within and outside the district exert a combination of carrot and stick influences (Sorauf, 1992; Marshall, 1998). Although candidates of the respective parties may conform to positions proposed by party leaders in the legislature because these positions are in line with their own policy preferences, they may also need to do so to get campaign funding and campaign support from the national (or state) party organizations or from activists. On the one hand, activists may offer substantial financial support to candidates who express strong support for more extreme policies espoused by activists. On the other hand, funding from national sources may not be forthcoming to candidates who stray too far from positions that groups associated with the party regard as acceptable.

For legislators looking to their future, another potential incentive to take positions consistent with those of the national party is that candidates who do not reflect the party's brand may anticipate lack of acceptance into the governing structure should they reach Congress. If their party controls their own state, the policies espoused by state party leaders may also matter, since incumbent candidates may wish to avoid party retaliation in the form of being redistricted out of their seats.

Constraints on candidate positioning may be particularly pressing if a district is competitive, in which case support from outside the district may be more crucial to reelection. But the conflict between national party positions and activists may be minimal if the activists exert a major role in shaping the party's candidate pool and if they are powerful enough to potentially mount a credible challenge even to party leaders seen as deviating too far from ideological purity, as in the threat that was made by Tea Party activists to mount a primary challenge to Speaker John Boehner (Boatright, 2013). However, even if the likelihood of primary defeat in any given election is low (in 2018, for example, only four House members were beaten in a primary, and no

26   WHERE DID POLARIZATION COME FROM?

Senators), the *threat* of primary challenge—even one they expect to win—may be enough to keep legislators in line (or induce them to retire).

Voter perceptions must also be taken into account. Yet another reason that candidates may avoid straying too far from their party's national ideology is that such independent positions may not be credible to district voters, who suspect that, if elected, the candidate will be pressured by the national party leadership to adhere to the national party line rather than to conform more closely to the views of the district electorate. There are numerous examples of this phenomenon, including the 2013 Markey–Gomez contest for US Senator in Massachusetts to fill the unexpired term of John Kerry. According to a *New York Times* article on this election (June 26, 2013; A13), the losing Republican candidate "could not convince enough Massachusetts voters that he would vote independently of the national Republican party."

2.3. Analysis of Constraints of Party Discipline versus Pressures for Convergence to the Median Voter

We seek to model party polarization in a two-party legislature, allowing for both constituency-specific and national effects. We assume that national party positions are tied to the ideological preferences of the set of House members elected from each party and that there are constraints on the degree of deviation from national policy positions allowed to House candidates. We will refer to such a party restriction as a *national party constraint*, or simply *constraint* for short. Among other effects, such constraints affect how easy it is for candidates of the two parties to be competitive in any given district, a condition that may draw them away from the district median.

As noted in Chapter 1, a number of authors (e.g., McCarty et al., 2006; Theriault, 2008; Butler, 2009) have studied the effects of national party position and district ideology on changing patterns of polarization. Ansolabehere, Snyder, and Stewart (2001) find empirical evidence that national ideology has historically been much more important than district ideology in determining candidate stance. Analyzing House candidates from 1874 to 1996, Ansolabehere et al. (136) conclude that Congressional candidates

primarily espoused the ideology associated with the national party, moderating very little to accommodate local ideological conditions. District-by-district competition exerts some pressure on candidates to fit with their constituents, and there have been times in American history when this pressure has been more acute than others. From the 1940s to 1970s candidates became much more responsive to district interests, but that degree of responsiveness waned in the 1980s and 1990s.[3]

Thus, responsiveness to district ideology was observed to be higher toward the middle of the 20th century, during the era in which partisan polarization in Congress was at or near its lowest ebb. On the other hand, when district candidates follow the national party lines, generally Republicans will be elected in Republican districts and Democrats in Democratic districts, so that the two party cohorts will form polarized groups.

Hussey and Zaller (2011, 336) find that, between 1876 and 1940, members of Congress (MCs) "were almost exclusively responsive to the agendas of their parties, regardless of the partisanship of the districts that elected them. Since the 1940s, MCs may have become more responsive to the partisanship of their voters, but still appear to give more allegiance to party agendas than voter preferences." In particular, as illustrated by figure 11.5 in Hussey and Zaller (2011, 325), the effect of the MC's party was found to be highest—that is, in our terms, the partisan constraint was tightest—about 1900 and again about 2000, whereas it was least—that is, the partisan constraint was most lenient—during the middle decades of the 20th century.

We have updated the Hussey-Zaller data, using (normalized) presidential two-party vote share for the Democratic presidential candidate in the most recent past election as a proxy for the ideological location of the median voter in the district. The relationship between DW-NOMINATE score and presidential vote share (see Figs. 2.1A and B) is roughly linear, so initially, in this chapter, we focus on linear relationships. Indeed, as is evident from Figure 2.1, on average the DW-NOMINATE gap between a Democratic winner and a Republican winner from districts with similar Democratic presidential vote share is roughly constant regardless of the level of that vote share.[4] In particular, this gap represents the degree to which winners of opposite parties elected from similar districts offer distinct policy positions.

---

[3] Reproduced with permission, from Ansolabehere et al. (2001). In particular, these researchers find that Republicans became district-responsive in the 1930s and the Democrats in the 1960s, with both parties peaking in district-responsiveness in the early 1970s. Both of these partisan peaks in district-responsiveness occurred primarily before the recent dramatic upswing in party polarization.

[4] See sections 3.1.2 and A3.2 for analysis of a relatively small but significant quadratic effect.

(a)

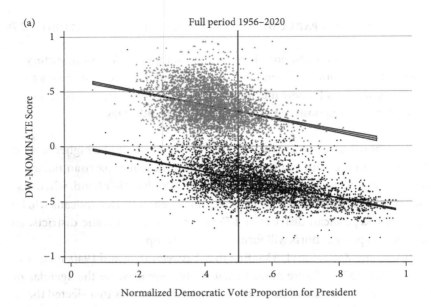

(b)

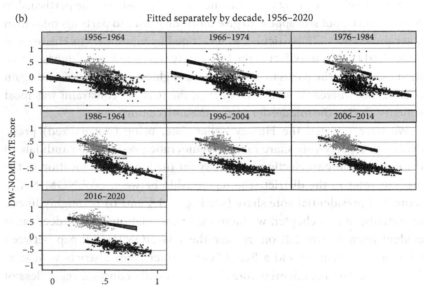

Graphs by era

Figure 2.1. DW-NOMINATE Scores versus Ideology (Normalized Presidential Vote Share), by Party, for US House Members, Fitted by Linear Regression

Notes: The plots present linear regression lines for DW-NOMINATE scores versus the normalized Democratic vote proportion for president in the House member's district (i.e., the district's Democratic presidential vote share minus the national Democratic presidential vote share). Black dots indicate Democratic House members, and gray dots Republican members. The data in part A are for the full period of 1956–2020, with sample sizes of 5,507 for Republicans and 7,084 for Democrats; the data for part B are identical, but separated by the eras noted in the figure. The vertical line at 0.5 in Figure 2.1A represents identical Democratic presidential vote shares at the national and district level. The shaded regions around the lines represent 95 percent confidence intervals.

Empirical Result 2.1. The gap between Republican and Democratic scores in similar districts is large, in fact as large as the difference in scores of members of the same party whose (normalized) vote shares in their districts vary by as much as 40 percentage points (see Fig. 2.1A).

Empirical Result 2.2. As we move by decade from the 1950s to the present (see Fig. 2.1B), the gap between candidates of opposite parties elected from districts with similar presidential voting patterns has grown substantially. Or, to put it another way, holding constituency characteristics roughly constant, ideological difference between candidates of opposite parties at the district level has increased over time, at the same time as ideological polarization between the Congressional delegations of the two parties (see Fig. 1.1) has grown.

2.4. Modeling Effects of Party Constraints: One-Sided and Two-Sided Constraints

In this section we report theoretical findings that arise from two kinds of constraints on the ideological leeway that parties permit their candidates to locate away from the national party position. These findings will be compared with the empirical record.

As we have argued, any national political party has competing motivations that may affect incentives that it offers, or restraints that it may impose, on candidates of that party at the district level. If primarily motivated to gain and preserve control over the legislative agenda, a rightist party may disfavor candidates taking moderate or leftist positions because such candidates if elected may not support—in fact may oppose—the party agenda. Extreme rightist candidates, on the other hand, may be tolerated because they are likely to be loyal supporters under a two-party system, since their positions are remote from those of the other party. Such motivations may be modeled by assuming that the party exercises a *one-sided* constraint, reining in candidates or opposing the nomination of candidates who drift too far in the *moderate* direction.

Alternatively, a party that is most sensitive to maintaining the credibility of its brand may expect candidates to be nominated that do not deviate too far in *either* direction from the ideal position that reflects its brand. These alternative motivations suggest a *two-sided* constraint, under which a center-right party, for example, is resistant to candidates either too moderate or too conservative. Mirror-image motivations apply to a center-left party.

30 WHERE DID POLARIZATION COME FROM?

To summarize: Under a *one-sided constraint*, candidates may offer positions more extreme than the party position but not too moderate. Under a *two-sided constraint*, candidates are limited to offering campaign platforms that are neither too moderate nor too extreme relative to the party position.

We now specify more explicitly the ideological range mandated by the national party constraints, in order to discern in which districts it is feasible for a party's candidates to be competitive. We focus here on the assumption of one-sided constraints; that is, Republicans are allowed to be more extreme to the right and Democrats allowed to be more extreme to the left, but candidates of each party are restricted in the direction of moderation. (The effects of two-sided constraints are considered in Appendix A2.2.) Suppose for the moment that, on a 0-to-100 Left-Right scale,[5] the national Democratic position is at 40 and the national Republican position is at 60.

Example 1. Suppose that each candidate is allowed a tight leeway of only 5 units in the moderate direction from the party position. Accordingly, the Democratic candidates are permitted any location between 0 and 45 while Republican candidates are allowed any position between 55 and 100. We assume that each candidate tries to get as close to the district median as possible under the circumstances.

In this example, there are three categories of district medians: (1) The district median lies in the interval from 0 to 45, meaning that the Democrat can locate at the district median but the Republican cannot, so the Democrat can be expected to win. (2) The median location lies between 45 and 55, and thus neither candidate is allowed to be at the district median, so the choice will be between a Democrat at 45 and a Republican at 55. (3) The district median lies between 55 and 100, with only the Republican candidate able to locate at that median, and thus the Republican can be expected to win.

This example illustrates the forced choice that voters may need to make between two candidates, neither of whom is close to the median, in situations where the party discipline constraint is relatively strong. Furthermore (see calculations in section A2.1.1 of the Appendix of this chapter), the gap between the means of the Republican and Democratic delegations in the House—following a single election—expands from the initial 20 points to 50 points, more than doubling the degree of polarization. Following a second election, that gap expands even further to 58 points. In other words, the tight

---

[5] For convenience, we speak here of a 100-point scale to avoid frequent use of decimals in the 2-point (−1 to +1) DW-NOMINATE scale.

HOW DOES PARTY DISCIPLINE GENERATE POLARIZATION? 31

constraint imposed on party members generates a major increase in polarization in the House, which is augmented even further in the following election.

Example 2. Now, imagine an alternative situation in which each candidate is allowed a greater leeway of, say, 20 units from the party position. In this case, the Democratic candidates are permitted any location between 0 and 60, while Republican candidates are allowed any position between 40 and 100.

In this second example, there are again three categories of district medians, but the types of outcomes are not all the same: (1') The district median lies in the interval from 0 to 40, meaning that the Democrat can locate at the district median but the Republican cannot, so the Democrat can be expected to win. (2') The district median lies between 40 and 60, meaning that *both* candidates can locate at the district median and each has an equal chance to win. (3') The district median lies between 60 and 100, so only the Republican candidate can locate at that median and he or she is thus expected to win.

In this case, the gap between the means of the Republican and Democratic delegations in the House expands from the initial 20 points to 48 points (see A2.1.1 for the calculations), and a second election expands that gap slightly further to 50 points. Thus, even a looser constraint imposed on party members generates significant increases in polarization in the House.

In section A2.1, we develop a model that formalizes and extends the ideas suggested by the examples above. We provide there the mathematical machinery to demonstrate several theoretical propositions about the effects of national party constraints on polarization in the US House, specifically the *post-election gap* between the mean locations of the two party delegations. We express these propositions here in general terms; more precise statements and proofs can be found in section A2.1.[6]

> **Theoretical Proposition 2.1.** For any plausible value of the party constraint, the party delegation means become decidedly separated—that is, the legislature is polarized.
>
> **Theoretical Proposition 2.2.** For each fixed level of the constraint, the post-election gap and hence the party delegation means settle quickly to limiting values—that is, an equilibrium is approached after only a few elections. The post-election gap at equilibrium is independent of

---

[6] The model we develop is based on Merrill, Grofman, and Brunell (2014).

the starting values. If the party constraint is lax, this *gap at equilibrium is small* and the party delegations overlap; but if the party constraint is tight, the *gap is large*. Thus, tight constraint leads to widely separated party delegations.

Figure 2.2 depicts the mean locations of each party delegation at equilibrium as a function of the leeway permitted by the party constraint. This figure supports the statements in Theoretical Proposition 2.2 (see section A2.1.3 for the proof).

Theoretical Proposition 2.3. When the party constraint is lax, the variance among the members within each party delegation is large—that is, each party delegation is heterogeneous and the two overlap substantially. Conversely, if the party constraints are tight, this variance is small—that is, each party delegation is homogeneous and the two are highly separated (see section A2.1.4 for the proof).

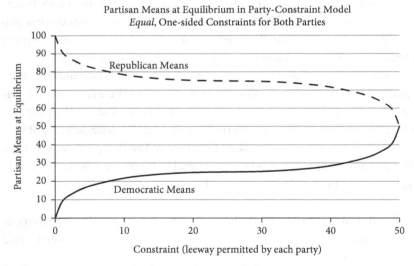

Figure 2.2. Party Means Under Equal One-Sided Party Constraints

Notes: For each degree of constraint (indicated on the horizontal axis), the model projected positions for the means of the party delegations at equilibrium are indicated by the values on the two curves. For example, under a tight constraint of 10 units on the 100-point scale (i.e., one tenth of the scale length), the Democratic delegation mean will settle at about 20 and the Republican mean at about 80—that is, at highly polarized positions. Note that for any plausible level of constraint, the model-projected Republican and Democratic mean positions are widely separated, but that the degree of party separation is largest when the party constraints are tight—that is, when the leeway permitted by the constraints is small.

This model-projected pattern can be compared with the historical record shown in Chapter 1 in Figure 1.1, in which—just as in the model projections—as the partisan means diverge, generally each party delegation becomes more concentrated, accentuating the effects of polarization. Figure 1.1B shows that intraparty variation was at its lowest at approximately the times that partisan separation was greatest (at two successive turns of the century), while intraparty variance was greatest when partisan separation was least (approximately mid-century or shortly thereafter). Thus, the empirical pattern follows the theoretical findings of our model: namely, strong polarization reflects high separation between narrow distributions of partisans, and low polarization represents reduced separation and broad (overlapping) distributions.

2.5. Effects of Asymmetry in the Strengths of the National Party Constraints and Its Potential Strategic Use

We now relax the simplifying assumption that the partisan constraints of the two parties are equally strong, in order to investigate the consequences in the asymmetrical case in which one party's constraint may be tighter than that of the other party. A number of recent authors have provided evidence that the Republican Party, which has historically been the less diverse of the two parties, today exerts far greater pressure for ideological conformity than does the Democratic Party (see, e.g., Hacker and Pierson, 2006; Seo and Theriault, 2012). Mann and Ornstein (2012), in particular, see the present problems of Congressional gridlock as being far more due to the Republicans' ideologically grounded intransigence than to similar hardened attitudes on the left.[7] Indeed, Tea Party activists threatened to campaign against incumbents who fail to show sufficient ideological purity, and this threat extended even to party leaders (Boatright, 2013); more recently, the same threat has been posed by Trump loyalists. As noted above, hardline Republicans in the 2021–22 House ostracized those House members of their own party, such as Rep. Liz Cheney, who voted to impeach President Trump. And a number of those members chose to retire or were forcibly retired by opposition from Trump loyalists in the primary.

---

[7] See also Theriault and Rohde (2011).

Let us suppose, as an example, that the Republican Party has a tighter constraint than the Democratic Party. Figure 2.3 depicts the mean locations of each party delegation at equilibrium as a function of the Democratic Party's level of constraint (leeway), with the Republican leeway set at one half that of the Democrats. The size of the gap between the party means is similar to that under equal constraints; however, when constraints are unequal, as indicated above, the gap remains substantial for more relaxed levels of Democratic constraint, because the other party still has a relatively tight constraint. (For example, by design, when the Democratic leeway approaches 50, the Republican leeway is still less than 25.)

But perhaps more notable is that, although the size of the partisan gaps is not greatly different from that in the equal-constraint scenario, the partisan means are decidedly asymmetrical when constraints are unequal, as we see in Figure 2.3. Replacing equal with unequal constraints transfers marginal seats from the party with the tighter constraint (in this example, the Republicans) to the party with the looser constraint (the Democrats). But this effect shifts the distributions of both partisan delegations in the direction of the party with the tighter constraint. For example, in Figure 2.3, the Republican mean is nearly twice as far from the center of the scale as the Democratic mean.

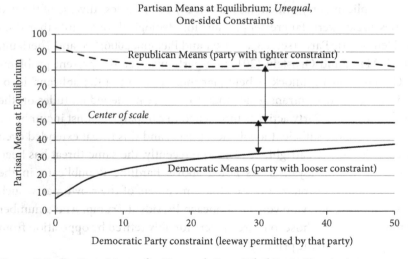

Figure 2.3. Partisan Means for Unequal, One-Sided Party Constraints

Notes: The Republican party constraint is set at half the Democratic party constraint. As indicated by the two arrows, the model projected positions at equilibrium for the party with the tighter constraint is substantially more extreme than that of the party with the looser constraint.

HOW DOES PARTY DISCIPLINE GENERATE POLARIZATION? 35

According to the model, in this example, the Democratic delegation attains a strong majority of the seats by the second election (see Merrill et al., 2014, for further plots and details).

To investigate the potential strategic use of constraint strength, let us suppose that initially both partisan constraints are strong, but equal. If exogenous conditions are such that one party (say, the Republicans) wins a legislative majority, the opposition party (the Democrats) has an incentive to relax its constraint in order to help win marginal seats and improve its chances of becoming the majority.[8] At the same time, a homogeneous and polarized majority party provides the conditions for delegating procedural tools to the party leadership, leading to legislative efficiency and even more party discipline (an issue we return to in Chapter 6). As we have seen from Figure 2.3, this is not likely to have a large effect on the polarization gap, but the evidence from that figure suggests that the Democratic delegation is motivated to moderate (i.e., move toward the center) and win a majority, whereas the Republican delegation may become more extreme—that is, both parties will shift to the right. In Chapter 3 we will explore this curious phenomenon, which we have labeled Polsby's Paradox, under which a party attaining a majority typically moves in the direction of the minority party.

Carrying this scenario forward: Other things being equal, if the Democrats by relaxing their constraint do regain a majority, the Republican Party should have an incentive to loosen its constraint as well, leading eventually to less polarization.[9] Thus, we come full circle. Strengthening constraints leads at first to more and more polarization, which, if asymmetric in nature, can motivate relaxation of those constraints and hence reduced polarization. In this sense, polarization can be expected to follow a cyclic pattern, as we see in the historical record. We summarize as follows:

Theoretical Proposition 2.4. While asymmetry in the strength of the constraints maintained by the two national parties can have relatively little direct effect on the degree of partisan separation, this asymmetry

---

[8] For example, in 2018 the Democratic Party did indeed relax its constraint and support moderate candidates, leading to its successfully regaining control of the US House.

[9] In the Senate, there is an additional asymmetry between the parties that reduces the incentive for the Republican Party to relax its constraint to seek more votes. Small states tend to be more conservative (in part because many are largely rural) but select just as many Senators as large states. As a result, the median of the set of state median voters is substantially to the right of the median national voter. Thus, to win a majority of Senators, the Republican Party needs to attract the median of the set of state median voters, a more conservative goal than the median of all national voters.

36 WHERE DID POLARIZATION COME FROM?

can shift both partisan delegations decidedly in the direction of the party exercising the tighter constraint.

Proofs, under appropriate assumptions, of the theoretical propositions stated above are found in this chapter's Appendix. Section A2.1 presents the basic model of constraint effects and investigates in detail the consequences of a (one-sided) constraint. Section A2.2 investigates the consequences of assuming, instead, a two-sided constraint (constraints in both the moderate and extreme directions), associated with primacy of maintaining a partisan brand. In section A2.3, we consider the asymmetrical case in which the respective party constraints are unequal in strength. These results have important implications for the structure of political competition at the constituency level and the nature and possible asymmetry of party polarization in the legislature.

2.6. The Linkage of Homogeneity within Parties and Distance Between Parties

This chapter represents an effort to investigate, under simplifying assumptions, the relationships between national party constraints on district candidates and polarization in the resultant legislature. Understanding how and why legislative polarization levels might change is important for a number of reasons. Party divergence affects the capacity of a legislature to find common ground and the motivation of the dominant party to seek the common interest, as made evident, for example, in the US House in 2021 and 2023 as the government struggled to raise the debt ceiling.

Furthermore, differences in policy-oriented versus office-winning motivations within a dominant party can affect the ability of that party to pass its programs. Consider, for example, the 2017 failure of the Republican Party to repeal Affordable Health Care (Obamacare), and its internal divisions over how much to spend on building a wall between the United States and Mexico. The effects of party divergence are exacerbated if either or both party delegations are ideologically concentrated. When this is the case, polarization degrades representation for moderate voters by tending to make every vote into a choice between polar opposites, neither of which represent moderate voters' wishes, inducing what Bafumi and Herron (2010) call "leapfrog representation."

HOW DOES PARTY DISCIPLINE GENERATE POLARIZATION? 37

Insofar as legislation reflects the ideology of the median legislator, under extreme polarization, even relatively small shifts over elections in the ideological location of the electorate can lead to wide swings in the legislative output when the partisan majority shifts (Grofman et al., 2001; Bafumi and Herron, 2010). Insofar as legislation reflects the majority party's median legislator—as the conditional party government model suggests will happen under polarized conditions (see Chapter 6)—the nature of legislation can tend to alternate even more wildly between two extremes. But, even if only one party is ideologically cohesive, with the other remaining relatively diverse, dramatic changes can arise from changes in party control, although the changes will not be as great as when both parties are ideologically cohesive. This is what we saw in 1994 (Grofman et al., 2001). Throughout most of the 20th century the Democrats were more of the "big tent" party and had less internal ideological homogeneity.

Our model generates changes in party polarization endogenously and predicts that partisan polarization will be coupled with tight intraparty ideology. We summarize below the results that we stated separately above:

Conclusion 2.1. When party discipline in both parties is tight, the gap between party-delegation means at equilibrium is large and both party delegations are narrowly distributed as well as highly separated from one another.

Accordingly, party differentiation and party cohesiveness go together. As noted earlier, this theoretical prediction of our model is fully borne out by the empirical evidence. As noted in Chapter 1, the partisan gap between the party delegations is significantly and negatively correlated with both the standard deviation for Democrats and the standard deviation for Republicans.

Furthermore, empirically, the link between party discipline and polarization can be strengthened by recourse to a procedure to estimate party influence (discipline) on roll-call voting in Congress, developed by Snyder and Groseclose (2000) and applied by them to the period 1871–1998 (see Fig. 2.4).[10] This objective measure of party discipline is significantly (and

---

[10] The procedure is intended to separate legislators' own preferences by assessing their votes on lopsided congressional votes, on which pressure is assumed not to be needed. See also McCarty et al. (2001) for a critique and Snyder and Groseclose (2001) for a rejoinder concerning the Snyder-Groseclose procedure. McCarty et al. argue that the effects of party discipline are embodied primarily in the ideal point of a legislator rather than exercised separated on each roll call and that the

38 WHERE DID POLARIZATION COME FROM?

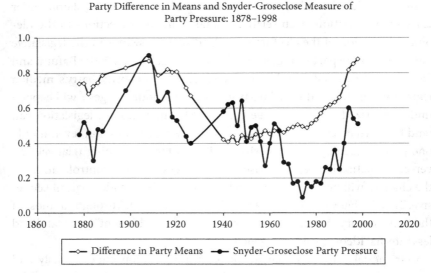

Figure 2.4. Gap between Parties and Snyder-Groseclose Measure of Party Pressure

Note: The Snyder-Groseclose measure of party pressure, or discipline, is positively correlated with difference in party means and negatively correlated with the pooled intraparty standard deviation, both significance at the 0.01 level or higher.

Source: Adapted in part, with permission, from Snyder and Groseclose (2000, Fig. 2).

positively) correlated with the partisan gap between Democratic and Republican delegation means, and significantly (and negatively) correlated with the pooled party standard deviation.[11] Hence, the Snyder-Groseclose measure suggests that when party discipline is strong, party delegations are internally concentrated and widely separated from one another—that is, the House is highly polarized.

Graphically, the time series of the Snyder-Groseclose measure of party discipline shows substantial similarities with the difference between the partisan mean DW-NOMINATE scores (see Fig. 2.4), although the two are by no means identical. (The Snyder-Groseclose measure depends entirely on roll calls and does not directly measure discipline imposed

---

Snyder-Groseclose method overestimates the party-discipline effect. But both individual roll calls and ideal points (estimated from roll calls) are roll-call effects from party discipline, as Snyder and Groseclose (2001) point out.

[11] The correlation with the partisan gap is 0.39, significantly positive at the 0.01 level; while the correlation with the pooled party standard deviation is −0.49, significantly negative at the 0.001 level.

HOW DOES PARTY DISCIPLINE GENERATE POLARIZATION? 39

by activists and others outside Congress.) The plot for the Snyder and Groseclose measure shows that party pressure in the US House peaked in the first decade of the 20th century, then dropped—sharply at first, then gradually—to a low in the 1970s, then rose again rapidly until the 1990s, when their study ends. This pattern closely follows the historical trajectory of party discipline depicted by Pearson (2015) and summarized in the introduction to this chapter.

At the end of the 20th century and the beginning of the 21st, increasing ideological party branding, partisan sorting of the electorate, and the role of party activists substantially tightened the national policy constraint on within-district positions, widening the partisan gap at equilibrium and maintaining high partisan polarization in Congress. Whatever may have been the initial impetus for the tightening of such constraints—for example, gain in the ability of Republicans to be competitive in the South after the Democrats under Lyndon Johnson enacted major civil-rights and voting-rights policies—our model demonstrates that constraints on candidate positioning tied to national party positions can operate in a dynamic and self-reinforcing fashion. In particular, partisan differentiation can lead to pressures for additional polarization as the zone in which a given party can be competitive shrinks.[12] This effect is especially strong when parties exercise tight constraints on candidates that limit changes only in the direction of moderation. However, as noted earlier in Theoretical Proposition 2.4, relaxing one of our initial assumptions, namely symmetry in the level of constraint exercised by the two parties, can lead to a different expectation of the nature of party competition:

Conclusion 2.2. While asymmetry in the strength of the constraints maintained by the two national parties may have relatively little direct effect on the degree of partisan separation, it can shift both partisan delegations decidedly in the direction of the party exercising the tighter constraint.

---

[12] Stringent party discipline within a legislature can, in principle, lead to even greater polarization than the process we have described. Nevertheless, we would argue that in the single-seat plurality elections in the United States—unlike in European parliamentary systems where list PR methods give parties much greater control over their representatives—it is the forces that operate at the constituency level to determine the ideological variation within and between parties that are most determinative of the degree to which party discipline can be enforced. This will be reflected in the kinds of bills and amendments that come up for a vote.

40 WHERE DID POLARIZATION COME FROM?

While the party-constraint model is perhaps most useful in explaining how party polarization might be expected to increase over time, it also helps us understand conditions of party overlap:

Conclusion 2.3. If the discipline by which national parties constrain the positioning of district candidates is sufficiently loose, so that district candidates can deviate greatly from national policy norms, then party delegation distributions will be broad and close to each other.

Thus, loose constraints lead to extensive overlap of party policy distributions and party means that are not too far apart. In that case, the gap at equilibrium is low and parties are much less polarized. Historically, in the US Congress, extensive wiggle room was the norm during the mid-20th century, when conservative Southern Democrats and liberal Northern Republicans—both of whom deviated greatly from national party means—were electable. Consequently, during this period Congressional partisan delegations were relatively unpolarized. Here, regional variation linked to a Civil War legacy allowed for a "four-party" situation: Northern Democrats, Southern Democrats, Northern Republicans, and Southern Republicans.

The theoretical results of this chapter suggest that lessening the restrictions of party discipline has the potential to reduce both of the characteristics of polarization: wide separation between parties and intraparty concentration. If the constraints differ in strength, the party with the weaker discipline has the potential to realize a majority in the legislature, providing the opposing party an incentive to relax its constraint as well, thus reducing polarization. We will return to the question of how polarization might be alleviated at the end of the book.

3

Why, Even in Highly Competitive Districts, Are Candidate Positions So Different?

3.1. Relation of Candidate Divergence to District Competitiveness

As we have seen in previous chapters, we have advanced well beyond the simple expectation, commonly attributed to Downs (1957), that two-party competition will result in convergence to the median. Two key modifications are the recognition that (1) there are strong competing incentives for party divergence, paralleling Downsian pressures for party convergence; and, (2) competition in multiple legislative constituencies complicates the standard Downsian logic.

Likewise, empirical work provides compelling evidence of divergence between, for example, US Senators of the same state (Poole and Rosenthal, 1984), or House members elected successively from a given district who come from opposite parties. Similar nonconvergence results are found in Grofman, Griffin, and Glazer (1990), Snyder (1994), Erikson and Wright (1997, 2000), Burden (2001, 2004); Lee, Moretti, and Butler (2004), and Clinton (2006).

The implications of national party constraints, developed in Chapter 2, would project that insofar as national parties are polarized and ideologically far apart, strict constraints should keep district candidates from assuming moderate positions, even in competitive districts where the median voter is moderate by national standards. Thus, we would expect that divergence between opposing candidates in each district would increase as national polarization increases. At the same time, we might expect that the degree of accommodation to the local electorate would vary with the degree of competitiveness within the district. In particular, it seems possible that representatives from safe seats could more safely disregard the views of minority-party

---

How Polarization Begets Polarization. Samuel Merrill III, Bernard Grofman, and Thomas L. Brunell, Oxford University Press. © Oxford University Press 2024. DOI: 10.1093/oso/9780197745229.003.0003

42 WHERE DID POLARIZATION COME FROM?

voters in their constituencies and afford to take more extreme positions expected by their national parties than could representatives from marginal seats. Hence, when elections are expected to be very close, it still seems plausible (à la Downs) that candidates of each party might moderate their positions toward those of the median voter in the district. Yet even this limited claim has found only partial empirical support, and even that varies over time.

For example, Ansolabehere, Snyder, and Stewart (2001, 136) find that "competition exerts some pressure on candidates to fit with their constituents, . . . but that degree of responsiveness waned in the 1980s and 1990s." Moreover, there is a recent body of US political journalism (see, e.g., Miniter, 2005; Nagourney, 2003) suggesting that, when confronted with (potentially) very close contests, instead of reaching out to centrist voters, candidates seek to mobilize their own support base in terms of turnout and campaign support by espousing noncentrist positions which are especially attractive to their own party's supporters. For example, Lucy McBath beat Karen Handel in 2018 in Georgia's 6th Congressional district. Handel was a solid textbook Republican, voting with her party 96 percent of the time. Lucy McBath is an African-American who prioritized gun control and racial justice after her teenage son was killed in a shooting in 2012. This district is largely affluent and white and had not been represented by a racial minority until McBath's victory. Neither of these two candidates was running from the center, as they offered very clearly distinct policy perspectives to the voters in the district.

On the theoretical level, Krasa and Polborn (2018) have provided a compelling argument as to why relatively moderate districts may elect extreme representatives. Suppose that voters significantly recognize and value the possible effect of their vote for their local Congressional candidate on the prospects that their party win a majority in the US House. In that case, a party with a modest majority in the district has the leeway to nominate an extreme local candidate who will still be expected to win in the district.

To see this, suppose, for example, that the median voter in a district is moderately conservative and that the national Republican position is very conservative but still closer to the district median voter than that of the national Democratic party.[1] Insofar as voters make their local choice on the

---

[1] Although we may speak in this book of winning the median voter nationally, winning party control of the House is more closely associated with winning the median of the district medians, which need not be the same as the national median of all voters. In fact, given the present geographical

basis of their national party preference, a moderately conservative median voter is motivated to vote for the local Republican in spite of her/his extremity, because doing so furthers the voter's goal that their party achieve majority control in the House. A moderate median voter in the district is hence only a limited constraint on the local Republican candidate, permitting the Republican primary electorate (and/or local party leadership) to nominate a candidate who represents an extreme partisan faction and can still win the general election. Hence, nationalization of Congressional elections augments the relevance of the party-constraint model introduced in Chapter 2. When elections in the Congressional district are nationalized, party discipline from party leaders and/or activists arising at either the national or local level can enable extreme candidates to be elected.

3.1.1. Empirical evidence

Using the first dimension of DW-NOMINATE scores for the US House and Senate, Adams et al. (2013) analyze, for the period 1956–2004, how the degree of ideological polarization between the parties varies as a function of district ideology, defined in terms of Democratic presidential support in the district. We update that analysis through the Congress elected in 2020. The simplest findings accord with expectations. In general, the more Democratic-leaning the district at the presidential level, the more liberal are the representatives from the district. Again, as expected, Representatives from opposite parties who are elected from districts of similar ideology display sharply different legislative voting records for any given level of (Democratic) presidential support. Accordingly, Democrats elected from such districts are, on average, considerably more liberal than Republicans elected from similar districts.

Surprisingly, however, Adams et al. also find, and we confirm, that the ideological difference between the (winning) candidates of the two parties is often at least as great in districts that, in presidential support terms, are the *most* competitive—a finding that contradicts the intuitive expectation that the pressure for policy convergence is greatest when the election is most

---

concentration of Democrats in many metropolitan districts as well as the results of gerrymandering, the median of the district medians is substantially to the right of the median of all voters in the nation (Klein, 2020). This is one reason why the median (and mean) of the Republican delegation in Congress has been able to move further right than the median of the Democratic delegation has moved left.

44   WHERE DID POLARIZATION COME FROM?

competitive.[2] This empirical analysis suggests that candidates may be just as divergent from one another when the election is most competitive as when a race is lopsided.

In election contexts that one might think give candidates the strongest possible incentives to maximize their electoral support, the winning candidates tend to present radical policies *relative to the center of district opinion.* Note that this finding does not imply that the most competitive districts elect the most extremist members of Congress. Rather, it indicates that Democrats and Republicans elected in competitive districts may be at least as polarized *relative to each other,* but not necessarily more extreme than those elected in lopsided districts.

Why might candidates be as dissimilar, or more so, when the election is expected to be most competitive? The intuition can be grasped by considering the *least* competitive election context—namely, that in which all citizens in the electorate identify with the same party. If, say, all citizens are Democratic partisans, then the Democratic candidate will appeal on policy grounds to these partisans, and so will the Republican candidate because he or she has no Republican partisans to whom to appeal. Therefore, margin-maximizing candidates will converge to identical positions in this "perfectly" uncompetitive scenario; and, by extension, they can be expected to converge to similar positions for partisan contexts that strongly favor one party over the other.

By contrast, in competitive districts each candidate's optimal strategy is to appeal in large part to his/her own partisan constituency, which motivates increased divergence of the candidates' positions. To see better why this might be, we will return to a formal theoretical explanation for this behavior in section 3.2 (and later in Chapter 5). But first we describe the empirical evidence in more detail.

3.1.2. Data analysis for the US House

As indicated above, our empirical analysis is patterned on that of Adams et al. (2013), but updated from members of Congress elected during the period

---

[2] We focus on winners because idiosyncratic factors may drive the ideological location of the candidate of the minority party in uncompetitive seats, and our interest is in how different from the ideological location of the median voter a candidate can be and still be able to win the district. We treat idiosyncratic candidate characteristics and incumbency advantages as effectively washing out when comparing the set of Democratic and Republican winners from districts with the same ideological characteristics (as inferred from presidential election outcomes).

1956–2004 to cover the period from 1956–2020. The DW-NOMINATE scores for this analysis, as well as for other analyses throughout the book, were obtained from the website https://voteview.com/data (accessed 2-20-2022).[3]

Figure 2.1 in Chapter 2 plots (the first dimension of) DW-NOMINATE scores for US House members against the (district-specific) normalized Democratic vote share in the district in the contemporaneous presidential election.[4] Plots (similar to but updated from those in Adams et al., 2013, and using DW-NOMINATE scores computed from the static scores algorithm) are presented for the full period 1956–2020 in Figure 2.1A; plots broken down by subperiods (eras) are shown in Figure 2.1B (see Chapter 2 for these plots). In each plot, the area to the left of the vertical line represents Republican districts (i.e., those in which the district Democratic presidential vote was less than the national Democratic vote), while the area to the right of the vertical line represent Democratic districts (those in which the district Democratic presidential vote was greater than the national Democratic vote). The fitted lines in Figure 2.1—performed separately for each party— are based on linear regressions of the DW-NOMINATE scores against the district ideology (along with a dummy variable for districts from the South).

As expected, the fitted line for each party slopes downward, both for the full 1956–2020 period and for each of seven subperiods. For each party, all of these downward slopes are statistically significant at the 0.001 level and are substantial. Furthermore, the gap between the winners from the two parties is substantial; for instance, the pooled data for the full period suggests that, on average, a Republican Congressperson from even a 70 percent Democratic

---

[3] In this book we use the *static* scores in the voteview data, because *dynamic* DW-NOMINATE scores (https://legacy.voteview.com/dwnomin.htm) are not available for House members elected more recently than 2012. We would have preferred to use dynamic scores, were they available, because dynamic scores reflect ideological changes of individual legislators over time in successive Congresses (using a linear model), whereas static scores estimate a single fixed value for each legislator. Because both ideological changes in individual legislators and replacement of legislators have both been found to affect the partisan distribution of ideology (Bonica and Cox, 2018; Theriault, 2006, 2008), dynamic scores would appear to be more appropriate for our analyses, if they were available. See Appendix A3.1 for a plot showing a substantial and asymmetrical difference between static and dynamic mean scores through 2012, as well as discussion of empirical studies that may account for this difference. Accordingly, analyses based on dynamic scores would likely show even greater divergence between the parties in Congress, reflecting extremism of the Republican delegation.

[4] Specifically, the normalized Democratic vote proportion for president is equal to district presidential vote share minus the average presidential vote share over all districts. For midterm Congressional elections, the presidential vote from two years earlier was used. Levendusky, Pope, and Jackman (2008) find that, in the 1990s, the presidential vote appears to be an excellent proxy for district-level partisanship, as Congressional and presidential election outcomes have become more highly correlated over the period they analyze (1952–2000).

46   WHERE DID POLARIZATION COME FROM?

district can be expected to be just as conservative as a Democratic member from a 30 percent Democratic district.

However, one might suspect that a quadratic analysis (i.e., one fitting the data for the respective parties by parabolas) would reveal an inward bow of the curves, so that the gap between the curves would be smaller in the middle where the two parties are more competitive. But, *to the contrary*, quadratic analysis (see Fig. 3.1A and B for the fitted parabolas, and section A3.2 for the analytic details) demonstrates that, in fact, the gap between winning candidates of the two parties is *as great* or even greater in competitive districts as in more lopsided ones.

3.1.3. Implications of candidate divergence in competitive districts

In summary, these findings cast considerable doubt on any simplistic claim that more evenly balanced electoral competition in a district prompts candidate convergence across party lines. Moreover, the substantive conclusions largely generalize across time periods and they are consistent across the House and Senate (see section A3.2). As expected, the evidence indicates that elected officials' legislative voting records respond to district ideology, and that Democratic House members are substantially more liberal than Republicans when controlling for district ideology. But no consistent evidence is found that the degree of ideological polarization between Democratic and Republican House members is smallest in the most competitive districts. In fact, if anything, the data suggests the opposite pattern: that over the past 60 years partisan polarization has often been as *great* or greater in districts that are most competitive (see section A3.2). This latter finding is contrary to the intuition that political competition exerts maximal pressures on politicians to moderate their positions when this competition is most intense—that is, in highly competitive districts.

A practical implication of the latter result is that it casts doubt on whether using redistricting to draw more competitive districts for members of the House will bring the politics of moderation to Congress (cf. Brunell, 2008, and Brunell and Grofman, 2008). Indeed, the results suggest that Democratic and Republican Representatives elected from competitive districts (as defined by the presidential vote) may be at least as ideologically far apart from each other as when they are elected from districts that are lopsidedly Democratic or lopsidedly Republican at the presidential level.

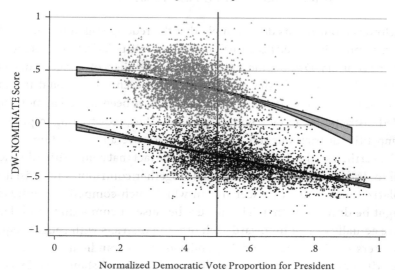

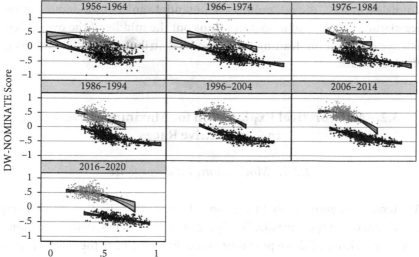

Figure 3.1. Quadratic Regression for DW-NOMINATE Scores versus Ideology (Normalized Presidential Vote Share), by Party, for US House Members

Notes: The plots present quadratic regression curves for DW-NOMINATE scores versus the normalized Democratic vote proportion for president in the House member's district (i.e., the district's Democratic presidential vote share minus the national Democratic presidential vote share). Black dots indicate Democratic House members, and gray dots Republican members. The vertical line at 0.5 in Part A represents identical Democratic presidential vote shares at the national and district level. The shaded regions around the lines represent 95 percent confidence intervals.

48 WHERE DID POLARIZATION COME FROM?

However, our results do not imply that the redesigning of districts to be more competitive would necessarily increase overall polarization in Congress. On the contrary, Democratic and Republican members of Congress in competitive districts, while sharply different from each other, would in most cases be less extremist than those who would have been elected in more lopsided districts, as can be seen in Figure 3.1. Thus, redistricting to produce competitive districts might reduce, not increase, overall polarization.

Nevertheless, the findings suggest that the fact that competitive districts fail to draw the competing candidates together contributes to legislative polarization relative to a scenario in which such competing candidates might be drawn together. This occurs because, if competing candidates were actually drawn in toward each other in districts with roughly equal numbers of Democrats and Republicans, these candidates—including the winners—would likely be moderates by national standards. By contrast, their tendency to be drawn apart to moderately extreme positions, and in the last two decades to quite extreme positions (as shown by the empirical results above), erodes the potential ranks of moderates in the legislature. The loss of moderates thins out the middle of the overall legislative distribution, leading to a bimodal distribution of all members of the legislature.

3.2. A Theoretical Explanation for Maximum Divergence in Competitive Races

3.2.1. Motivations for divergence

We have seen empirically in section 3.1 above that the two major-party nominees in competitive districts typically take widely separate positions, and that neither of these positions is ideologically near the median voter in the district. To better understand why vote-maximizing candidates in close elections might rationally take positions far from the district median, we model the complex interactions of political competition, partisan loyalties, and incentives for voter turnout. Our intention is to provide an explanation of why candidates may mobilize their voter base to turn out by adopting positions attractive to the party faithful, rather than trying to attract the median voter by moving toward the center. Note that the arguments for candidate divergence in this theoretical section do not

WHY CANDIDATE POSITIONS ARE SO DIFFERENT? 49

depend on national party constraints (as discussed in Chapter 2), but rather support *additional* motivations for district candidates not to converge to a central position.

Should the degree of competitiveness of a race affect the tendency to motivate divergent party strategies? One might expect intuitively, as suggested in the previous section, that safe, uncompetitive seats would permit and encourage noncentrist strategies, especially by the dominant party, while competitive seats would intensity the Downsian logic to converge to the median. If we can show, even in highly competitive races and for electorates that include substantial proportions of Independents, that office-seeking candidates have substantial incentives to appeal to their partisan constituency—that is, that the intuition above is *incorrect*—then this implication fundamentally alters the expectations of the Downsian model. Accordingly, having found empirical evidence for the following hypothesis, we seek a theoretical explanation in the following section:

Hypothesis 3.1: The divergence between vote-maximizing candidates' optimal positions is at least as great when the Democratic and Republican constituencies are at or near equal size as when the partisan distribution is unequal.

This expectation is counterintuitive and certainly not consistent with the traditional journalistic versions of Downsian theory. Rather, we might expect the centripetal pull of the median voter to be most relevant when an election is likely to be close.

3.2.2. A spatial model with partisan loyalty and abstention due to alienation

We develop a spatial model that features a two-candidate election involving one Democratic and one Republican candidate, who choose positions along a unidimensional liberal–conservative ideological continuum to maximize votes; the candidates' positions are denoted by D and R, respectively. Following Adams, Merrill, and Grofman (2005), we employ a probabilistic, multivariate voting model that incorporates components of issue voting, partisan loyalty, and abstention due to alienation. Voters are influenced by (1) their proximity to the candidates' ideological positions (specified by

50 WHERE DID POLARIZATION COME FROM?

an ideology-salience parameter); (2) their partisan loyalties (specified by a partisan-salience parameter); and (3) a random variable representing unmeasured influences on the vote. We further assume that citizens' turnout decisions depend on whether they find either of the candidates sufficiently attractive to impel them to turn out to vote (specified by an alienation-threshold parameter, and a random variable representing unmeasured influences on turnout). We assume that the voter distribution consists entirely of three groups of citizens: a *Democratic constituency* consisting of citizens who identify with the Democratic party, a *Republican constituency* consisting of citizens who identify with the Republican party, and a set of Independents.

> **Proposition 3.1 (Competitive Polarization):** Under the conditions above, it can be shown that
>
> a. The candidates' equilibrium positions lie between those of the overall mean voter and the means of the respective partisan constituencies,[5] and
>
> b. The distance between the candidates at equilibrium is at least as great when the two partisan constituencies are equal as when they are unequal.[6]

We will look at how, via effects on the expected closeness of the election, candidates' strategic behavior is affected by the size of each of these constituencies and the candidates' respective degree of mobilization.[7] More specifically, under the conditions of Proposition 3.1, when voters display partisan biases and other conditions are held equal, the following relationships hold:

---

[5] This result is consistent with previous spatial modeling work with probabilistic voting and variable voter turnout (Enelow and Hinich, 1989).

[6] Proposition 3.1 is stated in more detail in section A3.3 in the Appendix to this chapter. The proof is given in Adams et al. (2010, Theorem 1 and Corollary to Theorem 1). The Proposition also provides explicit formulas for Nash-equilibrium strategies for each of the two parties. In this setting, Nash-equilibrium strategies are positions toward which we can expect (office-seeking) candidates to approach as they seek to maximize their expected vote margins over their opponent.

[7] Butler (2009) develops a comparable model, assuming that partisans support their party for non-policy reasons but may abstain if the candidate is too far toward the center and that swing voters vote in a Downsian fashion. Using district-level estimates of the voter distribution, he explains polarization among candidates in terms of the location and size of candidates' bases and proportion of swing voters and focuses on change over time as these variables have changed.

WHY CANDIDATE POSITIONS ARE SO DIFFERENT? 51

1. The more extreme the position of the candidate's partisan constituency, or the larger the candidate's partisan constituency, the further the candidate diverges from the center in the direction of this constituency.
2. The larger the proportion of Independent voters in the electorate, the less the candidate diverges from the center.
3. For a fixed proportion of Independent voters, the divergence between the candidates' equilibrium positions is greatest when the Democratic and Republican partisan constituencies are of equal size; furthermore, the degree of candidate divergence declines monotonically as the proportions of Democratic and Republican partisans become more different.

Why, specifically, are margin-maximizing candidates motivated to shift away from the center in the direction of their partisans, as indicated in conclusions (1) and (2) above? The reason is that the marginal change in a candidate's probabilities of attracting her own partisans' votes via policy appeals is higher than is the marginal change in the probability of her attracting votes from the rival candidate's partisans. This conforms to common sense: the more uncommitted the voter's decision to turn out to vote for a candidate, the more the candidate will take the voter's preferences into account (Erikson and Romero, 1990). Conclusion (3) above implies that the policy distance between the candidates' equilibrium positions increases as the proportions of Democratic and Republican partisans become more nearly equal, and that candidate divergence is maximized when there are equal proportions of Democratic and Republican partisans in the electorate—that is, that *candidate polarization is greatest when the election is most competitive*.

The implication of conclusion (3) thereby directly contradicts the conventional wisdom that competitive elections motivate candidate convergence toward the center of the general electorate. Optimal (vote-maximizing) candidate positions in this abstention model are plotted in Figure 3.2 as a function of partisan composition of the electorate, with one third of the electorate assumed to be Independents, illustrating this implication.

Thus, we have both empirical and theoretical evidence that opposing party candidates in competitive districts are expected to be separated from one another just as much in competitive districts as in uncompetitive ones (and maybe even more so). But the separation itself is driven by polarizing factors

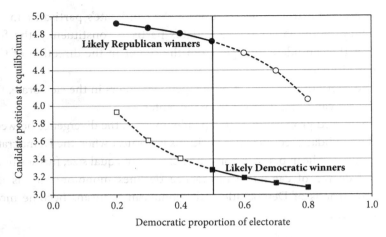

Figure 3.2. Optimal Candidate Positions as a Function of Partisan Composition of the Electorate

Source: Adapted from Adams et al. (2010: Figure 1).

Notes: Partisan distributions are assumed normally distributed on a conventional 1–7 scale, with means $\mu_D = 3$ and $\mu_R = 5$, and standard deviations $\sigma_D = \sigma_R = 1$; independents constitute one third of the electorate. Solid symbols indicate candidates whose expected vote share is at least 50 percent of the electorate—that is, those candidates who are most likely to be elected. Open symbols indicate candidates less likely to win election. Parameter settings are provided in section A3.3.

including party discipline, extremism of activists, heterogeneity among district electorates, primary elections, and many other factors.

3.3. The Polsby Paradox

Next we look at the evidence for what we will call the Polsby Paradox: that the direction of change of the median of the party making the (net) seat gains can be opposite from the change in direction in the overall chamber median. In other words, Democratic gains can shift the Democratic median to the right even while the chamber median is moving to the left, just as the opposite can occur with Republican gains.

We make the simplifying assumptions that between-party replacements tend to come from districts whose median member is ideologically between the two party medians, and that the new incumbent is to the left of

WHY CANDIDATE POSITIONS ARE SO DIFFERENT? 53

the previous incumbent if a Democrat replaces a Republican, but to the right of the previous incumbent if a Republican replaces a Democrat. Further, assuming that a within-party replacement occupies the same ideological location as his/her predecessor, then:

Proposition 3.2 (Polsby Paradox). Under the above assumptions:

a. If the proportion of Democrats increases, then the Democratic Party median moves to the right while the chamber median moves to the left, thus decreasing the gap between the chamber median and the Democratic Party median. At the same time, since the proportion of Republicans is decreasing, the Republican median is moving to the right, so thus the gap between the chamber median and the Republican Party median is increasing.

b. If the proportion of Republicans increases, then, for analogous reasons, the Republican Party median moves to the left while the chamber median moves to the right; thus the gap between the chamber median and the Republican Party median decreases, while the gap between the chamber median and the Democratic Party median is increases.

The logic behind Nelson Polsby's argument (personal communication, 1986) is that gains from each party come, on balance, from defeating the most vulnerable incumbents of the other party. These, by and large, are the moderate members of the party, who are elected to seats in districts from whose median voter they are ideologically divergent and hence that "should be" (or "should have been") captured by the other party. In accord with this logic, when a party makes electoral gains, it will, on average, pick up districts that are ideologically less extreme than the ones the party already holds (cf. Brunell, Grofman, and Merrill, 2016a).[8] However, if there is a time trend involving change within one party—say, with new Republicans moving on average to the right of those they replace, and even Republican incumbents trending in a rightward direction—then these assumptions are violated, and we may get the Polsby Paradox applying to only one party.

---

[8] Note, too, that the Polsby Paradox also applies if we consider means rather than medians. Under the assumptions we are using, the party medians and the party means should always be moving in the same direction. If there are Democratic gains, then both the Republicans and Democrats move in the same direction, to the right. If there are Republican gains, then both the Republicans and Democrats move to the left.

54   WHERE DID POLARIZATION COME FROM?

A quick way to check the expectations of the Polsby Paradox is to look at the correlation between the Congress-to-succeeding-Congress changes in the Democratic Party median and in the Republican Party median. According to the logic of the Polsby Paradox, this correlation should be positive. In fact, we find that for the period 1956–2010 the correlation is 0.59. However, there are some differences in the various periods, especially between the period 1945–1976, where the correlation is −0.95, and the period 1978–2010, where the correlation is 0.84. These differences between the two periods reflects the postwar period, in which the parties had significant ideological overlap and many of the more conservative Democrats were in safe seats in the South.

Because of the current asymmetry between the Democratic and Republican parties in having "moderate" incumbents whose seats might change hands, and because there is a long-term time trend in which Republicans, both new and old, are moving in a more conservative direction (see Mann and Ornstein, 2012), the Polsby Paradox is now visible only for Democrats. For Republicans, the long-term time trend swamps replacement effects. This phenomenon is what Mann and Ornstein label *asymmetric polarization*.

To demonstrate this fact, for each of the parties separately we provide a regression of Congress-to-Congress change in that party's DW-NOMINATE scores on Congress-to-Congress change in that party's seat share, along with a year variable to capture time trend. Table 3.1 reports the results for four subperiods of the entire period we are investigating: for 1864–1944, for 1946–1976, for 1978–1992, and for 1994–2010. Table 3.1 indicates that the Polsby Paradox fits the Democratic Party quite well, though it does not describe the ideological location of the party median for the GOP that well at all.[9] As the Democrats grow in number, they become more moderate; when they lose seats, they become more liberal. The Republicans follow a less distinct pattern; indeed, over the decades since 1974, the Republican median has trended more and more conservative regardless of whether the GOP gains or loses seats.

Another way to get a handle on the evidence for the Paradox is to look at years that produced large changes in the partisan complexion of Congress.

---

[9] We also examined the relationship between party delegation size and party ideological medians for state legislative chambers. The results mimic those for the US House: When the Democrats increase their seat share, their party median moves to the right. For the Republicans, as they increase their seat share, their party median either does not move much or moves to the right.

WHY CANDIDATE POSITIONS ARE SO DIFFERENT?   55

Table 3.1. Regression of Congress-to-Congress Change in a Party's DW-NOMINATE Scores on Congress-to-Congress Change in That Party's Seat Share, Along with Year Variable to Capture Time Trend: for 1864–1944, 1946–1976, 1978–1992, and 1994–2010

	1864–1944	1946–1976	1978–1992	1994–2010
Democrat Seat Difference	.0005*** (.0001)	−.0004* (.00016)	.0001 (.0001)	.0007*** (.00001)
Constant	.0029 (.005)	−.0087 (.005)	−.0027 (.002)	−.0019 (.0017)
Republican Seat Difference	−.00005 (.00005)	−.00006 (.00005)	−.00006 (.0003)	.00001 (.0001)
Constant	−.0017 (.0024)	−.0053* (.0018)	.0245*** (.004)	.0295*** (.0044)
N	44	16	8	9

Note: (*) denotes significance at the 0.05 level; (**), at the 0.01 level; and (***), at the 0.001 level.

Table 3.2. Democratic and Republican Gains in the US House in "Big-Shift" Years, Stratified by Moderates and Non-Moderates

			Democratic Gains			Republican Gains	
Congress	Election Year	House	Moderates: DW > −0.25	Liberals: DW < −0.25	House	Moderates: DW < 0.25	Conservatives: DW > 0.25
104	1994	−54	−41	−13	54	−7	61
110	2006	31	16	15	−30	−1	−29
111	2008	24	18	6	−24	0	−24
112	2010	−63	−48	−15	62	0	62

Note: "DW" specifies DW-NOMINATE score.

Table 3.2 depicts this phenomenon in the US House for recent "big shift" years. In the 1994 election, the Democrats lost nearly half (41 out of 88) of their moderates (DW-NOMINATE score > −0.25) but less than 10 percent (13 out of 170) of their nonmoderates. Similarly, in 2010 Democrats lost nearly 70 percent (48 out of 71) of their moderates, but again less than 10 percent (15 out of 186) of their nonmoderates. As a consequence of this disparate loss of moderates in 1994, the Democratic median shifted from −0.33 in the 103rd Congress to −0.38 in the 104th Congress, while the Republican median shifted from 0.40 to 0.46 between the same two Congresses. Here the Democratic shift was in the predicted direction (i.e., more liberal), while the GOP became more conservative after the large seat gain. Between 2008 and 2010 the Democratic median shifted from −0.347 to −0.398, while the Republican median shifted from 0.657 to 0.671. Here again, the Democrats shifted in the predicted direction, but the Republicans, despite picking up many "moderate" seats, became more conservative after the large seat gain. Turning now to years of Republican loss: In the elections of 2006 and 2008, Republicans lost a total of 54 seats, only one of which was classified as a moderate (DW-NOMINATE score < 0.25). As a consequence, between 2004 and 2008 the Republican median shifted from 0.581 to 0.657, while the Democratic median shifted from −0.382 to −0.347. So both parties in this case moved in the expected conservative direction.

3.4. Discussion: Implications of the Theoretical and Empirical Findings

We have shown that, even in the absence of the considerations that most previous theorists have advanced to explain candidate divergence (the desire to appeal to special-interest groups and party activists, the need to win primary elections, and so on), office-seeking candidates have incentives to diverge sharply from the center of the general electorate. Our theoretical and computational results, which suggest that candidates can, under realistic conditions, maximize their vote margins in general elections by presenting policies designed to appeal to their partisan constituencies, is relevant to the extensive literature on elections and representation.

The value of our theoretical results is that they provide a plausible rationale for the empirical findings in section 3.1 that legislators tend to represent their core supporters at the expense of their geographic constituency: namely, that this is an electorally optimal strategy. Thus, the analyses in this chapter lead to three primary conclusions:

Conclusion 3.1. Empirically, winning Congressional candidates of the two parties from ideologically comparable districts tend to be at least as ideologically divergent in competitive districts as in noncompetitive ones.

WHY CANDIDATE POSITIONS ARE SO DIFFERENT? 57

Conclusion 3.2. A spatial model, accounting for party loyalty and the threat of abstention, implies that positions similar to those observed in Conclusion 3.1 constitute optimal strategies for office-seeking candidates.

Conclusion 3.3. When a party wins more seats in Congress, the overall median moves in the expected direction (left for Democrats and right for Republicans), but the party median of the winning party typically moves in the opposite direction (rightward for Democrats and leftward for Republicans).

Our emphasis on the centrifugal effects on candidate strategies associated with voter turnout in a partisan electorate is one that is increasingly shared, both by the popular media and by campaign managers (see Miniter, 2005; Nagourney, 2003; Milbank and Allen, 2004). Thus, Matthew Dowd, a senior adviser to George W. Bush's reelection campaign, stated in the summer of 2003 that "there's a realization, having looked at the past few elections, that the party that motivates their base—that makes their base emotional and turn out—has a much higher likelihood of success on election day" (quoted in Nagourney, 2003).[10] More recently, when President Trump was asked about reaching out to swing voters for his 2020 reelection bid, he remarked "I think my base is so strong, I'm not sure I have to do that" (Bennett, 2019). And Stanley Greenberg, a Democratic pollster who advised the presidential candidates Bill Clinton, Al Gore, and John Kerry, argues (Greenberg, 2005, 91–92) that, in order to win elections,

> The starting point for both Democrats and Republicans is to make sure that they take into battle the core of loyalists that this era has bequeathed them. But since neither party's core support or base is big enough to assure victory, each struggles valiantly to make more of it—in the first instance, by growing the groups that are the most loyal, by fanning the passions on each party's lead issues to achieve even greater unity in their voting and more energy and greater turnout at the polls.

The empirical and theoretical results we have presented are exactly in tune with the arguments advanced by the political professionals quoted above. By shifting their policies away from the median voter's position in the direction of their partisan constituency's policy preferences, candidates increase the

---

[10] This remark is also quoted in Peress (2008).

58 WHERE DID POLARIZATION COME FROM?

unity in their partisan ranks, as Greenberg emphasizes, but simultaneously energize their base to turn out to vote, as both Dowd and Greenberg emphasize. The importance of our theoretical arguments is that they illuminate why the turnout gains that candidates obtain from targeting their base are likely to outweigh the vote losses among moderate voters that noncentrist positioning would seem to entail. In particular, in a partisan electorate, voters' candidate preferences are rarely in doubt. Since moderate Democratic and Republican partisans will support their party's candidate at high rates even when these candidates propose radical positions, candidates have leeway to shift away from the center, in order to boost turnout among their habitual supporters.

Thus, we have shown that the strategic logic of candidate positioning in a partisan electorate with variable turnout is dramatically different from the strategic logic that obtains when we disregard voters' partisan loyalties (cf. Hinich and Ordeshook, 1970). And, most importantly, we have been able to account for a seemingly counterintuitive but empirically observed phenomenon. The finding is that, even though candidates of both parties adjust their politics slightly away from national party positions to more closely fit the ideological distribution in the district being contested, in closely competitive districts Republican and Democratic candidates in such districts remain at least as far apart as they are in highly homogeneous districts that tend to be safe for the candidates of one party or the other. We will expand on these results in Chapters 4 and 5, in which we will account specifically for how ideological heterogeneity among districts, voter loyalty, and the role of activists reinforce polarization. In the latter chapter we will introduce the notion of the Downsian ceiling, which helps us account for elections in which polarization is so severe as to make appealing to one's base preferable as a vote-maximizing strategy to appealing to the median voter in the constituency.

4

Heterogeneity across Districts and within-District Partisan Gap and Proclivity

4.1. Introduction

In this chapter, we address the question of the relative contribution of structural factors to the development of polarization. Specifically, we will specify the level of polarization in the US House of Representatives as an explicit function of three factors: (1) heterogeneity across districts (the ideological heterogeneity of district median voters), (2) district-specific partisan gap (the distance between candidates of different parties in the same or ideologically comparable districts), and (3) partisan proclivity (partisan tendency in choosing between candidates ideologically equidistant from the median voter). The second of these factors, district-specific partisan gap is keyed to the constraints of national parties and activists (as outlined in Chapter 2) and related to party loyalty and the threat of abstention (as previously analyzed in Chapter 3).

The key empirical finding, reinforced by two alternative methods of calculation, is that, while changes in each factor have contributed significantly to the extremely high-level polarization of the present-day US House, more than 80 percent of the polarization as well as about 70 percent of the growth in that polarization from the late 1950s through 2020 can be attributed to a dramatic increase in the second of these factors: the partisan gap at the district level. The model on which these empirical results are based is taken from Brunell, Grofman, and Merrill (2016b); the empirical results have been updated through the 117th Congress (elected in 2020 and serving during 2021 and 2022), so the dataset now covers House members serving during the period 1957—2022.[1] Now, six decades after Downs (1957), the most

---

[1] Data source: https://voteview.com/data (accessed Feb. 20, 2022).

How Polarization Begets Polarization. Samuel Merrill III, Bernard Grofman, and Thomas L. Brunell,
Oxford University Press. © Oxford University Press 2024. DOI: 10.1093/oso/9780197745229.003.0004

60   WHERE DID POLARIZATION COME FROM?

plausible theoretical models strongly suggest that, in two-candidate contests, we should expect some degree of divergence from the median voter's ideological location.[2] We have argued this case quite explicitly. First, in Chapter 2, we showed theoretically that polarization in the House can be generated by party discipline focused on candidates competing in district elections, and that the level of that polarization can be enhanced with increased party discipline. Second, in Chapter 3, we concluded both empirically and theoretically that, given party loyalty and the threat of abstention due to alienation, the optimal strategies of partisan candidates are not only quite separate but are at least as separate in competitive districts as in lopsided ones. In particular, we have provided extensive empirical evidence that this has been the case in US elections for House members for more than half a century.

In US House races, not only do candidates diverge from the position of the median voter in each district, but, as we have seen in Chapter 2, the magnitude of the differentiation varies over time and is influenced by national party expectations. In that chapter we cited the findings of Ansolabehere, Snyder, and Stewart (2001, 136) that over the period 1874–1996 Congressional candidates mostly followed national rather than local party ideology, except from the 1940s to the 1970s, when national pressures lessened and candidates became more responsive to district interests. As we saw in Figure 1.1A, one extreme of party differentiation occurred around 1900; this differentiation then diminished in size to the point that the two parties were most nearly convergent a little past the mid–20th century, the period identified by Ansolabehere et al. as most district-responsive. Today, during a period of often oppressive national party discipline, we once again have extreme polarization, at a level not seen since the end of the 19th century. Indeed, ideological polarization and accompanying partisan enmity are arguably the driving forces of the past several decades of US electoral history. In Chapter 3 we argued that within each district the highly divergent ideological positions of the two major-party candidates may be electorally optimal, as a consequence of party loyalty and the threat of abstention.

Why might we expect changes in polarization in the US Congress over time? McCarty et al. (2006, 5–10) note that polarization in the Congress has correlated closely with increased income inequality and immigration. Fiorina et al. (2005), however, emphasize that recent increases in legislative

---

[2] See, e.g., Aldrich, 1983; Aldrich and McGinnis, 1989; Adams, Merrill, and Grofman, 2005; also empirical work on the United States in, e.g., Poole and Rosenthal, 1984; Bafumi and Herron, 2010.

PARTISAN DIVERGENCE WITHIN AND AMONG DISTRICTS   61

polarization can be linked to the ideological sorting of partisans in the electorate generated both by geographic mobility and by changes in the regional bases of the parties. They argue that explaining polarization does not require us to posit a growing policy extremism on the part of voters. Theriault (2008) agrees that polarization in Congress is in part due to geographical sorting of the electorate, but argues that there are also important changes at the elite level, such as instititional and procedural changes in Congress that enhance the capacity of party leaders to motivate party members via incentives such as campaign financing and committee assignments. Lebo et al. (2007) and Koger and Lebo (2012) emphasize reciprocal strategic calculations by party leaders and officeholders on both sides of the aisle in scheduling votes in which members from vulnerable districts must balance the need to pass or block legislation calculated to improve their party's image against concerns about their own reelectability.

Buchler (2018) notes that, in the presence of polarization, many conservative Republican (and liberal Democratic) members of Congress (MCs) are faced with a collective-action problem that arises because their sincere preferences are very conservative (in the Democrats' case, very liberal), whereas moderation might help their reelection prospects if their districts are not so extreme. These legislators can solve this collective-action problem if they empower their party leadership to discipline nearly all of their party's MCs to vote the (extreme) party line. Although this might result in some electoral loss, it can be minimized by letting leadership allow a few MCs in truly competitive districts to vote with their district on specific bills, and perhaps by gerrymandering to reduce the number of such competitive districts. Thus, roll-call voting in practice may largely follow party lines.

4.2. A 3-Factor Decomposition of Legislative Polarization

In this section we will attempt to tease out and quantify the links between electoral polarization at the district level and legislative polarization at the Congressional level. In Chapter 2, we developed a model that relates legislative polarization with constraints on district candidates' ability to locate at ideological positions far from the national party stance as perceived by voters and at odds with positions taken by activists involved in the candidate-selection process. This model suggests that divergence between the mean Democratic and Republican locations in Congress, as well as intraparty

62 WHERE DID POLARIZATION COME FROM?

homogeneity of a party delegation, go hand in hand with the tightness of any tether that compels district candidates to adopt the stance of their national party. In this chapter we focus on the separation aspect of legislative polarization; in Chapter 6 we will also consider intraparty variation.

As before, we will use, as a measure of the degree of legislative polarization, the *legislative gap*—that is, the difference between the mean (ideological) locations of the Republican and Democratic delegations in the legislature. Our aim is to specify this quantity as an explicit function of three components:

(1) *district heterogeneity*: the standard deviation over districts of the ideological locations of median voters
(2) *district-specific partisan gap*: the (mean) ideological difference between the candidates of the two parties in each district or in ideologically comparable districts
(3) *partisan proclivity*: the likelihood that a constituency with a given median will, *ceteris paribus*, elect a Republican rather than a Democrat (or vice versa) even if both candidates are ideologically equidistant from the median voter in the district

We will present results for a model in which (a) the distribution of ideological medians across districts is symmetrically distributed, and (b) the partisan proclivity function is linear and is similar for both parties. We state our result in Proposition 4.1:

> **Proposition 4.1.** Under the assumptions above, the legislative gap is a nonlinear function which is proportional to the sum of two quantities: namely, the district-specific partisan gap, and the product of the partisan proclivity and the *square* of the district heterogeneity.
>
> **Proof.** See this chapter's Appendix (section A4.1) for the full analytic statement of the proposition and reference to the proof.

Thus, under the conditions given above, Proposition 4.1 shows that the legislative gap increases with district heterogeneity, with district-level partisan gap, and with partisan proclivity. In particular, the legislative gap has an additive component equal to the district-specific partisan gap. Furthermore, the remaining component of the polarization gap in the legislature is proportional to the mean partisan proclivity (for a fixed distribution of district medians) and proportional to the *square* of the standard deviation of the distribution of district medians (for a fixed partisan proclivity function). In particular, the effect of squared district heterogeneity on polarization in the House is further multiplied by the partisan proclivity.

Accordingly, aside from the effect of the district-specific partisan gap, when the standard deviation of the district-median distribution doubles, the remaining component of the partisan gap in the legislature increases by a factor of four. As voters become more ideologically sorted along geographical lines, constituencies of MCs become more ideologically divergent from one another. Because of the effect of the squared standard deviation, Proposition 4.1 suggests that increased district ideological heterogeneity can have a strong (more than linear) effect on partisan polarization in the legislature.

4.3. Measuring the Three Factors Identified in Proposition 4.1 That Affect the Legislative Gap

We now present empirical measures for the three factors that we have identified as the foundational factors affecting the level of legislative polarization.

4.3.1. *District heterogeneity*

Our approximation to district heterogeneity is the standard deviation of normalized, two-party presidential vote shares across Congressional districts.[3] Because the relevant factor in Proposition 4.1 is the *squared* standard deviation, estimates for the squared standard deviation (variance) of the district medians are provided in Table 4.1 (in column 2), for the full period 1956–2020 and for each of seven subperiods. Note that the squared standard deviation of the district medians more than doubles from 141 in

---

[3] The presidential vote share in each district is normalized by subtracting the national presidential vote share. Note that proxying district medians by normalized presidential vote share reverses the direction of the scale, because a median voter on the left corresponds to a high Democratic presidential vote share. If the district voter distribution is uniform on an interval of unit length, the district median is exactly the Republican proportion of the vote.

Table 4.1. Empirical Estimates for Model Factors: 1956–2020

Era	Variance of District Medians	District-Specific Partisan gap: d	Mean Partisan Proclivity	Legislative Gap: Estimate from Proposition 4.1	District Partisanship	Legislative Gap: Estimate from Regression
(1)	(2)	(3)	(4)	(5)	(6)	(7)
1956–2014	178	28.8	0.538	31.9	6.2	35.0
1956–1964	141	24.9	0.448	26.1	2.6	27.5
1966–1974	143	24.8	0.341	26.3	3.6	28.3
1976–1984	134	26.0	0.461	28.0	4.5	30.5
1986–1994	147	28.3	0.490	31.0	5.9	34.2
1996–2004	197	32.4	0.642	36.2	7.1	39.5
2006–2014	235	33.5	0.779	39.2	8.7	42.2
2016–2020	295	36.3	0.837	41.9	7.7	44.0

Notes: A 100-point scale is used for m; regression terms have been multiplied by 50 to convert from the 2-point DW-NOMINATE scale to the 100-point scale. The estimate for the legislative gap from Proposition 4.1 (column 5) is computed from equation (A4.2): *Legislative gap* $= 0.08 \times (\text{mean partisan proclivity}) \times w\sigma_M^2 + d$, specified in section A4.1 of this chapter's appendix. The estimate from regression for the legislative gap (column 7) is computed from equation (A4.5): $\bar{y}_R - \bar{y}_D = (a_R - a_D) + b(\bar{x}_R - \bar{x}_D)$, given in section A4.4.

PARTISAN DIVERGENCE WITHIN AND AMONG DISTRICTS   65

1956–1964 to 295 in 2016–2020; that is, the partisan heterogeneity among Congressional districts has become much more pronounced.

4.3.2. District-specific partisan gap

Our second factor is the ideological difference between Republicans and Democrats elected from the same or ideologically comparable constituencies. The gap between a Democrat and a Republican from similar districts is dramatically highlighted when an MC of one party is replaced by an MC of the opposite party in the *same* district. Focusing on Democrats who were replaced by Republicans, and vice versa, in the following Congress over the period 1982 to 2004, Brunell et al. (2016a) find that the mean change in DW-NOMINATE scores for the 103 Democrats replaced by Republicans was 0.671 (on a scale with a range of 2.0) and the mean change for the 54 Republicans replaced by Democrats was –0.669. Thus, the average change in districts with partisan replacement during this period was approximately one third of the entire width of the scale.

To estimate in general the gap between Democratic and Republican winners in comparable districts, we first regress, separately for the winners of each party, the first dimension of DW-NOMINATE scores against the two-party presidential vote share, for the full period and by subperiod (see, e.g., Hussey and Zaller, 2011). The results suggest that an assumption of common slopes for the two parties is plausible; under this assumption, the *difference between the regression intercepts* for the two parties is used as a measure of the district-specific partisan gap. Figure A4.1 (see appendix) shows this data for the full period and by subperiod, together with separate regression lines for each party under the assumption of common slopes for both parties. See section A4.2 and Table A4.1 for estimation of the underlying regression parameters, including a rationale for our assumption of common slopes for the parties.

Our estimates for the district-specific partisan gap are given in column 3 of Table 4.1, for the full period 1956–2020 and for each of seven subperiods (see section A4.2 of this chapter's appendix for details). What is striking here is that the estimate for the district-specific partisan gap (on a 100-point scale) increases from 24.9 in 1956–64 to 36.3 in 2016–2020, nearly a 50 percent increase over the period of our study.

66 WHERE DID POLARIZATION COME FROM?

Note that the estimates of district-specific partisan gap reported in Table 4.1 are comparable to our earlier estimates based only on districts in which an MC was replaced by a member of the opposite party. This can be seen by comparing the partisan gap in Table 4.1 for the periods 1986–1994 (31.0) and 1996–2004 (36.2) with the earlier estimate based on partisan replacement alone for the period 1982–2004 (about 33.5 when the 2-point DW-NOMINATE scale is converted to the 100-point scale). This observation provides confirmation that the estimates obtained from using presidential vote shares as a proxy for district medians are plausible.

4.3.3. Partisan proclivity

Partisan proclivity is the likelihood that a constituency with given median voter ideological location would elect, say, a Republican, given that the two candidates are on opposite sides of and equidistant from that median. We estimate *mean partisan proclivity* as the average deviation of the probability from 0.5 (representing equal party probabilities) that a party wins in a district if each party offers either identical policy platforms at the location of the median voter or platforms at equal distance to the left and right of that median.[4]

Using equation (4.1) to calculate the value of mean partisan proclivity, we show in Table 4.1, column 4, the estimates of the mean partisan proclivity for the elections from 1956 to 2020. As expected, what we find is increasing partisan proclivity over time, particularly in the most recent years of the study, with the most recent subperiod reflecting a more than 80 percent increase over that of the earliest period. That is to say, it becomes more and

---

[4] Analytically, *mean partisan proclivity* is defined as $\dfrac{2}{100} \int\limits_0^{100} |P_R(m) - 0.5| \, dm$, where $P_R(m)$ is the probability (for the Republicans) that that party wins in a district with median voter at m (and similarly, for Democrats). This quantity is estimated from the data by first partitioning the districts in each election into 20 five-percentage-point bins according to the normalized presidential vote. For the ith bin, aggregated for each 10-year period and separately for the entire period of study, we determine the number n_i of districts and the proportion $P_R(i)$ electing a Republican. For each time period, the deviation of this proportion from 0.5 is averaged over districts and used to estimate the *mean partisan proclivity* (see Brunell et al., 2016b, for further details). Thus, the estimate for *mean partisan proclivity* is

$$\left(\frac{2}{\sum_i n_i} \right) \sum_i \left(n_i |P_R(i) - 0.5| \right). \tag{4.1}$$

PARTISAN DIVERGENCE WITHIN AND AMONG DISTRICTS   67

more predictable which districts will be won by Democrats and which by Republicans. Though this reinforces the trend we earlier noted of an increased heterogeneity among the districts, it is a distinct phenomenon, since we can, in principle, observe a rise in ideological differentiation of the districts without that being reflected in a rise in *constituency-specific* partisan proclivity.

4.4. The Relative Importance of the Three Factors on Legislative Polarization since the 1950s

Proposition 4.1 provides a decomposition formula (the explicit form is given in equation A4.2 in section A4.1 in this chapter's appendix) for legislative polarization under the assumption that the partisan proclivity function is linear. Using estimates from this formula in Table 4.1, the estimated values of the legislative gap are presented in column 5 of Table 4.1. This formula estimates an increase of at least 60 percent in the legislative gap, from 26.1 in 1956–1964 to 41.9 in 2016–2020.[5]

Overall, our calculations suggest that, for the full period, 90 percent of the legislative gap is due to the district-specific partisan gap.[6] Similarly, for the subperiods, the percent of the legislative gap due to district-specific partisan gap ranges from 95 percent (for 1956–1964) to 85 percent (for 2006–2014). Thus, at this stage of the analysis, one of our key findings appears to be that by far the largest component of the gap between the partisan delegations is due to the ideological distance between MCs representing districts with similar ideology—that is, due to party. A much smaller component is due to differences in district ideology and partisan proclivity. Furthermore, as we can see by comparing the estimates in Table 4.1 for 1956–1864 and 2016–2020, the *growth* between these two periods that is due to the district-specific partisan gap (11.4) is 72 percent of the *growth* between the same two periods in the partisan gap in the House (15.8).

---

[5] The lower estimates of growth in polarization for several statistics reported in this book relative to those given in Brunell et al. (2016b) are primarily due to the use of the static DW-NOMINATE scores in this book in contrast to the dynamic scores used in our earlier work. See section A3.1 in the Appendix for a discussion of this issue.

[6] The ratio d/*legislative gap* = 28.8/31.9 = 0.90, or 90 percent, where d is the district-specific partisan gap.

68   WHERE DID POLARIZATION COME FROM?

4.5. Alternative 2-Factor Decomposition of Legislative Polarization

The observations above about the proportion of legislative polarization explained by the district-specific partisan gap depend on the accuracy of our estimates for the remaining two explanatory factors: namely, the variation of district medians, and the mean partisan proclivity. As we have seen, these estimates are compromised by the empirical fact that presidential vote shares are an imperfect proxy for the ideological location of the median voter. Furthermore, any nonlinearity of the partisan proclivity function $P_R(m)$ may alter the effects of the partisan proclivity on legislative polarization, in part because the linear form for the partisan proclivity function likely underestimates its true deviation from 0.5. In particular, as we have just seen, use of the formula in Proposition 4.1 may underestimate legislative polarization due to district heterogeneity and partisan proclivity when the district-median distribution is asymmetric. As a robustness check to address these concerns, we turn to an alternative decomposition, which depends entirely on regression of DW-NOMINATE scores but does not separate the effects of district heterogeneity and partisan proclivity.

We show that legislative polarization can empirically be decomposed into (1) district-specific partisan gap and (2) a second factor that, following Hussey and Zaller (2011), we will call *district partisanship* (not to be confused with district-specific partisan gap, defined earlier), which reflects both district heterogeneity and partisan proclivity. We then assess the relative impact of each factor in this alternative, 2-factor decomposition. Finally, we will compare the estimates of the legislative gap from the alternative decomposition with that implied by Proposition 4.1, a decomposition that in part employs different data. The details are in section A4.4 of this chapter's appendix.

The values from this alternative analysis are given in Table 4.1 (columns 6 and 7) for the full period 1956–2020 and for each subperiod. Note that, under this alternative approach, district partisanship nearly tripled its value while the district-specific partisan gap gained nearly 50 percent over the period of the study, so that the alternative estimate of legislative gap increased significantly (69 percent).

According to this alternative estimate of legislative polarization, the district-specific partisan gap accounts for 82 percent of legislative polarization, similar to but a bit lower than the estimate from the 3-factor

PARTISAN DIVERGENCE WITHIN AND AMONG DISTRICTS   69

decomposition above. Both estimates indicate that the lion's share of legislative polarization in the legislature can be traced to district-specific partisan gap.

We note that both formulas for the legislative gap use the same calculation for the district-specific partisan gap (and the weighting factor). But for the remainder of the calculation, the alternative decomposition uses DW-NOMINATE scores, whereas Proposition 4.1 does not. Because the 2-factor, alternative decomposition, assesses the proportion of the legislative gap explained by party using only regression from the data and does not depend on estimating district heterogeneity and partisan proclivity per se, the fact that the two estimates (one from the 3-factor model and one from the 2-factor model) are roughly similar reinforces confidence in the numerical results.

Likewise, as we can see by comparing the estimates from the 2-factor model (in column 7 of Table 4.1) for 1956–64 and 2016–20, the *growth* between these two periods that is due to district-specific partisan gap (11.4) is 69 percent of the *growth* between the same two periods in the legislative gap in the House (16.5).

4.6. Discussion

We have measured changes in each of the three factors that determine the legislative gap over the period 1956–2020 to see how each has contributed to the increased polarization over this period. What we find is that the striking increase in legislative polarization during the last half century is due not to a single factor but rather to a combination of all three of the factors identified in this study: namely, a growth in the heterogeneity between districts; an increasing divergence between the positions taken by winning candidates of opposite parties in ideologically comparable districts; and an increase in the likelihood that more conservative and more liberal districts will be safe for one party.

Consistent, however, with the findings of McCarty et al. (2009), by far the most important of these factors is the district-specific partisan gap, that is the ideological difference between House members of different parties from the same or similar districts. In our estimates of electoral effects, we attribute to this single factor over 80 percent of the legislative gap in the US House as well as about 70 percent of the *change* in this gap over the last 60 or so years.

70 WHERE DID POLARIZATION COME FROM?

General agreement between the estimates from two methodologies—which in part use different data—to estimate the proportion of the legislative gap explained by party lends further credence to the estimates.

The analyses, thus, lead to three primary conclusions:

Conclusion 4.1. The partisan gap inherent in legislative polarization can be specified as an explicit function of three factors: (1) ideological heterogeneity among districts, (2) divergence between candidates of different parties in the same or ideologically comparable districts, and (3) district-specific partisan proclivity in choosing between candidates ideologically equidistant from the median voter.

Conclusion 4.2. While changes in each factor have contributed to the extremely high level of present-day polarization in the US House of Representatives, about 70 percent of the growth in that polarization from the late 1950s through 2020 can be attributed to a significant increase in the second of these factors: party divergence at the district level.

Conclusion 4.3. Furthermore, under the assumptions of Proposition 4.1, the remaining component of this polarization is proportional to the *square* of the variation in district ideology, a quantity that is further multiplied by the partisan proclivity of the district. Both district heterogeneity and partisan proclivity have increased dramatically over the period of our study.

In this chapter we have treated the three factors as independent of one another, and we believe that this is a plausible approximation to reality vis-à-vis the relation of the first of our factors to the other two. Ideological sorting of voters into districts may well occur regardless of the degree of the district-specific partisan gap at either the district or the legislative level. However, the other two factors are almost certainly interrelated.

The distance between the platform a candidate offers and the preferences of the median voter in her/his constituency is constrained by national party positions, given a lack of credibility granted by voters to party candidates who claim to locate themselves far from the national party position. This distance is also constrained by the reluctance of party voters and activists to nominate candidates too far from the national position (see Chapter 2 and Winer et al., 2014), especially insofar as the national parties have already taken polarized positions.

When we consider Tea Party- or Trump-endorsed challenges to Republican incumbents, we can see direct examples of the difficulty facing candidates who seek to moderate their position away from the national party position so as to move closer to their own district's median. Even when such challenges are not successful, they may motivate candidates to move closer to the party's ideological line, lest they continue to face such costly challenges in the future. On the other hand, given generous "wiggle room" at the constituency level for a candidate to credibly espouse a position with a reasonable chance to attract the median voter in the district, then the party delegations in the legislature will not be far apart. This follows because most constituencies will be competitive for both parties, and thus the set of constituencies won by each party will be representative of a broader range of ideological locations. In Chapter 5, we will turn to the interactions with legislative polarization of voter loyalty, the role of activists, and polarization in the electorate.

PART II

CONSEQUENCES OF POLARIZATION

5

How Do Party Loyalty and Activists Encourage Mobilizing the Base?

5.1. Introduction

It seems clear that in the 2020 election President Trump pursued a strategy of mobilizing his base by taking extreme policy stances and demonizing his opponent, an approach that was intended to appeal to his base supporters and motivate them to vote. Indeed, in June 2019 President Trump (quoted in Hopkins, 2020) proclaimed explicitly that he thought he could win in 2020 solely by mobilizing his base. Many Republican House members are now following his approach and policy stands in order to appeal to his base.

But doesn't an extreme policy stance undermine electability? Studying the period 1956–1996, Canes-Wrone, Brady, and Cogan (2002) found that House candidates suffered by voting with their party rather than with their district. Utych (2020), however, used Bonica's (2014a) CFscores (which apply artificial intelligence methods to data about the sources of campaign contributions) to represent ideology for the period 1980–2012. He finds that, whereas moderates have historically enjoyed a large advantage over extreme candidates in House elections, this gap has disappeared in recent years, with the two groups now about equally likely to be elected. It appears that candidates in partisan contests in the United States now are often more concerned than they used to be about motivating high turnout levels among their key supporters (their partisan base) and creating excitement among activists (and donors) by taking relatively extreme positions, among other methods. Such a strategy contrasts with that of tailoring a platform to the views of the median voter in the constituency (Bartels, 2016).

But why? Has a change occurred to make it an optimizing strategy to focus on turnout and activation rather than on Downsian appeals to the pivotal voter? The answer we give is a simple one. As polarization between the party bases grows, we argue that so too does the value of making turnout

---

How Polarization Begets Polarization. Samuel Merrill III, Bernard Grofman, and Thomas L. Brunell,
Oxford University Press. © Oxford University Press 2024. DOI: 10.1093/oso/9780197745229.003.0005

76 CONSEQUENCES OF POLARIZATION

rather than policy moderation the linchpin of victory, even in (or perhaps even especially in) highly competitive districts. We formalize this intuition in terms of a simple neo-Downsian model. Under this model, parties may be motivated not to converge as in the usual Downsian setting but rather to diverge to positions closer to the median voter of their respective bases than to the overall median.

In Chapter 2 we presented a model in which strict national party discipline limits district candidates to divergent platforms, leading to the election of relatively extreme district candidates. These new legislators reinforce the extremity of their parties' Congressional delegations, and the cycle continues. Here we suggest a further set of dynamic and interlocked effects of polarization that will operate to reinforce the way in which polarization begets more polarization.

In this chapter, we also highlight two key consequences of party polarization in Congress: Polarization is likely both to increase partisan loyalties and to enhance the power of activists within the party. And, just as we posited a feedback loop between legislative polarization and party-platform differentiation at the district level, so too there are feedback loops between legislative polarization, party loyalty, and the role of activists; thus, once again, polarization breeds polarization. As polarization between the parties increases party loyalty, voters' partisan loyalties in turn influence the strategic choices made by parties. And again continuing the feedback loop, the strategic choices of parties affect voter attitudes. And so it continues.

We argue below that, when party polarization grows, voters with more extreme ideological positions are more likely to exhibit greater intensity about the election outcome than voters with more moderate views. Thus, the importance of activist views within each party should increase. One possible mechanism is that, as polarization grows, the willingness of extreme voters to commit funds and other forms of campaign resources increases relative to that of more moderate voters. Another mechanism is that activists seek to veto candidates who depart too far from the party position, and may mount successful challenges to incumbents in primaries; the threat of such primary challenges thus becomes a good reason for incumbents to toe the party line.

These two effects—increased party loyalty and enhanced action by extreme voters to bring about their desired election outcome—combine to encourage candidates to emphasize increased turnout of their own supporters as polarization increases. That is because, on the one hand, increased party loyalty means that making inroads into the other party's support base becomes more difficult; and, on the other hand, the increased importance of party activists makes it harder for parties to pull back from more extreme positions and appeal to more moderate voters. Thus, rather than extremism leading to at least one of the parties moderating its views to be more competitive, as we might expect from a purely Downsian perspective, it becomes very difficult—although still possible—for either party to deviate from appealing primarily to extremists.

In fact, in the presence of sufficient polarization between the party bases, we will show that party loyalty and the threat of abstention alone are sufficient to motivate optimal party strategies that diverge toward the median of their respective bases, a divergence that is further enhanced by the influence of activists.[1] In 2016 Donald Trump, once he won the Republican nomination, exploited party loyalty to maintain the support of most Republicans while he pursued an unconventional outsider and populist campaign that in many ways ran counter to traditional Republican tenets.

In this chapter, we make both theoretical and empirical arguments. The theoretical sections 5.2–5.4 are the heart of the chapter.[2] In section 5.2 we address the first two of three hypotheses showing why party loyalty should increase as the parties become more polarized, and why this polarization strengthens the expected influence of party activists within the party. In section 5.3 we introduce a third hypothesis and show under what conditions and why, as polarization between the party bases increases, party loyalty, along with the threat of abstention due to alienation, should lead parties and their candidates to prioritize mobilizing their base over persuading swing voters. We argue further that this effect should be enhanced by the increased influence of party activists. Section 5.4 summarizes the results from these three hypotheses, and section 5.5 presents empirical evidence that bears on the three theoretical propositions.

---

[1] Note that we are making a distinction between polarization between party positions (as in Congress) and polarization between party bases (in the electorate). There is general agreement that party bases in the electorate have become substantially more polarized in recent decades, regardless of whether that has been caused by ideological change by individual voters or by voters sorting into parties along ideological lines.

[2] This development parallels that in Merrill, Grofman, and Brunell (2022).

78 CONSEQUENCES OF POLARIZATION

5.2. Modeling the Effects of Polarization on Party Loyalty and the Importance of Party Activists

5.2.1. Party loyalty and the strength of partisan identification

We indicated in the introduction two reasons why increased polarization between the parties in Congress should be expected to lead to greater strategic emphasis on mobilizing the base rather than appealing to the middle. The first is the expectation that growing polarization increases party loyalty among those who remain within a party; the second is the expectation that growing polarization increases the importance of party activists within the party. Our first hypothesis addresses the first of these expectations.

> **Theoretical Hypothesis 1: As polarization within Congress grows, *ceteris paribus*, party loyalty and the strength of partisan identification as a predictor of voting also increase.**

Why should party polarization in Congress increase party loyalty? In the usual one-dimensional spatial model, note that the voter's perceived difference in utility between the two candidates (that is, degree of preference) is a function of that voter's own position and the ideological location of the two parties. We assume that a voter weights movement away from herself by ideologically distant candidates more heavily than movement away by ideologically proximate candidates.[3] It follows (see section A5.1 for the details) that, *ceteris paribus*, unless a voter is exactly ideologically equidistant from the candidates, that voter's utility difference between the candidates increases as the candidates spread apart. The latter is expected with greater polarization in Congress, which leads to increased ideological distance between Congressional candidates. Thus, party loyalty should increase with increased legislative polarization.

Adams et al. (2017) provide empirical evidence from the 2010 Congressional elections that "moderate voters weigh candidates' policy/ideological positions far less than non-moderate voters." This result helps substantiate the theoretical expectations outlined in the previous paragraph.

---

[3] This differential weighting can reflect the tendency for voters to be more influenced by negative information about parties they oppose than positive information about parties they support; that is, more extreme positions by a candidate tend to activate the opposing party's base to turnout in opposition more than the candidate's own party's base to turnout in support (Hall and Thompson 2018).

These researchers also cite numerous findings from both psychology and political science that, as individuals' preferences become more extreme, their views intensify. See, especially, Van Houweling and Sniderman (2005), who report experimental research in which subjects reporting moderate views discounted candidates' ideologies when compared to noncentrist participants. Furthermore, Simas (2021) provides empirical evidence from House elections to show that ideological extremity of candidates is associated with higher ratings for their competence and integrity, suggesting that, in a polarized setting, "voters may still find value in positions even if they do not match their own."

5.2.2. *Extreme voters are motivated to show greater intensity about the outcome*

Theoretical Hypothesis 2: As polarization in Congress grows, *ceteris paribus*, voters with more extreme ideological positions increasingly exhibit greater intensity about the election outcome than voters with more moderate views. Thus, the importance of activist views within the party is enhanced.

For a fixed pair of candidates, extremist voters are more affected by polarization than nonextremist voters, because *as a voter takes a more extreme position, that voter's utility differential between the candidates increases* (details in section A5.1). Or to put it another way, voters with more extreme ideological positions are likely to show greater intensity about the election outcome than voters with more moderate views, and this difference in intensity increases as polarization between parties (or their candidates) grows. A plausible implication of this result about differential impacts is that, as party polarization grows, extreme voters become increasingly willing to commit funds and other forms of campaign resources relative to more moderate voters.

Svolik (2020), using analysis of a survey experiment, shows that voters in polarized societies are willing to trade off democratic principles for partisan interests, and that this willingness increases with the intensity of their partisanship. Using an experimental approach, Graham and Svolik (2020) find that electorates that are polarized or that lack crosscutting cleavages are less punishing of candidates who undermine democratic principles. In particular, they find that voters with extreme or intense policy preferences are

80 CONSEQUENCES OF POLARIZATION

willing to sacrifice democratic principles at higher rates than centrist and moderate voters, because the former are unwilling to forgo partisan and policy attachments in return for upholding democratic ideals.[4] This finding reinforces our theoretical expectation that the influence of those with more extreme views will also grow with polarization.

5.3. Increased Motivation of Parties to Focus on Turnout of Voters in the Party Base

5.3.1. Persuasion versus focus on one's own supporters

Theoretical Hypothesis 3: As polarization between the support bases of the respective parties grows beyond a threshold, and in the presence of party loyalty in that electorate, there is an increased tendency for candidates to strategically position themselves nearer the median of their own supporters and seek to increase the turnout of these supporters, as compared to offering a moderate platform intended to gain votes from centrist voters.

To address Hypothesis 3, we highlight the voters who identify with a party to the point of not seriously considering voting for the other party, a group that we refer to as the party's *base*.[5] In turn, we show that, as polarization between the party bases increases beyond a threshold, spatial positions of the parties that maximize vote-share migrate from being at or close to the overall median voter to being closer to the respective party base medians. Thus, divergent party appeals to the respective bases become more valuable by comparison with Downsian appeals to the center. To see this, we will focus on how appeal to the base affects turnout vis-à-vis how appeal to moderate or

---

[4] On the other hand, Independents and partisan "leaners" may support more democratic candidates enough to defeat undemocratic ones regardless of their partisan affiliation. In 2022, candidates for Secretary of State in battleground states who focused their campaigns on denial of the results of the 2020 presidential election underperformed and lost. A survey by Citizen Data found that split-ticket voters in the 2022 elections often expressed concern about policies dangerous to democracy. In a closely divided electorate, a few such voters can have a major impact and could be a harbinger for reaction to extremists (see Homans et al., 2022).

[5] We have also argued that increased polarization in Congress should lead to increased influence by activists and that voters with more extreme ideological positions should display increased intensity about the election outcome relative to those with more moderate views. However, we do not assume these latter implications in proving Theoretical Hypothesis 3.

centrist voters affects vote share. For simplicity in this section, we will refer to polarization between the party bases as simply *polarization*.

This last issue has been addressed empirically by Hill (2017), who employed election returns and administrative data to assess effects of persuasion of swing voters and changes in the composition of the electorate (i.e., changes in turnout) in pairs of successive elections in Florida during the period 2006–2010. Without disaggregating House, Senate, and gubernatorial elections, Hill found that switching parties between elections led to a mean change of 4.1 percentage points in party support, while changes in the composition of the electorate between elections produced a mean change of 8.6 percentage points. But there was wide variation in each of these measures among contests. For just the 34 of these contest pairs involving US House elections, the median effects can be determined from Figure 3 in Hill. The median effect of change of composition (i.e., in turnout) in House races is almost three times the corresponding median effect for switching voters (7.4 percentage points for changing composition versus 2.6 percentage points for switching).[6] Investigating the possible differential effects of open versus incumbent House races (not discussed by Hill) could help further refine answers to the composition/switching question.

Analyzing House races in 2006–2014, Hall and Thompson (2018) find that extremist party nominees are penalized in general elections, and provide suggestive evidence that their loss of vote share is mostly due to turnout.[7] Further evidence (which, in their words, is "somewhat imprecise") suggests that this loss of vote share by extremist nominees is mostly due to higher turnout by the opposing party. Muñoz and Meguid (2021), in the context of French presidential elections, find that party polarization leads to significantly higher turnout for voters close to one party and far from another—that is, for generally more extreme voters.

---

[6] The data for Hill's analyses are restricted to one (although large and heterogeneous) state and to two pairs of election dates. A more recent study by Hill, Hopkins, and Huber (2021), using similar methodology, finds that in four of six states studied, swing voters had considerably *more* effect (than changes in composition) on the outcome of the 2016 *presidential* election; however, that study does not cover *Congressional* elections. As Hill (2017) notes, characteristics of different candidates in successive elections play an important role in party switches by swing voters. Such candidate effects seem likely in the 2016 presidential election between Donald Trump and Hillary Clinton, so it is unclear how much inference for House elections we can draw from the 2016 presidential election.

[7] Note that extreme nominees of a dominant party in a district can often afford to lose vote share without jeopardizing victory in the general election.

82   CONSEQUENCES OF POLARIZATION

5.3.2. Responding to the threat of abstention

To address the turnout-versus-persuasion issue—and hence Theoretical Hypothesis 3—directly, we consider a simplified version of the abstention model we introduced in Chapter 3 (subsection 3.2.2), also described in Adams et al. (2005, Ch. 7) and Adams et al. (2010). As in Chapter 3, we consider three groups of voters: those who identify with the Democratic Party and don't consider voting for the Republican candidate (the Democratic base); those who identify with the Republican Party and don't consider voting for the Democratic candidate (the Republican base); and Independents, who do not identify with a party but do use spatial cues in determining their vote.[8] (There are other voters, who do not identify with a party and who vote non-spatially, and thus cannot be appealed to directly through spatial positioning. These voters are excluded from the initial analysis but will be discussed later.)

Motivated by Theoretical Hypothesis 1, we assume that partisanship is so strong that, because of partisan loyalties, all partisan voters prefer their party's candidate to the other party's candidate. Furthermore, each partisan voter's turnout depends only on evaluation of their party's candidate.[9] We assume that the voter votes for the candidate of her party if the distance to that candidate is less than an alienation threshold, denoted by A; otherwise, the voter abstains. In particular, if the Democratic and Republican candidates are located at D and R, respectively (see, for example, Fig. 5.1A), then a Democratic voter votes for the Democrat if the voter lies between $D - A$ and $D + A$, and otherwise abstains. (Other aspects of the figure will be described later.) Similarly, a Republican voter votes for the Republican if the voter lies between $R - A$ and $R + A$, and otherwise abstains.

In section A5.2 of the Appendix to this chapter, we show that a Nash equilibrium[10] occurs if the Democratic candidate, by moving to the right, would lose from her base the same number of votes to abstention as she gained from Independents to whom she would be closer, while a mirror-image statement

---

[8] Butler (2009) analyzes a similar model (see also subsection 3.2.2 above), with three groups of voters (a Democratic base, whose members either vote for the Democrat or abstain; an analogous Republican base; and centrist voters, who vote spatially and are termed swing voters). Butler assumes that parties seek to maximize their probability of winning, whereas we assume that they seek to maximize their respective vote shares, a very similar goal in close contests. Using regression analysis, Butler focuses on the evaluation of empirical hypotheses.

[9] An alternative that we do not pursue is that each partisan also takes into account the ideological distance between the two candidates in determining whether to vote.

[10] A Nash equilibrium is a pair of simultaneous positions, one for each party candidate, such that neither candidate can improve its vote share by unilaterally changing its position.

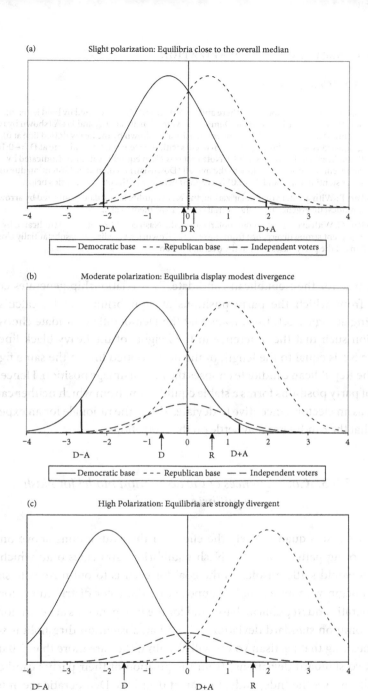

Figure 5.1. Nash Equilibria (at D and R) for Democratic and Republican Candidates for Varying Degrees of Voter Polarization
Source: Merrill et al., 2022.

84 CONSEQUENCES OF POLARIZATION

Figure 5.1 (*Continued*)

Note to Part A: Equilibrium locations (here and in Parts B and C) are denoted by bold lettering and arrows. The difference between the Democratic voter density at D-A and D+A (shown by two heavy black lines) is equal to the Independent density at 0 (shown by the heavy dotted line at 0), thus satisfying Equations A5.1. Thus, equilibrium occurs with the Democratic candidate at $D = -0.10$, and the Republican candidate at $R = 0.10$. Note that this Nash equilibria at ±0.10 (indicated by arrows) represent positions very close to the overall (Downsian) median at 0. Abstention due to alienation (abstention threshold $A = 2.0$) is assumed here and in the other scenarios below.

Note to Part B: With greater voter polarization, the Nash equilibria at ± 0.60 (indicated by arrows) represent modest divergence from the overall (Downsian) median at 0.

Note to Part C: With even greater voter polarization, the Nash equilibria at ± 1.60 (indicated by arrows) represent strong divergence from the overall (Downsian) median at 0, substantially closer to the medians of the party bases than to the overall median.

holds true for the Republican candidate. This relationship generates equations from which the party positions at equilibrium can be calculated. Looking at Figure 5.1, this means that the Democratic candidate chooses a position such that the difference in the heights of the heavy black lines in Figure 5.1 is equal to the length of the heavy dotted line in the same figure, and the Republican candidate chooses the mirror-image position. Hence this pair of party positions forms a stable equilibrium, from which neither candidate has an electoral incentive to deviate. This is the rationale for an expectation that the candidates may settle on these positions.

5.3.3. Consequences of the abstention model for Nash equilibria: Examples

Next, we assess quantitatively the effects of the assumptions above on the likely voting patterns and the Nash equilibrium strategies onto which the parties would settle, insofar as the goal for each is to optimize vote share. Let us begin with an example: Suppose that the voter distributions for the Democratic and Republican bases and for the Independents are each normal with common standard deviation = 1, and an abstention threshold is set at 2.0, meaning that partisan voters will abstain if they are more than 2.0 units (i.e., two standard deviations) from the position of their party's candidate. Initially, we set the Independent mean at 0 and the Democratic mean to be the negative of the Republican mean. It follows by symmetry that $D = -R$ at equilibrium. Figures 5.1A, B, and C depict different degrees of polarization defined by setting the Republican mean at 0.5, 1.0, and 2.0, respectively (and the Democratic means at the mirror images of these values). We will

MOBILIZING THE BASE 85

Table 5.1. Nash-Equilibrium Locations as a Function of Proportion of Independents and Medians of Party Bases

Proportion of Independents		0%	5%	10%	20%
Median of Democratic Base	Median of Republican Base	Nash-Equilibrium Locations			
−0.5	0.5	± 0.50	± 0.31	± 0.10	± 0.00
−1.0	1.0	± 1.00	± 0.81	± 0.60	± 0.15
−2.0	2.0	± 2.00	± 1.81	± 1.60	± 1.15
		Downsian Ceilings			
		± 0.00	± 0.19	± 0.40	± 0.85

Note: An abstention threshold of $A = 2.0$ is assumed.
Reproduced with permission from Merrill et al., 2022.

refer to these values as specifying slight, moderate, and strong polarization. Furthermore, for the initial example, we set the proportion of Independents at 10 percent, with the remainder divided equally between the two parties, so that each base is 45 percent of the total. Table 5.1 summarizes the Nash-equilibrium party locations in relation to the medians of the party bases.

Note that, for slight polarization, Nash-equilibrium positions for both parties are almost Downsian (i.e., convergent), at ±0.10 (Fig. 5.1A). For moderate polarization, equilibrium locations are modestly divergent, at approximately ±0.60 (Fig. 5.1B). But for strong polarization (Fig. 5.1C), the Nash-equilibrium locations, at ±1.60, are highly non-Downsian and divergent. In fact, these last positions are much closer to the partisan medians than to the overall median. Note that the relationship between the divergence of the partisan voter distributions and the divergence of the Nash equilibria is not linear.

Next, we vary the proportion of Independents. Raising the percentage of Independents to 20 percent draws the parties inward, as expected, reducing divergence at equilibrium, leading to Downsian Nash-equilibrium values at the overall median for slight polarization, close to Downsian-equilibrium positions at ±0.15 for moderate polarization, but divergent strategies at ±1.15 for strong polarization. On the other hand, lowering the proportion of Independents to 5 percent leads to divergence for all three degrees of polarization.[11] If we eliminate Independents altogether, then the Nash-equilibrium locations are simply the respective partisan voter medians.

[11] Although self-placement data by respondents in surveys, such as the American National Election Studies, may suggest a larger percent of Independents or moderates than modeled here,

86 CONSEQUENCES OF POLARIZATION

Finally, we consider a scenario in which one party—say, the Republicans—has a larger base, which is more extreme than that of the other party. Furthermore, the Republicans decide to appeal strongly to their base, positioning themselves at their party-base median instead of pursuing their equilibrium strategy, while the Democrats maintain their optimal strategy. Section A5.3 presents an example of this scenario in which the Democrats win the election. This scenario may have occurred in the presidential election of 2020, in which Donald Trump focused almost entirely on appealing to his base, whereas Joe Biden appealed not only to his base but also to uncommitted voters including moderates, and won. Section A5.3 explores several other modifications of the basic assumptions of the model.

5.3.4. The Downsian ceiling and its relation to Nash equilibria

Divergence at equilibrium is plotted in Figure 5.2 against divergence of party bases for each percent of Independents indicated above. Note the nonlinear relationship for each fixed proportion of Independents: Downsian convergence is maintained until the divergence of each party base median (from the overall median) reaches what we will call the *Downsian ceiling*, after which divergence of party strategies does increase linearly. Values of the Downsian ceiling are provided in Table 5.1 (see also sections A5.3 and A5.4).

Note that, for our example using normal densities, once the medians of the party bases exceed twice the Downsian ceiling, the equilibrium positions are closer to the party base medians than to the overall median, a state of affairs we might interpret as suggesting that each party candidate is focusing more on its base than on moderates in the center. In section A5.4 in the Appendix of this chapter, we show that these conclusions about the Downsian ceiling persist when normal densities are replaced by any symmetric, unimodal distributions (for which, as in the normal distribution, the mean and the median are identical). That is to say, the linear relationship (beyond the Downsian ceiling) between the equilibrium strategies and the partisan medians, as well as the positions of the equilibria relative to the partisan

---

the analyses in Adams et al. (2017) discussed above suggest that moderates are less likely to employ proximity in their vote choice than non-moderates. Thus, the proportion of moderates who vote spatially—those we classify as Independents—may be substantially less than those who appear to be moderates. Furthermore, we might expect that the proportion of Independents would decrease as polarization increases.

MOBILIZING THE BASE 87

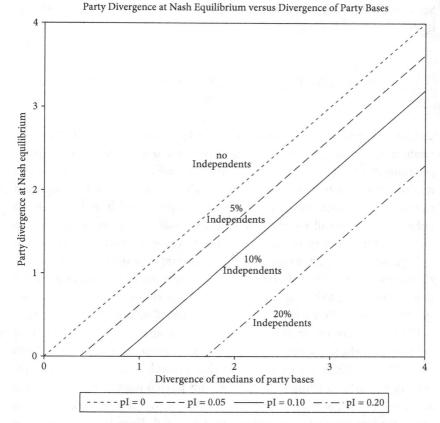

Figure 5.2. Relation of Divergence at Nash Equilibrium to Divergence of Party Bases

Note: Party divergence at equilibrium becomes progressively more nonlinear (vis-à-vis party base divergence) as the proportion of Independents rises. Normally distributed party bases and an abstention rate with threshold = 2.0 are assumed.

Source: Merrill et al., 2022.

and overall medians, continue to apply in this wider setting. In particular, for any symmetric, unimodal party-base distributions we show that:

- If the distance of each party-base median from the overall median is more than twice the Downsian ceiling, then the strategic position of each party at Nash equilibrium is closer to the party-base median than to the overall median.

88 CONSEQUENCES OF POLARIZATION

See Corollary 1 in section A5.4 for an analytic statement of this result and its proof.

5.3.5. Summary of findings relating to Theoretical Hypothesis 3

To summarize our analyses supporting Theoretical Hypothesis 3: When the electorate is significantly polarized, our primary conclusion is that optimal party positions at equilibrium are also highly polarized and nearer the respective medians of the party bases than to the overall voter median. In fact, beyond a Downsian ceiling below which both equilibrium positions fall, in the Downsian fashion, at the overall median, each party's equilibrium position diverges in lockstep with the divergence of the median of its base. That is to say, beyond the ceiling, the party's optimal position moves just as much as the median of its base. Furthermore, when the polarization between the party bases exceeds twice the Downsian ceiling, the parties' optimal strategic positions are nearer to the respective medians of the party bases than to the overall median of the electorate.

If, in fact, there are no Independents (who use spatial cues), the equilibria fall exactly at the partisan base medians. As the proportion of Independents rises, the equilibria are drawn somewhat inward, but even with 20 percent Independents (unlikely under strong polarization), those equilibria are closer to the party-base medians than to the overall medians, as long as the party-base medians are sufficiently separated. Even if the party bases are located asymmetrically (see section A5.3), the locations of the party equilibria largely track the party-base medians. But if one party hews too close to its partisan base, the opposing party—even if its base is smaller—still has a chance to win. On the other hand, varying the abstention threshold (see A5.3) has a relatively small effect on candidate equilibria.

In our analysis so far, we have disregarded citizens who do not use spatial cues and have dealt instead with the effects of abstention or vote choice by spatially motivated voters. Many non-spatially oriented citizens may not be policy-oriented at all but may instead be more susceptible to nonpolicy appeals.[12] Still, these citizens likely have some effect on a party's

---

[12] The vote choices of many voters who provide centrist responses to liberal–conservative questions on surveys such as the American National Election Studies either do not reflect or only weakly reflect ideology (Adams et al., 2017), thus inflating the proportion that appear to act as centrists or moderates.

MOBILIZING THE BASE 89

spatial strategies. For citizens who are not spatially motivated but who can be considered part of one of the party bases, turnout can be influenced by appeal from the candidate of the base party in a more diffuse way that is still correlated with spatial position, or at least the direction of that position. When parties are polarized, such appeals are likely to be highly partisan, may depend on excoriating or demonizing the opposing party and its candidates, and may involve doubling down on the extreme positions and rhetoric used to appeal to more ideologically spatially oriented members of the base.

5.4. Conclusions from Theoretical Analysis

Previously, in supporting Theoretical Hypothesis 1, we argued that, in the presence of legislative polarization, party loyalty and strength of party identification are more predictive of vote choice than in a less-polarized setting, Democratic identifiers being more likely to vote for the Democratic candidate and Republican identifiers to vote for the Republican. Furthermore, Theoretical Hypothesis 2 suggests that more extreme voters may be more inspired to influence the outcome, and their strength of preference increases with the degree of polarization. However polarized the general electorate may be, activists are likely to be more motivated to participate in the campaign and be more strongly polarized—that is, more extreme in their respective directions. Whereas activists are unlikely to abstain from voting itself, they may well abstain from active campaigning or may not provide campaign contributions if they judge their party's candidate to be too moderate (or too extreme). Hence, to a significant extent, parties and candidates may adjust their positioning according to the actions of activists rather than to the expected vote choices and turnout by the overall electorate.

Thus, polarized voters and especially activists are likely to perceive large differences between the candidates, a tendency that is more pronounced for extreme voters, who are likely to show more intensity about the outcome than more centrist voters. In turn, parties and candidates have reason to appeal to voters who have the most utility at stake, voters who are more likely to be extreme. Furthermore, strong partisans are resistant to persuasion by the opposition even if the latter's candidates move toward the center.

In addressing Theoretical Hypothesis 3, we have seen that, when voters are polarized and party loyalty is high, each party optimizes its vote share

90   CONSEQUENCES OF POLARIZATION

by assuming a position, not close to the median of the electorate at large, but rather close to the median of its partisan base. In fact, insofar as the party responds especially to activists rather than to its overall base electorate, it may campaign from an even more extreme position close to the median of its activists. In situations where the two parties are highly competitive, such strategies would, in fact, be most imperative. *This is exactly opposite to the expectation we would infer from the usual Downsian perspective.*

In the following sections we turn to some empirical evidence about the effects of polarization on changes in party loyalty, the influence of extremists, and the strategy of appealing to one's own base.

5.5. Empirical Evidence for the Effects of Polarization on Party Loyalty

Empirical Hypothesis 1: As polarization within Congress grows, *ceteris paribus*, party loyalty and the strength of partisan identification as a predictor of voting also increase.

In section 5.2.1 above, we provided a theoretical argument to support Theoretical Hypothesis 1—namely, that polarization should increase party loyalty and the strength of partisan identification as a predictor of voting. As polarization within Congress grows, in either House or Senate, the policy preferences of the median legislator of either party will diverge further and further from the preferences of the overall median voter. In fact, we demonstrated the seemingly counterintuitive result that the strength of party preference—that is, party loyalty—for each voter can increase even if the party in Congress is moving away from the position of the voter, as long as the other party is also moving away in the opposite direction.[13]

We will test Theoretical Hypothesis 1 empirically in three ways. As legislative polarization has grown, we should expect that

---

[13] Grynaviski (2006) has made a closely related argument. He asserts (323): "[I]f party unity is high, then party labels will provide a useful signal to voters about candidate characteristics and identifications with the parties will be strong, but if party unity is low, then party attachments will be weak." He uses this argument to conclude that we should see changes in the consistency of party loyalty over time as a function of polarization.

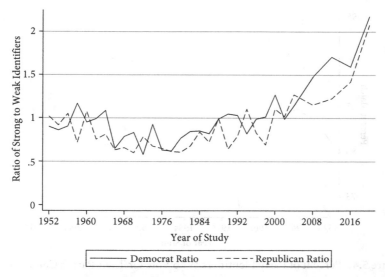

Figure 5.3. Ratio of Strong Identifiers to Weak Identifiers by Party, 1952–2020

a. within each party the ratio of strong party identifiers to weak party identifiers has grown;
b. the proportion of party identifiers who support their party (e.g., at the presidential level) has grown; and
c. the proportion of voters who cast a split ticket for House member and president has declined.

Re Empirical Hypothesis 1a: Within each party, the ratio of strong party identifiers to weak party identifiers has grown.

Grynaviski (2006, Table 2) reports by decade the proportion of respondents in the American National Election Studies who identify themselves as strong partisan identifiers, weak identifiers or Independent leaners, or as pure Independents. Grynaviski (2006, 340) concludes from this table that "during the 1960s and 1970s, the proportion of respondents who considered themselves strong party identifiers declined from its peak levels in the 1950s. Similarly, the proportion of respondents who considered themselves pure Independents almost doubled from its low in the 1950s to its high in the 1970s. Then, as party unity began to grow, the trends in the strength of partisan identification also reversed, with growing numbers of strong partisan identifiers and declining numbers of pure Independents

92 CONSEQUENCES OF POLARIZATION

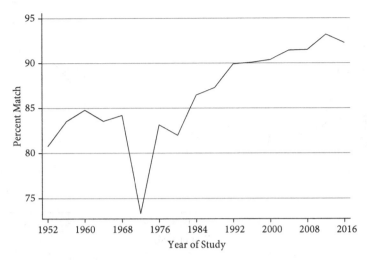

Figure 5.4. Percent of Party Identifiers Who Vote for Their Party's Candidate for President

through the 1980s and 1990s." When we extend the data to a more recent period, as shown in Figure 5.3, the pattern for pure Independents relative to party identifiers is not clear (data omitted for space reasons), but the key result is that an initial drop in the ratio of strong identifiers to weak identifiers within each party was followed by a sustained increase in that ratio since the 1970s.[14]

Re Empirical Hypothesis 1b: The proportion of party identifiers who support their party (e.g., at the presidential level) has grown.

Figure 5.4 depicts the proportions of party identifiers who vote for their party in presidential elections. The data indicate that that proportion has consistently increased since the 1970s, thus supporting Hypothesis 1b.[15]

---

[14] For both Democrats and Republicans, the increasing slope of the strong to weak ratio since 1975 is significant at the 0.001 level and is significantly different from the slope before 1952 (we use 1975 as the cut-point in this and subsequent analyses to represent the 1970s). The increase in the ratio of strong to weak identifiers holds, even if the proportion of independents is not constant.

[15] The increasing slope since 1975 is significant at the 0.01 level and is significantly different from the slope before 1975.

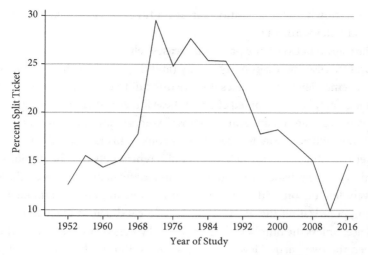

Figure 5.5. Percent of Voters Reporting Voting a Split Ticket for President and House

Re Empirical Hypothesis 1c: The proportion of voters who cast a split ticket for House member and president has declined.

Figure 5.5 demonstrates an increase in the proportion of split-ticket votes for president and House member (see, e.g., Brunell and Grofman, 2009) before the 1970s, followed by a sustained decrease in that proportion since the 1970s. This supports Hypothesis 1c.[16]

5.6. Summary

We have shown that polarization at the party level will increase party loyalty among those who identify with a party and increase the strength of partisan identification as a predictor of voting. In fact, party loyalty can increase even when the party in Congress is moving away from the position of the voter, as long as the other party is also moving away in the opposite direction. We

---

[16] The decline since 1975 is significant at the 0.001 level, whereas the previous rise from 1952 to the mid-1970s is significant at the 0.05 level.

94 CONSEQUENCES OF POLARIZATION

have also shown that polarization can affect the relative influence of activists and moderates within a party.

Polarization between the parties increases reliance on extremist voters for electoral success, increases party loyalty (and disproportionately so for voters with extreme views), and makes it more difficult to convert supporters of the opposing party. The combined effect of these forces is that increased polarization leads to greater reliance on one's "own" voters to provide winning margins as the most efficient way to affect the outcome. This is especially relevant in competitive situations in which turnout differences between the supporters of each party can be critical to victory, and in circumstances in which there are relatively few uncommitted voters. Even in noncompetitive situations, with growing polarization the primary appeal of a candidate is likely to be to her own base, unless the number of uncommitted voters is large relative to the gap between the two parties' levels of base support. But, in the presence of party loyalty and sufficient polarization between the party bases, the threat of abstention alone implies that optimal party strategies are nearer the medians of the party bases than to the overall median of the electorate.

Based on both theoretical and empirical evidence, we draw three major conclusions:

Conclusion 5.1. Party loyalty and the strength of partisan identification grow as a predictor of vote choice with increased polarization between party positions.

Conclusion 5.2. Extreme voters demonstrate greater intensity about the election outcome than more moderate voters as polarization between party positions increases, thus enhancing the importance of activist views within the party.

Conclusion 5.3. As polarization between the party bases grows beyond a specified point, parties and their candidates are motivated to position themselves nearer the median of their own supporters than the overall median, and to focus on turnout rather than seek to persuade centrist voters by offering a moderate platform.

Thus, and arguably most importantly, we offer the processes described in this chapter as an answer to the question of why appeals to the base are far more common than they used to be. Quite simply, as polarization—either between the party positions or between the party bases—increases, the strategic utility of catering to the party base goes up as well.

6

Consequences of Polarized Politics

6.1. Electoral Competition, Voter Choice, and Congressional Decision Making

As we have shown previously, party differentiation at the constituency level and polarization in roll-call voting within Congress are reciprocally linked. The central argument of this chapter is simple: Changes in polarization strongly link to many other well-known phenomena whose associations with polarization deserve further study. Some of these links, such as increases in party loyalty and in the influence of activists and greater reliance on a strategy of mobilizing the party's electoral base, were discussed in Chapter 5, and some in other chapters, but most are mentioned in this chapter for the first time. Our goal is to provide a more unified discussion of topics that are often treated in isolation from one another in the literatures of legislative politics and party competition. Although our list of factors is by no means exhaustive, we hope to tease out expected linkages, linkages that have either previously not been noted or, if noticed, have not been treated together or theoretically grounded. In this discussion we take polarization as the independent variable, though, of course, we recognize the potential for reciprocal causality for some of the effects we consider.

The specific electoral phenomena we discuss in this section include within-district and within-Congress policy divergence, reduction in the number of competitive districts, split-ticket voting, and regional realignment. Furthermore, we relate the constrained ideological choices available to voters to the ongoing debate about whether or not polarization in Congress is entirely elite-driven and the reasons why we can elect legislators who are more ideologically extreme than the voters whom they represent. Within Congress, we note in the following section that polarization can be linked to striking policy reversals in periods of one-party dominance of Congress and the presidency, and linked to gridlock in eras of divided government. We relate these concepts

How Polarization Begets Polarization. Samuel Merrill III, Bernard Grofman, and Thomas L. Brunell, Oxford University Press. © Oxford University Press 2024. DOI: 10.1093/oso/9780197745229.003.0006

96 CONSEQUENCES OF POLARIZATION

to legislator-centric versus party-centric government and the power of a concentrated minority. Polarization may also provide incentives to eliminate super-majoritarian rules. Section 6.2 deals with implications of polarization for electoral competition and voter choice, while section 6.3 treats its possible consequences for Congressional decision making.

6.2. Consequences for Electoral Competition and Voter Choice

We hypothesize five consequences for electoral competition resulting from the growth of polarization within Congress:

1. Within each constituency, the ideological distance between the platforms offered by candidates of opposite parties increases.
2. Polarization within Congress may increase without any change in the ideological location of the voters within constituencies.
3. The set of districts in which there can be viable partisan competition shrinks.
4. Split-ticket voting (between votes for, say, the president and the House member) declines.
5. Regional realignment is likely because the ideology of the median voter in a district is strongly linked to region.

We explore each of these hypotheses in turn.

Hypothesis 6.2.1: As polarization within Congress grows, within each constituency the ideological distance between the platforms offered by candidates of opposite parties will increase.

As we argue in Chapter 2, as polarization within Congress grows, the party-discipline model of political competition implies that, within each constituency, the ideological distance between the platforms offered by candidates of opposite parties will increase, because the range of feasible ideological locations available to each party's candidates is limited by distance from the national party position.[1]

---

[1] Recall that we proxy national party position by the mean ideological location of the parties in Congress since this reflects the policies that each party seeks to see implemented.

CONSEQUENCES OF POLARIZED POLITICS   97

Because candidates do not, as in the simplest Downsian model, converge to the views of the median voter in the district, our more nuanced neo-Downsian model (see Chapter 3) offers a theoretical explanation for the "leapfrog politics" highlighted by Bafumi and Herron (2010),[2] in which, under plausible conditions, non-median strategies can be optimal and replacement of an incumbent with a legislator of the other party can lead to a dramatic change in the ideology of the district's representative.

The implication of this pattern of replacement is that the candidates who win party primaries increasingly come to mirror the national position of the party. Successful candidates thus come over time to look more extreme as "candidate wiggle room" declines—that is, as the length of the tether from national party positions and activist preferences tightens at the same time as the national party position becomes more extreme relative to that of the other party.

Hypothesis 6.2.2: Polarization within Congress can increase without any change in the ideological location of the voters within any constituency.

One of the puzzles of present-day politics is how we can elect ever more ideologically extreme legislators even though, arguably, voters are not endorsing more extreme positions than they used to (Fiorina, 2017). One answer that has been given to this puzzle is that it is not a puzzle at all. Voters—especially activists—have indeed come to take more extreme views, and so it is not surprising that their representatives are also more extreme (Abramowitz, 2010). Although polarization at the elite level may be happening first and at a more extreme level, voters are taking their cues from elites in their own party. A second answer is that indeed it is a puzzle, but the appearance of polarization comes from voter sorting into political parties, so that issues such as abortion, which once upon a time did not distinguish supporters of the two parties, now generates a veritable chasm between the supporter bases of the parties (Gidron et al., 2021; Fiorina et al., 2005). According to this argument, voters as a whole are not more extreme, but voters within each party look ever more distinct from those of the other party ideologically. Related to the partisan sorting disagreement is an argument that geographic sorting is occurring as voters more likely to vote for a given party move to areas of

---

[2] Earlier work such as Poole and Rosenthal (1984) also noted this phenomenon. But, of course, it has only grown more acute over time.

98 CONSEQUENCES OF POLARIZATION

their own state or to other states that reflect the ideology of their party. Thus, states and constituencies become more ideologically homogeneous in terms of partisanship.

The answer we give to this puzzle is that we can elect legislators who diverge faster from the ideological center than do the voters whom they represent, because, as polarization grows, the logic of the party-constraint model forces voters into making constrained choices between two candidates, at least one of whom (and often both of whom) is moving further and further away from the median voter in the constituency. The model supposes a natural dynamic in which, absent countervailing forces, polarization begets polarization in Congress. Thus, our response to the puzzle emphasizes that polarization within the legislature is induced not only by nationalization of the electorate and empowerment of leadership but by the constraints on the choices offered voters. We can elect legislators who are more and more ideologically extreme relative to the voters whom they represent because national party desiderata and the logic of the model force voters into making constrained choices between two candidates, at least one—and often both—of whom are quite ideologically distant from the median voter in the district.[3]

The national party can afford to compel candidates to be more extreme than their districts, because, under polarization, voters with allegiance to that party have come to nationalize their vote, often casting it primarily to help their party control Congress rather than considering which candidate they most agree with on policy. Still, when such extreme candidates are elected and become legislators, they may face the collective-action problem mentioned in section 4.1: Vote sincerely for extreme positions, or vote strategically to appeal to their district. If all vote strategically, their party's extreme legislation, which they favor, may be defeated. They solve the collective-action problem by empowering their caucus leadership to force just as many of them as necessary to pass extreme legislation (Buchler, 2018), or by voting with their party on procedural votes but with their district on substantive votes (Pearson, 2015).[4] Thus, the polarization-begets-polarization cycle comes full circle. Party discipline necessitates extreme choices by the district electorate; in turn, the legislators elected voluntarily seek party discipline

---

[3] Thus, we can remain agnostic about whether voters are actually more extreme than they used to be, since the legislators they elect are dancing in a spiral of polarization begetting polarization in Congress.

[4] Legislators can usually rely on their caucus leaders to arrange procedural votes so that substantive votes that are controversial are avoided.

CONSEQUENCES OF POLARIZED POLITICS   99

to cast extreme votes in Congress. Furthermore, district candidates who might prefer to moderate their votes face the prospect of challenges from activist forces in the district that support, and insist on enforcing, the national ideology.

Hypothesis 6.2.3: As polarization within Congress grows, *ceteris paribus*, the set of districts in which there can be viable partisan competition shrinks.

Polarization makes some districts, typically those with a strong majority of supporters of one party, essentially unwinnable for the other party, in part since that party's candidate cannot offer a credible policy position as close to the median voter in the constituency as can the candidate of the other party. Thus, *ceteris paribus*, we expect to see a decline in the number of districts that change partisan control over the course of a decade. Of course, as legislative polarization increases, it is not necessarily the case that there will be fewer marginal constituencies (Mayhew, 1974; see also Jacobson, 1987; Ansolabehere, Brady, and Fiorina, 1992), since that will depend upon factors such as the nature of redistricting (e.g., levels of partisan gerrymandering vs. incumbency-protection gerrymandering). Nonetheless, on balance we would expect to see fewer competitive districts when constraints on candidate ideological locations tighten. In particular, other things being equal, because of the tightening constraints described above, only in districts where the median voter is ideologically centrist relative to the *national* party positions can we expect frequent party alternation in office.

Figure 6.1 plots the percentage of House seats in which the House candidates are within 10 percentage points of one another (i.e., 55 percent–45 percent or closer). We see a clear linear trend downward between 1952 and 2016, which largely but not entirely supports the hypothesis, since the time trend predates the era of polarization. The linear trend is statistically significant at $p < 0.001$.[5]

---

[5] As polarization within Congress grows we might also expect average victory margins to increase, or fewer districts to change hands over the course of a decade. Such a pattern, however, is obscured because party-discipline constraints on candidate locations are not the only factors affecting expected victory margins or the proportion of districts close enough to be vulnerable to change in party control. For example, if redistricting creates seats with margins nicely tailored to crack opposition strength but not to waste votes for the party in control of the redistricting process, then average victory margins can decline. Similarly, the results would also be affected by what happens in open seats and by incumbent-protection gerrymanders.

100 CONSEQUENCES OF POLARIZATION

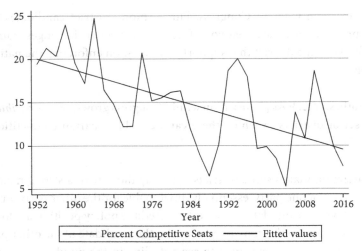

Figure 6.1. Percent of Competitive House Seats, 1952–2016
Note: Competitive seats are those decided by 10 points or less (55–45 or closer).

Hypothesis 6.2.4: As polarization within Congress grows, split-ticket voting (between, say, the president and the House member) declines.

The fact that polarization will, at the district level, generate candidates who look more like the national image of their party and less like the median voter in their own constituency strongly suggests that, *ceteris paribus*, split-ticket voting should decrease. As we saw in Chapter 5, split-ticket voting outcomes for the House and the President (see Fig. 5.5) have gone down from highs of over 40 percent of Congressional districts in the 1970s and 1980s, to less than 10 percent in the most recent elections. As we noted in that chapter, the decline since 1975 is significant at the 0.001 level, whereas the previous rise from 1952 to the mid-1970s is significant at the 0.05 level; thus, Hypothesis 6.2.4 is clearly confirmed. Split-ticket voting represents a bipartisan act on the part of the voter; its decline as a result of polarization reinforces partisanship, furthering polarization.

Another kind of split-ticket voting is shown by time-series data on the number of states with Senators of opposite parties. Until such time as realigning trends make more Southern and Western states competitive again for Democrats (Brunell and Grofman, 2018), we expect to see the number of states with Senators of opposite parties declining. This is exactly what we observe in Figure 6.2. Divided delegations peaked in the mid-1970s, with

CONSEQUENCES OF POLARIZED POLITICS   101

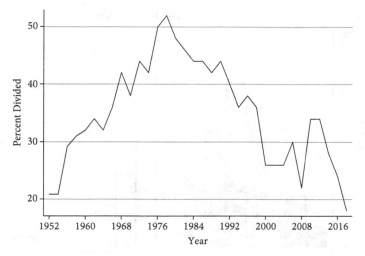

Figure 6.2. Divided Senate Delegations, 1952–2018

over half the states being represented by one Republican and one Democratic Senator at the same time. Since then, the percentage of states with mixed Senate representation has declined nearly every election. In 2018 fewer than 20 percent of the states had a delegation of opposite-party Senators. The decline since 1975 and the previous rise from 1952 to the mid-1970s are both significant at the 0.001 level.

Hypothesis 6.2.5: As polarization within Congress grows, a regional realignment is likely.

As candidates look more like the national image of their party and less like the median voter in their own constituencies, regional realignment can be expected. Most obviously, predominantly White constituencies in the South (but not Black-majority or -near-majority districts) are now unlikely to elect even conservative Democrats, because the identification of a candidate with the liberal Democratic party makes victory virtually impossible. The two histograms in Figures 6.3A and B, which portray the distribution of DW-NOMINATE scores for members of Congress from the US South in 1980 and 2016, clearly show this trend. There are more Democrats and moderates in 1980, whereas in 2016 there is clear party differentiation, with

102 CONSEQUENCES OF POLARIZATION

(a)
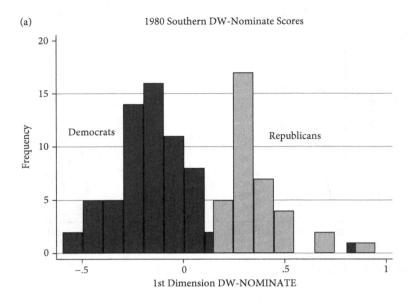

(b)
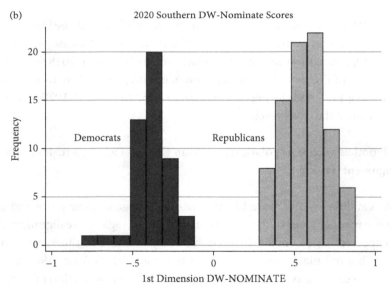

Figure 6.3. Distributions of Southern House Members

the region's Democrats becoming more liberal and its Republicans far more conservative.

6.3. Consequences for Congressional Decision Making

We state four hypotheses for Congressional decision making that are related to polarization within Congress:

1. Legislator-centric government is associated with significant partisan overlap and relatively stable policy outcomes keyed to the chamber median, whereas party-centric (strong-party) government is associated with significant party separation and legislative outcomes that track the majority-party median and oscillate greatly.
2. During periods of significant partisan overlap, the chamber median legislator can be closer to the median legislator of the *minority* party than to the *majority*-party median if the relative concentration of the minority party is sufficient to compensate for its low seat share.
3. Striking policy reversals typically occur when control of government flips back and forth between dominance of both Congress and the presidency by first one party and then the other; whereas gridlock is likely in eras of divided government. In particular, change in party control affects not just the ideological location of legislators at the median but also super-majoritarian pivots, and thus a polarized environment can generate large increases in the range of issues facing gridlock.
4. The dominant party—depending upon expectations about the likelihood of divided government and which party is most likely to control the Senate—may push to eliminate super-majoritarian rules in the Senate.

As polarization within Congress increases, virtually all issues will be viewed through the filter of party loyalty and take on a wholly partisan flavor. As parties polarize within Congress, we see fewer bills in Congress that generate bipartisan support, fewer instances of bill cosponsorship across party lines, and much more disputatious hearings in committee and subcommittee, as well as strong party-line voting both before and after bills get to the floor. Hyper-polarization entails an increasing number of votes with

104   CONSEQUENCES OF POLARIZATION

virtually no party crossover, an absence of substantive debates centered on the question of what is effective policy, and party posturing on issues which, in another era, could have been matters of compromise. This is exactly what we see happening today on issues from immigration reform to the use of face masks to better cope with a pandemic. In this light, we explore each of the hypotheses above in turn.

6.3.1. Legislative-centric versus party-centric government

Hypothesis 6.3.1: Legislator-centric government is associated with significant partisan overlap and relatively stable policy outcomes keyed to the chamber median, whereas party-centric (strong-party) government is associated with significant party separation and legislative outcomes that track the majority-party median and oscillate greatly.

The swings between polarization and party overlap can help illuminate a question that has been debated in the Congressional literature concerning underlying determinants of roll-call voting and party competition in the House and Senate. One approach—the party-centric—emphasizes majority-party control (Kiewiet and McCubbins, 1991; Cox and McCubbins,2005); whereas the *legislative-centric* approach emphasizes the policy preferences of individual legislators and/or the structure of committees (Krehbiel, 1998). In the first approach, the ideological location of party medians (especially the majority-party median) is critical to the nature and passage of legislation; in the second, it is the ideological location of the chamber (floor) median (and other pivot points) that is most important.

The concept of *conditional party government* (see Aldrich, 1995; Aldrich and Rohde, 2000; Rohde, 2010; Cox and McCubbins, 2005) can be thought of as reconciling the two approaches by regarding both the chamber and the party medians as important, but with the relative importance of each varying over time as conditions such as the level of polarization change. As a unifying perspective, we express the relationship between party-based and more autonomous voting patterns as a continuum between total polarization (as one polar endpoint) and total party overlap (as the other polar endpoint). The former represents the pure party-centric model; the latter, a purely legislator-centric pattern. The period 1950–1970, on which so many of the classic articles and books on Congress (Matthews, 1960; Ripley, 1975; Polsby,

1968) were based, reflects a case of high overlap that is far from the party-centric pole of the continuum and is in fact highly atypical. Today's climate, in which a majority party may only bring to a vote bills that are supported by a majority of its own caucus (the "Hastert Rule"), represents the party-centric pole of the continuum.

In the pure party-centric model, the majority party attempts to rule alone, voting on and passing only bills that are supported by a majority of its caucus. Hence, from a Downsian perspective, the median voter of the *majority caucus* is determinative of which alternative is chosen for a vote, and party discipline by the majority party ensures that it will pass. Under the purely legislator-centric model, the full chamber considers the alternative on an equal basis and, again in a Downsian perspective, the *chamber* median is determinative of what is brought forward and passed.

The pivotal legislator on which a legislature has reason to focus is, in a sense, analogous to the optimal position for a party to take in seeking electoral support. As we have seen in Chapter 5 in our arguments for appealing to one's base, the best office-seeking strategy for a party in a general election often lies intermediate between the overall and party median, and more toward the latter as polarization increases.

Just as a party in a general election adjusts its strategy under the threat of abstention due to alienation on the fringes of its support, a majority party in Congress must adjust its strategy to the threat of recalcitrant blocs of extreme or moderate voices within the party delegation. This effect was evident when the Democratic majority in the House in 2021 had to bargain with both a moderate bloc uneasy with the cost of the Build Back Better bill and a progressive bloc that was prepared to withhold support for a related bill until a vote on Build Back Better was guaranteed. Note that in both the legislative and general-election setting, the party is effectively bargaining with the legislators/voters who lie at the cusp of abstention on each of its flanks. In principle, a Downsian ceiling (beyond which a party would shift its focus toward its own median legislator) could be constructed for party strategies in a legislature, but in practice the party focus would depend on the size and political viability of the discontented blocs, among other idiosyncratic factors.

In the Conditional Party Government (CPG) model, Aldrich and Rohde (2000) define the "conditional" aspect as the "degree to which the preferences of party members are similar within each party (particularly the majority), and different between the parties." Accordingly, the degree of party government should increase with separation between the parties and with

106 CONSEQUENCES OF POLARIZATION

homogeneity of each party—that is, it should increase with legislative polarization as we have defined it in Chapter 1 of this book. To capture this measure of polarization analytically, we define the *separation index* of the parties as the *ratio* of divergence to variance, specifically the ratio of the difference in party *medians* to the sum of the party *standard deviations*.[6] Hence, the separation index increases as the party medians recede from one another and as they become internally more homogeneous. Using this measure, we next show that the relation between chamber and party medians (and hence the relation between legislator-centric and strong party government) is highly correlated with the degree of polarization of the party delegations in the House.

Figure 6.4A plots both the party medians and the chamber medians in the House over the period 1856–2020. It is apparent that, whereas the patterns of the Republican and Democratic medians are each relatively smooth throughout the period, that of the chamber medians bounces back and forth between values near one of the party medians (typically that of the majority party) until about 1930, and again from about 1990 onward. During the intervening era from about 1930 to about 1990, however, the chamber medians are relatively stable and remain near the midpoints between the medians of the two parties.

Figure 6.4B plots the separation index over the period of our study. Clearly, this measure shows that polarization was pronounced before 1930 and after 1990, the same periods during which the chamber median tracked the majority-party median. On the other hand, polarization was much more limited from the 1930s through the 1980s, when the chamber median was intermediate between the party medians. Hence, high polarization is clearly correlated with strong party government, whereas low polarization corresponds to legislative-centric government.

As we have seen, majority-party medians are critical determinants of legislative output during strong party government, while chamber medians are critical to legislation under legislator-centric government. To track legislative outcomes more explicitly and relate them to chamber and party medians, we turn to a measure of policy *outcomes* developed by Poole and Rosenthal (2007, fig. 4.1) that gauges the spatial location of the winning policies in a

---

[6] Although we have expressed party separation in terms of means in the rest of the book, we speak here of medians because of their role in determining pivotal legislators, both within parties and in the chamber as a whole.

CONSEQUENCES OF POLARIZED POLITICS 107

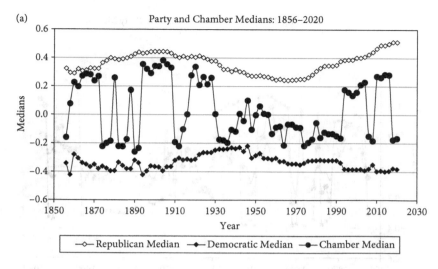

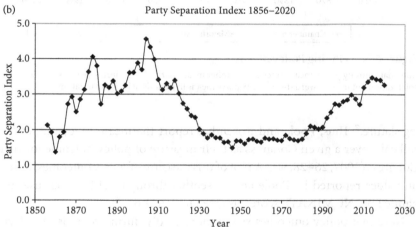

Figure 6.4. Relations of Party Medians to Chamber Medians and Measures of Separation, 1856–2020

Note: Party separation in the legislature is defined as the ratio of the distance between the party medians to the sum of the intraparty standard deviations—that is, *party separation* = $\frac{M_2 - M_1}{\sigma_1 + \sigma_2}$, where M_1 and M_2 are the party medians and σ_1 and σ_2 are the standard deviations for Democrats and Republicans, respectively. We assume $M_1 < M_2$.

108   CONSEQUENCES OF POLARIZATION

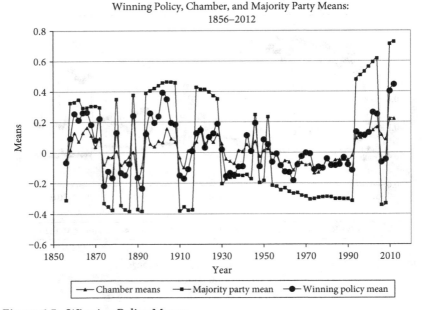

Figure 6.5. Winning Policy Means
Note that winning policy means track the chamber means fairly closely during periods of low polarization but move toward the majority party means in periods of high polarization.

legislature.[7] Thus, Poole and Rosenthal report the mean policy output for roll calls over a given Congress as their measure of policy outcome for that Congress (2007, 26–28, 90). A plot of this measure of policy outcomes, based on values reported by Poole and Rosenthal through 2012 (which use dynamic DW-NOMINATE scores) is given in Figure 6.5.[8]

Note that policy outcomes swing more wildly during periods of polarization. By contrast, during the non-polarized period 1931–1990, policy outputs are less volatile than during the eras before and after these dates. Although the policy-outcome series is strongly correlated with the chamber

---

[7] To obtain this measure for roll calls with two outcomes (such as bill passage and status quo), Poole and Rosenthal (2007) estimate both legislator locations and roll call cut-points, as well as the signal-to-noise ratio. The latter permits estimates of the locations of the two possible outcomes (which are equidistant from the cutpoint). This step is then reversed, re-estimating the locations of legislators and cutpoints. The whole process is then iterated, maximizing the probabilities the process assigns to the observed votes, until stability is attained. The estimated coordinate for the policy outcome is that of the winning alternative.

[8] Unfortunately, medians are not always available in the empirical literature, so at times we must rely on means; Poole and Rosenthal (2007) provide only the policy outcome means (not medians). Substantively, both distance between party medians and distance between party means are measures of separation between parties. Chamber medians, however, are far more volatile than chamber means.

CONSEQUENCES OF POLARIZED POLITICS 109

means (correlation = 0.84), policy outputs are even more strongly correlated with the majority-party means (correlation = 0.89) and negatively correlated with the minority-party means (correlation = –0.85).[9]

6.3.2. The power of a concentrated minority

Hypothesis 6.3.2: During periods of significant partisan overlap, the median legislator of the minority party can be closer than the majority-party median to the chamber median if the relative concentration of the minority party is sufficient to compensate for its low seat share.

Strong party government depends upon the ability of the majority party to command the loyalty of the overall median legislator.[10] In section A6.1 of the Appendix to this chapter, we lay out a statistical model—based on normal distributions for both parties—that elucidates how party medians and chamber medians are interlinked. Using this framework, we analyze (section A6.2) the situations where the chamber-median legislator (and ideologically similar legislators) are not members of the majority party—specifically, where the minority-party median is closer to the overall chamber median than is the majority-party median. In this situation, the minority party may be able to offer policy options to the median legislator that s/he will find more palatable than those offered by the majority party.[11] We provide specific analytic conditions for this situation to occur.

Accordingly, we investigate empirically to see if, at some points in the history of the US Congress, the seemingly perverse situation actually occurred in which the chamber-median legislator (or legislators close to that median) was a member of the minority party. This phenomenon should be less likely

---

[9] Policy outcomes, however, are substantially more volatile than the chamber means (in fact, the standard deviation of the outcomes is nearly twice that of the chamber means). Even so, the policy outcomes—often tempered by divided government and other factors—are considerably less volatile than the majority party means (policy outcomes have a standard deviation about half that of the majority party means).

[10] This need was on prominent display when the majority Democrats in the 117th Senate (elected 2020) worked anxiously to gain the support of Senators Manchin and Sinema, who occupied chamber median positions for the Build Back Better bill under Reconciliation procedures, eventually achieving a measure of success in the form of the Inflation Reduction Act. House moderates played a similar, but less demanding, role in the closely-divided House.

[11] Cf. Feigenbaum, Fouirnaies, and Hall 2017.

110   CONSEQUENCES OF POLARIZATION

when there is a considerable gap between the party delegations, or when one party has lopsided control of the chamber.

We identify the median member of the House in each of the Congresses from the 91st (elected 1968) to the 113th (elected 2012) and their party affiliation. Since we expect that there is a probabilistic element to identifying the median legislator, depending on exactly what floor votes took place, we have also identified the two members to the left of the median member and the two members to the right of the median member.

The recent polarization in Congress has virtually guaranteed that all five MCs closest to the median are from the majority party; in fact, in the 98th–113th Congresses, this is always the case. However, in earlier periods, when the parties did have some ideological overlap, we do see instances in which minority-party members (in this case Republicans) were very nearly the median members of the House. For instance, in the 92nd Congress (elected 1970), Republicans included three of the five members closest to the chamber median (Representatives Heckler, Conte, and Steele). In the 93rd Congress (elected 1972) the story is exactly the same. In the 97th Congress (elected 1980), two of the five MCs closest to the median were from the GOP. The years in which a member of the minority party has been one of the five "close to median" members of the House are disproportionately ones where the parties are ideologically close and/or where at least one of the parties is ideologically diverse.

6.3.3. Gridlock

Hypothesis 6.3.3: As polarization within Congress grows, striking policy reversals are likely when control of government flips back and forth between dominance of both Congress and the presidency by one party and then the other, whereas gridlock is likely in eras of divided government. In particular, change in party control affects not just the location of legislators at the median but also supermajoritarian pivots, and thus a polarized environment can generate large increases in the range of issues facing gridlock.

Polarization in the House does not occur in a vacuum. To understand fully its consequences, especially for public policy, we must look to the

CONSEQUENCES OF POLARIZED POLITICS   111

political context, especially the outcomes of presidential elections. For present purposes, the most important distinction is between unified and divided government. The effects of polarization should be very different between periods of unified control of Congress and the presidency and periods of divided government.

When politics is highly polarized and there is alternation between unified control by one party and then unified control by the other party, we expect to see striking policy reversals, or at least strong efforts to generate such about-faces, such as the Republican attempt to repeal Obamacare. In contrast, in periods of divided government, we expect gridlock, since each side may prefer to maintain an issue for campaign fodder rather than compromise to pass legislation, and neither side will allow the other side to "get credit" for policy changes widely favored by the public. Opportunities for gridlock are exacerbated by the supermajoritarian requirements in Senate rules and needed to override a presidential veto in both houses, as we discuss below. Gridlock effects may, however, be ameliorated insofar as the President can use executive orders and appointments when his/her party controls the Senate, even when the other party controls the House. Thus, for example, President Obama resorted to executive orders to implement the Clean Air Act and other measures, while President Trump reversed a very large number of his predecessor's orders, including Obama's Clean Power Plan for the environment, his halt to the Keystone oil pipeline, and his fuel-efficiency standards for automobile manufacturers.

Given high polarization within Congress, when control of Congress shifts, the ideological location of the median legislator changes dramatically (Fig. 6.4A), and even the supermajoritarian pivots (Krehbiel, 1998) can shift substantially.[12] As polarization increased and the distributions of the party delegations on the DW-NOMINATE scale have separated, changes in the median have increased strikingly, starting in the late 1970s and accelerating in the early 1990s and beyond.

The dynamics of supermajoritarian pivots, however, are not dependent on the movement of a single percentile. The location of the pivot required for override of a presidential veto, for example, switches back and forth between the 33rd percentile and the 67th percentile of the DW-NOMINATE scale, depending on whether the president is a Democrat or a Republican

---

[12] In contrast, the *mean* (as opposed to the median) ideology in Congress is much more stable. The mean absolute change (from Congress to Congress) of the House medians over 1940–2010 is 0.094, almost three times the corresponding statistic for the House means, which is 0.034.

112   CONSEQUENCES OF POLARIZATION

(see Fig. 6.6).[13] Because of the switches in the override pivot between these two percentiles each time the presidential party changes, the override pivot is highly volatile, even more so than the median. In particular, the override pivot was volatile even during the long period of almost continuous Democratic hegemony in the House from 1940 until the election of 1994, because the party of the president switched back and forth.

Perhaps the most significant aspect of the pivot positions and their volatility over time is the *gridlock interval* they specify. Here we will focus on the Senate, where the need for a cloture vote to end a filibuster creates an obstacle that is unique in the legislative process. In this setting we define the *gridlock interval* as follows.[14] Consider the DW-NOMINATE interval from -1.0 to $+1.0$, where -1.0 represents extreme liberal and $+1.0$ represents extreme conservative. Assume that each bill has a cut-point on the DW-NOMINATE scale and all Senators vote in accordance with their DW-NOMINATE scores. Under a Democratic president, the Democrats, to pass a bill, must get the votes of all Senators with a score lower than and including the 60th percentile of the DW-NOMINATE scores (to obtain cloture and thus end a filibuster or the threat of one), while the Republicans in the same Senate would need to get all the votes higher on the scale than the 33rd percentile (to override a presidential veto). In this case, the gridlock interval runs from the 33rd percentile to the 60th percentile. Any bill (other than a budget-related bill under Reconciliation) with cut-point strictly between these two goal posts will not succeed. Similarly, under a Republican president, the gridlock interval runs from the cloture pivot at the 40th percentile to the override pivot at the 67th percentile.

Strictly speaking, the override pivot requires a two-thirds majority in both Senate and House. Thus, the gridlock interval can be thought of as that interval within which no proposal can surpass the hurdles of House, Senate,

---

[13] Assuming that members of the House are voting ideologically, when the president is a Republican, overriding a veto requires amassing votes starting from the ideological left. Because the DW-NOMINATE scale increases from left to right, this defines the veto override pivot as the 67th percentile. On the other hand, given a Democratic president, override requires two-thirds of the members starting from the right, so that the override pivot is the 33rd percentile of the DW-NOMINATE scale. Of course, these assumptions can at times be overcome, but their relevance is greatly augmented by polarization, under which bipartisan legislation is much more difficult.

[14] Our definition is equivalent to that introduced by Krehbiel (1998, 38), who defines the *gridlock interval*, given a Republican president, as consisting of potential left-of-center status quo points for which a moderate-to-conservative legislative majority is unable to pass a more conservative policy because it would be killed by a liberal filibuster and potential right-of-center status quo points for which a moderate-to-liberal majority is blocked from passing a more liberal policy because a veto would be sustained. An analogous definition holds, given a Democratic president.

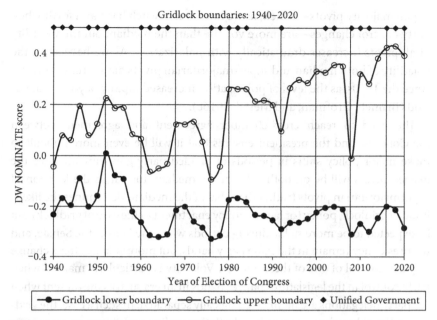

Figure 6.6. Gridlock Boundaries for President and Senate

and president to become law. However, for simplicity, we track—in Figure 6.6—the gridlock intervals accounting just for the president and Senate.

For each Congress, the upper curve in Figure 6.6 represents the pivot Democrats would need in order to pass legislation (i.e., the Republican "firewall"), while the lower curve represents the pivot Republicans would need to pass legislation (the Democratic "firewall"). For example, in 1995 there was a Democratic president and Republican Senate. Hence, the Democrats needed to reach (i.e., get the votes of all Senators up to) the 60th percentile in the Senate (0.266 on the DW-NOMINATE scale) to attain cloture and pass legislation, whereas the Republicans would have needed to reach the 33rd percentile (−0.263) to override a veto and pass their legislation. Congresses with unified government (i.e., president and Senate controlled by the same party) are indicated by black dots in the figure.

As seen in Figure 6.6, the width of the gridlock interval between the upper and lower curves has expanded rapidly from 1940 to 2020, particularly since the late 1970s. Typically in the neighborhood of 0.25 on the DW-NOMINATE scale in the 1940s, the width of the gridlock interval has hovered during the latest decade in the vicinity of 0.6, an overall twofold to threefold increase.

Super-majority pivots—which, as we have seen, switch back and forth when party control changes—are more volatile than the median, but the volatility of all pivots increases dramatically with polarization. As we have seen, the volatility of both median and super-majoritarian pivots has increased greatly since the 1970s, as the level of polarization increased rapidly beyond that period (Brunell, Grofman, and Merrill 2016c).

The need to reach cross-chamber agreement and agreement between the Congress and the president ensures that it will be even more difficult to make major policy shifts in periods of divided party government, since the needed pivots will be on both sides of the median. Insofar as the location of supermajoritarian pivots (rather than that of the median) determines the likelihood of gridlock, policy (or lack of policy enactment in the case of gridlock) can be expected to be more stable during periods when the House, the Senate, and the presidency remain in the same party hands, but more volatile after a change in party control of one of these entities. Volatility is particularly marked when party control in the legislature changes hands in an era such as the present when the party delegations are highly ideologically separated. In such a case, the gridlock interval lengthens markedly as both the median and supermajority pivots swing dramatically. See Figure 6.7, which illustrates the remarkably high correlation between polarization and the length of the gridlock interval.

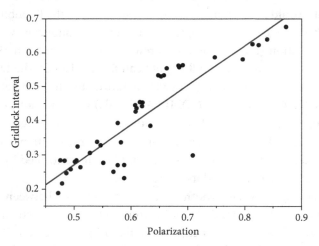

Figure 6.7. Relation of Width of Gridlock Interval to Polarization, for President and Senate, 1940–2020.

6.3.4. *Divided government and rescinding supermajoritarian rules*

Hypothesis 6.3.4: As polarization within Congress grows, depending upon expectations about the likelihood of divided government and which party is most likely to control the Senate, the dominant party may push to eliminate supermajoritarian rules in the Senate.

A possible exception to gridlock, involving transformative appointments to the judiciary and the bureaucracy, can occur under divided government when the same party controls the presidency and a majority in the Senate. If one party believes that the other party is unlikely in the foreseeable future to control both the presidency and the Senate, then it might be willing to rescind supermajoritarian rules. In fact, there are ways in which parties circumvent such requirements in the US Senate, with the most obvious example being the "nuclear option" that was used twice in the last decade to change the supermajoritarian rules in the Senate with respect to presidential appointments to the executive and judicial branches. In 2013 the Democratic majority led by Harry Reid of Nevada eliminated the ability to filibuster lower judicial appointments and executive-branch appointments. In 2017, the Republicans used the nuclear option to eliminate the filibuster for Supreme Court appointments (Wawro and Schickler, 2018). The Senate usually requires 60 votes to invoke cloture to stop a filibuster, and a two-thirds majority vote to amend the rules. The nuclear option is a work-around in which the majority leader raises a point of order to the presiding officer about the requirement, the presiding officer denies the point of order, and the denial is appealed by the majority leader and overturned by a simple majority vote.

Alternatively, a majority party can appeal to the parliamentarian to declare that a bill related to the budget satisfies the criteria for reconciliation, under which only a simple majority is needed for passage. Such a ruling was obtained on behalf of the Democrats' razor-thin Senate majority in 2021 for the Build Back Better bill and in 2022 for the Inflation Reduction Act.

6.4. Discussion

Empirically, during 1930–1990, party separation in the US House was consistently small and partisan overlap consistently large, while legislation was

CONSEQUENCES OF POLARIZATION

keyed to the legislator at the chamber median. By contrast, during approximately the years 1856–1930 and again from 1990 to the present, partisan overlap has been negligible and expected legislative outcomes have followed the majority-party median, swinging widely back and forth as first one party and then the other held the majority.

We highlight and compare *majority-party* medians—which are keyed to strong party government—and *chamber* medians—which are keyed to legislation under legislator-centric government. We have seen from Figure 6.4A that before about 1930 and after 1990, the chamber median was (relatively speaking) much closer to the majority median than was the case during the less polarized era from the 1930s through the 1980s. Thus, insofar as legislation tracks the *majority-party* median during polarized periods characterized by strong party government (1856–1930 and 1990–2020) but follows the *chamber* median during periods of partisan overlap and legislator-centric government (1930–1990), the contrast in the extremity of legislative activity between party-centric and legislator-centric eras is accentuated. The correlation between chamber and majority-party medians, furthermore, is found to be much stronger during periods of polarization (low partisan overlap) than during the period of high partisan overlap.

Finally, we highlight the conditions under which the capacity of the majority party to retain the support of the chamber median legislator—as strong party government requires—can be compromised. We show, however, that during periods of significant partisan overlap, the median legislator of the minority party can be closer to the chamber median than is the majority party median, if the relative concentration of the minority party is sufficient to compensate for its low seat share.

This theoretical expectation is generally borne out by the empirical record. Furthermore, again during periods of high partisan overlap, legislators that may hold a pivotal position in determining the content of legislation—including the median legislator as well as those located near that median—often belong to the minority party, thus providing power to that party.

7

Discussion and Conclusions

7.1. What We Have Learned

The guiding force toward polarization, as we have seen again and again in this book, is party discipline, which imposes constraints on the ideological positions that US Congressional candidates can assume, and in turn limits the political options from which voters can choose. These effects are exacerbated by party loyalty, the role of activists, voters' threat of abstention, and the desire for parties to compete in multiple districts with one national brand. Thus, our first major Conclusion is:

Conclusion 7.1. Tight national party discipline of House candidates in both parties generates district elections that choose party delegations to Congress that are ideologically widely separated from one another, while each delegation separately is ideologically narrowly distributed.

On the other hand, if the leeway permitted to district candidates by national parties is sufficiently relaxed so that district candidates can deviate greatly from national policy norms, then party delegation distributions are broad, ideologically close to each other, and overlapping. If there is asymmetry in the permitted leeway maintained by the two national parties, the degree of polarization is similar to that under equal leeway, but both partisan delegations can shift decidedly in the direction of the party employing the tighter constraint, and, *ceteris paribus*, the party with the looser constraint will win a majority.

As estimated by Snyder and Groseclose (2000) and tracked historically by Pearson (2015), the strength of party discipline began to decline from a high near the beginning of the 20th century. From World War II to the 1970s, both parties exercised relatively loose constraints, while the two party delegations overlapped on policy positions and were each relatively heterogeneous. During this period, the Democratic Party, composed of Northern and Southern wings, had the looser constraint and maintained a majority

How Polarization Begets Polarization. Samuel Merrill III, Bernard Grofman, and Thomas L. Brunell, Oxford University Press. © Oxford University Press 2024. DOI: 10.1093/oso/9780197745229.003.0007

118 CONSEQUENCES OF POLARIZATION

in the House throughout the period. Since the 1970s, however, both parties' constraints have tightened, as parties have increasingly expected their members to toe the party line, while polarization proceeded and each party became more homogeneous. Following the 1994 election, the erstwhile minority Republican Party greatly tightened its leash under Speaker Gingrich (whereas according to party-constraint theory alone, they should have relaxed it) and won a majority. Gingrich and other Republican leaders were able to do this in part because they nationalized support for Republican House candidates, convincing voters to cast their votes to secure a well-defined national, but party-specific, program rather than to vote for individuals that would represent their own local interests (Theriault, 2008).

Empirically, we provided evidence that:

> **Conclusion 7.2. Winning candidates of the two parties for seats in the House, especially in recent decades, tend to be at least as ideologically divergent—from the median voter in their district—in competitive districts as in noncompetitive ones.**

We have shown that, theoretically, a spatial model accounting for party loyalty and the threat of abstention implies divergent positions that constitute optimal strategies for office-seeking candidates. Moreover, additional components of polarization may increase with the *square* of the across-district variation in district ideology. Thus, these factors combine with party discipline to engender highly divergent party positions, even in competitive districts. Furthermore, we showed that, empirically,

> **Conclusion 7.3. The lion's share of the growth in polarization in the House in the past half century can be attributed to the dramatic increase in the divergence between party platforms at the district level.**

Addressing the consequences of polarization, we argued that:

> **Conclusion 7.4. As party polarization grows, activists (often with relatively extreme views) tend to exhibit greater intensity about the election outcome than non-activists (often with less extreme views), thus reinforcing the expected influence of party activists (and extreme views) within a party.**

DISCUSSION AND CONCLUSIONS 119

Furthermore:

Conclusion 7.5. Given sufficient polarization between the supporters of the two parties, party loyalty combined with the threat of abstention should lead not to Downsian convergence but to divergence of party positions closer to the medians of the respective party bases than to the overall median. Under such circumstances, parties and their candidates have reason to mobilize their base rather than appeal to centrists.

Furthermore:

Conclusion 7.6. Polarization decreases the number of competitive districts and the prevalence of split-ticket voting, even though Congress may be polarized without concomitant polarization by voters. At the same time, when unified government of one party is followed by similar control by the other party, legislative polarization generates sharp policy reversals as well as greatly increased gridlock during divided government.

Thus, the Congressional pendulum swings along a continuum from, at one end, legislator-centric government associated with significant partisan overlap and relatively stable policy outcomes keyed to the chamber median, and, at the other end, strong party government associated with party separation and legislative outcomes strongly correlated with the majority-party median.

During periods of significant partisan overlap, as we've demonstrated, the power of a minority party may be sufficiently concentrated to be ideologically closer to the chamber median than is the majority party. As a consequence, the minority party may be able to forge winning coalitions with members of the majority party, as when the cross-party conservative coalition of Northern Republicans and Southern Democrats in the mid-century was at the peak of its power.

In summary, we find:

Conclusion 7.7. Polarization generates reinforcing and exacerbating forces such that, even without conscious intent on the part of political actors, polarization tends to generate more polarization.

7.2. Long-Term Cyclical Time Trends Associated with Changes in Polarization

American politics have undergone long periods of polarization as well as a long period of overlapping party distributions. We have offered institutional and structural explanations for the rise of polarization in an effort to complement explanations based on substantive factors such as immigration and economic inequality or specific triggering events, such as the passage of the Voting Rights Act. As seen in the accordion-like pattern in Figure 1.1, we have gone from increasing polarization in the House (from about 1860 to 1900) to decreasing or stable levels of party separation (about 1910 to 1970) and back to a world of increasing polarization (beginning about 1970), at intervals that range from about 40 to 70 years.[1] But so far, there has been no evidence of a reversal of the trend toward polarization during the recent 50 years.[2] This raises the question addressed in the next section.

7.3. Can Polarization Be Reversed?

We began this book with a quote from the famous 1950 Report of a committee of the American Political Science Association, which called for a more responsible two-party system. Its goal was to establish "a centralized and logical system which will define alternative policies with clarity and will guarantee their execution through improved means of party discipline" (Schlesinger, 1951, 222). But we now need to rethink that goal. We have arrived at a level of what we call hyper-polarization that can best be characterized as a holy war that only extreme partisans want but which now has spread to the point that many ordinary voters are reluctant to see family marriages across party lines.[3] This is a conflict that, as in the Disney version of Dukas's *Sorcerer's Apprentice,* we apparently don't know when or how to stop. Even a million COVID deaths did not move us in the direction of moderation. But even extreme partisans may wonder about the desirability of our predicament, if for no other reason than that they can imagine someday being on the losing side.

---

[1] Given the entire time series, Brady and Han (2015) note that polarization is nothing new in American politics, then go further to suggest "it is the immediate post-World War II era that is really unusual" (141).

[2] See Hare, Poole, and Rosenthal (2015).

[3] "In 1980, only 5 percent of Republicans said they wouldn't want their kids to marry a Democrat. By 2010 that figure had risen to 49 percent" (Runciman, 2018, 57; internal citation omitted).

DISCUSSION AND CONCLUSIONS 121

Schlesinger's review expresses his grave doubts about the wisdom of the Report's advice. He suggests (222) that American political scientists are

infatuated with the British party system (as it is understood or misunderstood in the United States). The committee's proposals could hardly work without a reorganization of our parties on taut ideological lines. Yet one must question (as the report never does) not only whether such a reorganization is feasible, but also whether it is desirable. May not our existing system be better suited to the genius of a country considerably more far flung, diverse and heterogeneous than Britain? Is not the fact that each party has a liberal and conservative wing a genuine source of national strength and cohesion? The result is, of course, that no group can have the desperate feeling that all options are foreclosed, all access to power barred, by the victory of the opposition: there will always be somebody in a Democratic administration on whose shoulders business can weep, and even a Republican administration will have somewhere a refuge for labor.[4]

Schlesinger further asserts (222), in language that seems increasingly prescient: *"If the party division were strictly ideological, each presidential election would subject national unity to a fearful test. We must remember that the one election when our parties stood irrevocably on questions of principle was the election of 1860"* (emphasis added). As we look toward the presidential election of 2024, not only can we expect to see the parties standing irrevocably apart on questions of policy but we certainly will also see them irrevocably opposed even on questions of fact. This coming presidential election, like that of 1860, is a potentially precarious one for American democracy.

Accordingly, perhaps the most pressing question today in US politics is: Can polarization be reversed? We believe that the answer to that question is yes. There is compelling historical evidence, presented in multidisciplinary studies such as that of Putnam and Garrett (2020) and in the more direct evidence of the alternating patterns of DW-NOMINATE scores shown in Figure 1.1, that the United States can in principle reverse a pattern of increasing polarization. There is a long litany of factors that could affect and possibly mitigate polarization, such as changes in the demographic composition of the electorate, changes in national policies related to immigration or income inequality, new electoral rules and alternative voting procedures (including ranked-choice

---

[4] Reproduced with permission, from Schlesinger, 1951.

voting and proportional representation), the strengthening (or weakening) of party organizations, reform of internal Congressional rules such as the filibuster, and changes in the media and the internet.

Putnam and Garrett place the long-term cycle of polarization in a much larger context. They provide extensive evidence that the cyclic pattern of polarization from the late 19th century to the present is seen not just in politics and economics but also in culture. Furthermore, they emphasize the parallels between the Gilded Age of the late 19th century and the present time. They identify the Progressive Era of the early 20th century as the catalyst that reversed major trends in politics, economics, and culture, with culture (in their reckoning) as the driving force. To quote Putnam and Garrett (19–20):

> If ever there were a historical moment whose lessons we as a nation need to learn, then, it is the moment when the first American Gilded Age turned into the Progressive Era, a moment which set in motion a sea change that helped us reclaim our nation's promise, and whose effects rippled into almost every corner of American life for over half a century. Understanding what set those trends in motion, then, becomes of critical importance.

We agree with the Putnam-Garrett analysis that any shift away from polarization (and from other concurrent trends) will be long-range, requiring decades. While we do not disagree about the role that culture may have played as a leading indicator of economic and political change, we regard an investigation of the kinds of cultural forces that influenced the reversal of the polarization of the Gilded Age as outside the scope of this volume. Nor will we attempt to delve into all the likely consequences of changes in the proposed mitigating factors enumerated earlier. Instead, we will focus on three possible factors that might have a long-term effect on polarization that can be derived from our institutionalist perspective.

7.3.1. Asymmetric constraints

Suppose that the constraints exerted in our model by the national parties and activists on their candidates for Congress are initially tight and of equal strength, conditions that, as we have seen in Chapter 2, lead to polarization. If exogenous conditions are such that one party—say, the Republicans—wins a legislative majority, the opposition (Democratic Party) has an incentive to relax its constraint and support moderate candidates in order to help win marginal seats and thereby regain the majority. This change would render the constraints exercised by the two parties asymmetric in strength, and as we saw in Figure 2.3, the Democratic delegation should become more moderate while the Republican delegation should become more extreme.

In fact, that occurred in the US House elections in 2018, with electoral success for the Democratic party as it retook the House, and as expected, both party delegations shifted to the right, as described in the Polsby Paradox (Chapter 3).[5] In general, other things being equal, when the Democrats—by relaxing their constraint—regain a majority, the Republican Party in turn has an incentive to expand its support by loosening its constraint as well, an action that would yield more moderation for both parties, thereby over time generating a reversal of polarization. Of course, the Republicans retained the Senate in 2018, but they did lose both the Senate and presidency in 2020. Still, they did not moderate.

Again, more generally, the scenario—under which a tight-constraint party relaxes its grip when faced with a moderate opposition party—may be delayed because it begins with a majority party that operates under tight discipline. Such a party is likely to be internally homogeneous (Chapter 2), with a core of policy-oriented activists (Chapter 5), and hence to possess the attributes specified in conditional party government for strong party government (see Chapter 6), leading to legislative efficiency (from its point of view) and further tightening of its discipline. Thus, the timing when both constraints loosen may be difficult to predict and the tenure of polarization may be prolonged.

But, taking the long view, even if the center holds for decades and less-polarized government is maintained, such a flight to the center will itself eventually be reversed. Greater moderation leads to abstention due to alienation and the threat of third parties on the flanks, which has the potential to eventually reverse the trend toward moderation (Callander and Wilson, 2007). Thus, we have a mechanism for cycling between periods of ideological polarization and ideological convergence—likely one with irregular and lengthy periods, as has been the experience in the United States for the last century and a half.

---

[5] The mean first-dimension DW-NOMINATE score for Democrats moved right by 0.021 and that for Republicans moved right by 0.016 between the House delegations elected in 2016 and 2018.

7.3.2. Changes in redistricting mechanisms

We have shown that simply adding more competitive seats cannot cure polarization, since, when polarization is extreme, even districts with a moderate median voter may experience only a choice between relatively extreme candidates of the two parties. Nonetheless, extreme partisan gerrymandering has other pernicious effects, especially by raising the stakes of party control. With extreme partisan gerrymandering, parties may hold on to majority or supermajority control in state legislatures or Congressional delegations, even in the face of electoral tides running against them and even after losing a majority of the statewide vote. This lock on power provides strong incentives to ignore minority views within the legislature or even the views of a majority of the overall electorate, and to fall back on the argument that to the victor belong all the spoils.

7.3.3. Introduction of new ideological or issue dimensions generating crosscutting cleavages

Might a major party that finds itself in the minority, or an insurgent presidential candidacy with new issues rising to the fore, reduce polarization? The models in this book are based on an assumption of unidimensionality, and our empirical analyses have considered only the first dimension of the DW-NOMINATE scores. William Riker's book *Liberalism Against Populism* (1982) suggests a mechanism through which a major crosscutting second dimension could fracture existing coalition lines built around an existing dimension. One of Riker's basic themes is that the side that is losing has an incentive to introduce issues that divide the opposition; the slavery issue before the Civil War is the most famous example.[6]

Chatfield, Jenkins, and Stewart (2021), in a study of the early 20th century and its emergence from the previous Gilded Age, find that the Farm Bloc and the Progressive Caucus managed to become a force in Congressional politics with crosscutting agendas that expanded beyond agricultural issues

---

[6] This divide-and-conquer technique did help the minority win some legislative contests, but it did not resolve the ultimate question of slavery. Manipulation that employs amendments in the form of "poison-pills" intended to split an opposing coalition is also harder to organize in the era of polarization and strong party government. See also Park's (2022) argument that partisan manipulation of dimensionality fosters party polarization in Congress.

DISCUSSION AND CONCLUSIONS   125

to include anti-railroad, pro-labor, anti-isolationist, anti-Prohibition, pro-regulation, and pro-tariff sentiments. These groups became a thorn in the side of the traditional wings of both parties, especially that of the GOP, and eventually helped expand the New Deal coalition. The researchers note, however, that these cross-party coalitions were not multiracial and hence did not face certain barriers that exist today.

McCarty (2015) points out that by mid-century parties were divided on crosscutting dimensions: namely, race and region (which were tied together), on the one hand, and economic policy, on the other. Today, in the 21st century, both partisanship and racial identity affect voting. Rosenfeld (2017) suggests that a successful insurgent candidate for president wielding a crosscutting agenda could potentially lead to a broader transformation in the party system, and by rejuggling party coalitions could dramatically change the current pattern of polarization and generate a crosscutting cleavage. But what a second crosscutting dimension might be today is not at all clear, as cultural and economic issues have largely been rolled into a single ideological dimension.[7] Moreover, empirical evidence suggests that today's voters primarily change their issue positions to match their party rather than change their party to match their issue positions (Levendusky, 2009).

7.4. Coda

Overall, we are pessimistic about a reduction in hyper-polarization in the short run. We have strived to provide compelling evidence that a multiplicity of forces operates to reinforce polarization, and that a positive feedback loop ensures that polarization breeds more polarization.

It is possible that some catastrophic event or all-encompassing initiative might dramatically reverse the current trend, as the Civil War led to the end of slavery or as the New Deal and World War II led to economic recovery and a reduction for many decades in the level of economic inequality. Such events would not need to be intentionally designed to end partisan extremism.

---

[7] In 2016 Trump used his brand of populism and anti-globalism as wedges to fracture the old Democratic coalition to his advantage (see Buisseret and Van Weelden, 2020). Subsequently, however, he corralled and unified virtually the whole Republican Party, at least in the Congress, into his bloc of adherents, so his "new" issues may not have expanded in an enduring way the dimensionality of the ideological space.

126 CONSEQUENCES OF POLARIZATION

But we are skeptical of the likelihood of a tectonic event that could have such a salutary effect on polarization. The historical evidence points elsewhere. While polarization can be reversed, reversal of the present polarization trend will most likely be a very slow and highly incremental process. "Quick fixes" are wishful thinking.

APPENDIX TO CHAPTER 1

Literature Review on Causes of Polarization

This Appendix elaborates on the very brief literature review in Chapter 1 of past work on causes of polarization. Having reviewed past approaches we will be in a better position to articulate in the succeeding chapters the ways in which our own approach is distinctive.

A1.1. Long-Term Cyclical Time Trends Associated with Changes in Polarization

There are many variables whose movements have been linked to polarization by various scholars, but even when we have variables that manifest a similar pattern to Figure 1 (see, e.g., Figure 1.1 among others in Putnam and Garrett, 2020), disentangling causality is not easy.

McCarty, Poole, and Rosenthal argue that polarization in Congress (2006: Chapter 1) is linked to two major factors—(1) increased income inequality and (2) increased immigration—and that polarization in the electorate is linked to both (Chapter 3). As these authors note, the Gini index of income inequality in the United States has tracked polarization in the House quite closely since the 1940s, while the income share of the top one percent suggests that economic inequality has correlated with polarization since the second decade of the 20th century (see Figs. 1.1 and 1.2 in McCarty et al., 2006). The period of lowest polarization in the post–World War II era is also the period in which income inequality was lowest; while the Gini index of family income increased from about 0.36 in the 1950s and 1960s to about 0.43 by 2000 and has risen further since. See also Alexander and Magazinnik's (2022) study of income inequality and polarization and Shor and McCarty's (2022) study of polarization in state legislatures.

The mechanism that links income to party choice by voters, however, has been challenged by Abramowitz (2010). He points out that factors other than income—such as race, gender, marital status, and religious commitment—are more predictive of partisan voting than income. For example, in recent House and presidential elections, a large majority of lower-income whites who regularly attend religious services voted Republican; whereas a majority of upper-income whites who rarely or never attend religious services voted Democratic. Thus, although there is a strong longitudinal correlation between income inequality and partisan polarization, it appears problematic to argue that polarization is primarily a consequence of income inequality, particularly in recent decades. Moreover, partisan identification differences along lines of educational attainment have grown, and this effect is partially crosscutting with income. Today, those with a college education, and particularly those with a graduate degree, are more likely to be Democrats.

At the same time, McCarty et al. (2006, 9) also note that, from at least about 1880, the degree of Congressional polarization rather closely tracks the percent of the country that was foreign-born (see Fig. 1.3 in McCarty et al., 2006). These researchers note that, following a substantial period of immigration (much of it from southern and eastern Europe) during the late 19th and early 20th centuries, immigration was drastically slowed

128 APPENDIX TO CHAPTER 1

by World War I and the restrictive immigration acts of the 1920s. Consequently, the percentage of foreign-born dropped precipitously while the children and grandchildren of the late-19th-century immigrant groups were becoming "Americanized" and were taking their place in mainstream American politics, leading eventually to the election of America's first Catholic president in 1960. Following the liberalization of immigration rules in the 1960s, the foreign-born percentage again rose rapidly as immigration resumed, but this time largely from Mexico and Central America.

A1.2. Other Factors That Have Influenced the Growth in Polarization since World War II

Fiorina and Abrams (2009), like McCarty et al. (2006), identify immigration as a factor in continued polarization, but they also identify a number of other key demographic and cultural changes that they see as linked to increased polarization after World War II, including migration of African-Americans from the South to the North, the rise of the Sun Belt, the revolution in the role of women, and the politicization of evangelicalism. While trends in some of these factors do not seem to parallel what we see in Figure 1.1A, others might easily be viewed as potential *triggers* for an increase in polarization after the 1960s.

The rise, in the 1960s and 1970s, of the women's movement, the movement for gay rights, and the anti-abortion movement had combined effects that eventually led to a considerable sorting of party support based on those cultural issues. This was also the era of both antiestablishment culture and massive anti-Vietnam war protests, along with the ensuing backlash. It is certainly plausible to view these changes in the political environment as triggers for polarization, since they, too, fostered an "us versus them" mentality. At the same time, as recounted by Rosenfeld (2017), activists and politicians intentionally developed disciplined, responsible parties that became dominated by issue-oriented interest groups, leading to ever-growing polarization.

We would call particular attention to two landmark pieces of 1960s legislation: the Civil Rights Act of 1964 and the Voting Rights Act of 1965, the latter of which had profound effects beginning with the 1970s round of redistricting.[1] While the time trends predate the 1960s, it is not until the Nixon presidency that it becomes obvious that the two major parties had largely switched places with regard to race—with the Republicans no longer the party of Lincoln (Carmines and Stimson, 1989; Karol, 2009). The effects of this racial reversal soon became clear, signaled first by Barry Goldwater's success in several Southern states in 1964 and then by the George Wallace candidacy in 1968. With Republicans following what came to be called the "Southern strategy," the door was open to nationalized polarizing forces. The 1980s and 1990s were marked by a secular realignment in the American South, with many White Democrats simply switching parties in voting behavior if not in party identification, and many Democratic officeholders losing to Republican candidates in both the House and the Senate. By 1994, the once dominant Democrats lost their Southern wing (at least for majority-White districts), with parallel

---

[1] We also note that, thanks to the Supreme Court's insistence on "deliberate speed," the full impact on school desegregation of *Brown v. Board of Education of Topeka*, 347 U.S. 483 (1954) did not come until more than a decade later (along with the new role of busing and the protests that this decision triggered).

APPENDIX TO CHAPTER 1   129

but not quite as striking declines in Republican strength in the Northeast and later in the Far West.

With the withering away of the Democratic Party's conservative Southern wing, the race dimension increasingly became folded into unidimensional competition. Moreover, identity politics pursued by both parties, especially recently, has led to a racialized party system, with racial and ethnic minorities overwhelmingly identifying as Democrats, and many Whites (especially those in the South, those without a college education, those in rural areas, and those with conservative religious values) becoming Republicans. This racial divide strongly supports a bipolar structure to political competition (see, e.g., Glazer, Grofman, and Owen, 1989).

There has also been a change in the internal organization of the parties that can be directly linked to polarization—namely, a rise in the role of ideological activists and the rise of intentionally responsible parties. Well before blind support of President Trump became the hallmark of congressional Republicans, the party bases, and especially party activists, had become more and more intolerant of candidates, including long-standing members of Congress, who did not adhere completely to the developing national party line. Relatedly, polarization along educational and informational lines is certainly important in contributing to sorting in terms of party voting and party loyalty but also in terms of fundamental generational belief differences within the electorate—such as about the importance and efficacy of COVID-19 vaccinations, and about the unfounded claims that the 2020 election was stolen from Trump through massive electoral fraud, or that six million illegal aliens voted in 2016—distinctions that involve irreconcilable conceptions of reality. Moreover, changes in the nature of campaign financing have led to a greatly increased importance of donors with political agendas of their own.

APPENDIX TO CHAPTER 2

The Party-Constraint Model

A2.1. Modeling Changes in Polarization

A2.1.1. The basic party-constraint model for party polarization

As indicated in the main text, we model party polarization in a two-party legislature, allowing for both constituency-specific and national effects. We assume that national party positions are tied to the ideological preferences of the set of representatives elected from each party, and that there are constraints on the degree of deviation from national policy positions allowed to candidates. These national party constraints may prevent full convergence to the district median and hence affect how easy it is for candidates of the two parties to be competitive in any given district.

Our model assumes that

1. The median voter ideal points over districts follow a specified distribution on a [0–100] left-right continuum (with higher numbers indicating more conservative positions), similar to a scale such as ADA or ACU scores, or the first dimension of DW-NOMINATE scores.
2. The platform positions of Democratic and Republican candidates are located on the [0–100] continuum and do not change after the election. In any district, the platform of the Republican candidate is not to the left of the position of the Democratic candidate.
3. D and R denote the positions of the national parties, assumed initially to be equidistant from the midpoint of the scale. In the beginning and after any election, D and R are evaluated as the mean positions of the respective party's set of representatives in the legislature.

Accordingly, we introduce parameters W_D and W_R (using the scale of the [0, 100] continuum) to define the constraints (i.e., the length of the "tether" exercised by a party) on Democratic and Republican candidates, respectively, from their national party positions. In other words, in our model, we further specify either:

4A. *One-sided constraints*: The most liberal position that can be taken by any Republican candidate is $R - W_R$, and the most conservative position that can be taken by any Democratic candidate is $D + W_D$. That is, the Republican and Democratic candidates are restricted to $[R - W_R, 100]$ and $[0, D + W_D]$, respectively, or

4B. *Two-sided constraints*: Republican and Democratic candidates are restricted to policy positions in the line segments $[R - W_R, R + W_R]$ and $[D - W_D, D + W_D]$, respectively.

132   APPENDIX TO CHAPTER 2

In either case, we replace the lower bound with 0 and the upper bound with 100, if needed. Finally, in each district, the candidate closer to the district median voter wins.

To make the modeling more tractable, we initially make several further simplifying assumptions on assumptions 1–3 (which will be relaxed later):

1′. District median voters follow a continuous, *uniform distribution* on [0, 100].

2′. R and D are initially exogenously given, and symmetrically located around 50.

3′. $W_D = W_R = W$, and the value of this parameter is exogenously given.

These assumptions allow us to focus on the long-run effects of W on legislative polarization by holding fixed other factors that would affect polarization. For convenience, in the following examples, we will assume 100 seats.

Example 1. Under these simplifying assumptions, first suppose that $R = 60$ and $D = 40$, and suppose a tight constraint—say, $W = 5$ (see Fig. A2.1). To read the figure, note that the leeway allowed is indicated on the vertical axis. So for a leeway of 5 units, focus on the horizontal dashed line in the figure. The solid slanting line is the Democratic bound; its intersection with the dotted horizontal line represents how conservative a stance a Democratic district candidate can take, a value of 45 in this case. In any district whose median m lies in the range [55, 100], the Republican can locate at that median m but the Democrat cannot, so the Republican wins at location m. In the interval (50, 55], the Republican wins while constrained to locate at 55. Similarly, Democrats win for district medians in the interval [45, 50). Overall, the Republican mean is (45*77.5 + 5*55)/50 = 75.25 (and similarly, the Democratic mean is 24.75), yielding a partisan gap after this first election of 50.5. With House delegation means now at $R = 75.25$ and $D = 24.75$, after a second election, similar calculations show that the Republican and Democratic means become $R = 79.1$ and $D = 20.9$, with a partisan gap of 58.2. Thus, in this example, under our simplifying assumptions, the partisan-constraint model we have posited moves the parties significantly further apart from their previous positions at $R = 60$ and $D = 40$, for which the partisan gap was only 20—first to a gap of 50.5, then after a second election to an even larger gap of 58.2.

Example 2. Again, starting with $R = 60$ and $D = 40$, let us suppose a looser constraint—say, $W = 20$ (see Fig. A2.1). In districts whose median voter m lies in the range (60, 100], the Democratic candidate is restricted by the constraint from entering this interval, so the Republican can locate at m but the Democrat cannot. Hence, the Republican wins, taking a position at m. Similarly, within the interval [0, 40), the Democrat wins with a position at m. Within the central interval [40, 60], both candidates can locate at m, each winning with probability 0.5. Calculation shows that, following a first election, the party delegation means become $R = 74.0$ and $D = 26.0$, for a partisan gap of 48.0. But after a second election, the means change little, to $R = 75.2$ and $D = 24.8$, for a partisan gap of 50.6, somewhat less than the gap of 58.2 observed earlier under a tight constraint. As for the tight constraint considered earlier, party delegations that are initially only moderately separated (by 20 points) are drawn much further apart, but following a subsequent election, little further change occurs.

To unify the results suggested by the two examples above, let G be the pre-election gap between the Democratic and Republican means—that is, $G = R - D$. When $W \leq G/2$ (i.e., the permitted constraint or leeway $W \leq 10$ for the setting when $G = 20$), the Republican candidate wins at location $60 - W$ if $50 \leq m \leq 60 - W$ and s/he wins at m if $60 - W \leq m \leq 100$. These conditions and those for $W \geq G/2$ are summarized in Merrill et al., 2014: Table 1. Similar conditions for Democratic candidates are mirror images of these because of the symmetry.

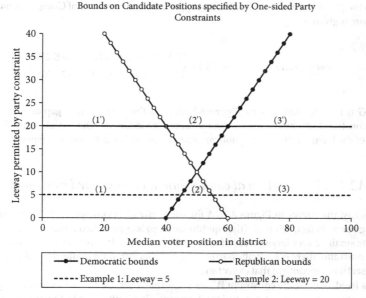

Figure A2.1. Bounds on Candidate Positioning

A2.1.2. Calculation of the post-election gap for a one-sided constraint

Initially let G denote the pre-election gap between the partisan means. For convenience in calculating mean partisan positions, we replace the continuum [0, 100] of our illustrative examples by a continuum of length 1 centered about 0—that is, the interval [−0.5, 0.5]. Thus, for D and R symmetrical about 0, if $W \geq G/2$, the mean Republican position is given by

$$\frac{1}{0.5}\left[\frac{1}{2}\int_{G/2-W}^{-G/2+W} m\,dm + \int_{-G/2+W}^{0.5} m\,dm\right] = 1/4 - (W - G/2)^2. \quad (A2.1a)$$

and, similarly, if $W \leq G/2$, the mean Republican position is given by

$$\frac{1}{0.5}\left[\int_{0}^{G/2-W}(G/2-W)\,dm + \int_{G/2-W}^{0.5} m\,dm\right] = 1/4 + (W - G/2)^2. \quad (A2.1b)$$

Note that, after the election, the difference between the Republican position and the Democratic position is the post-election gap between the Congressional party means, which, by symmetry, is twice the value of the expression in equation A2.1a (for $W \geq G/2$) and twice the value of the expression in equation A2.1b (for $W \leq G/2$). Thus, converting

134 APPENDIX TO CHAPTER 2

back to the [0, 100] scale, the *post-election gap*, which is our measure of Congressional polarization, is given by:

$$Post-election\ gap = f(G;W) = \begin{cases} 50 - 0.02(W - G/2)^2, & G \le 2W \\ 50 + 0.02(W - G/2)^2, & G \ge 2W \end{cases}, \quad (A2.2)$$

where G is the pre-election gap. Figure A2.2A plots the post-election gap as a function of the constraint, W, after each of several successive elections. The initial values for the means of the Democratic and Republican delegations are set at 40 and 60, respectively.

A2.1.3. Polarization at equilibrium for a one-sided constraint

Graphically, the curves in Figure A2.2A for successive elections appear to converge to a limiting curve; in fact, this limit (the equilibrium gap) is approached rather rapidly, except for quite small or very large values of the constraint.[1] Thus, it appears that for each value of the constraint, there is a specific partisan gap that becomes stable after several elections. In this section, we confirm that expectation.

For a fixed value of the constraint W, we show that, over a series of elections, the post-election gap converges to a limit, and we determine that limit—that is, the gap at equilibrium, denoted by $\bar{G}$:

$$\bar{G} = \begin{cases} 2W - 1 + \sqrt{2 - 4W}, & G \le 2W \\ 2W + 1 - 2\sqrt{W}, & G \ge 2W \end{cases}. \quad (A2.3)$$

To derive this result, note that each post-election gap becomes the pre-election gap for the next election. The sequence over elections of partisan gaps defined by repeated application of the function $f(G;W)$ defined by equation A2.2 (for fixed W) can be shown to converge when the gaps lie in an interval slightly smaller than the interval from 0 to 100—that is, as long as the distance between the parties is neither 0 nor the full length of the scale, and when W lies in an interval slightly smaller than from 0 to 50. The sequence $\{G_n\}$ where $G_{n+1} = f(G_n;W)$ and G_0 is an appropriate starting value, will converge if $\left|\dfrac{\partial}{\partial G} f(G;W)\right| \le K < 1$ for some K (Henrici, 1964: Ch. 4). Calculation of the derivative shows that this is true as long as G_n remains bounded away from 0 and from 100, and W remains bounded away from 0 and 50—that is, for any intervals of the form $\varepsilon \le G_n \le 100 - \varepsilon$ and $\varepsilon \le W \le 50 - \varepsilon$, for some positive ε. Thus, to determine the limit of the iterated sequence of post-election gaps, it suffices to solve the equation $G = f(G;W)$.

Denoting the solution of this equation by $\bar{G}$, we obtain equation A2.3.

---

[1] For W between 5 and 45, the post-election gap approaches within 5 units of its limit in two elections or less.

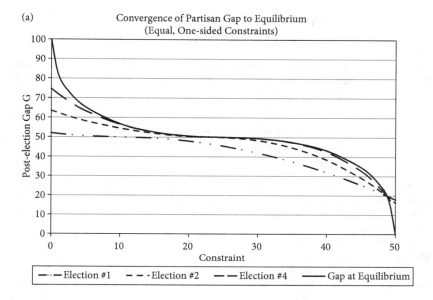

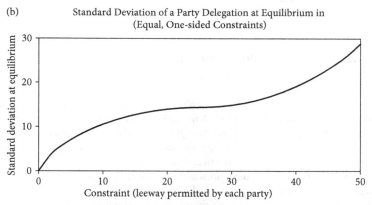

Figure A2.2. Post-Election Gap and Standard Deviation for the Party-Constraint Model after Successive Elections for a One-Sided Constraint

Notes: Before the first election, the means of the Democratic and Republican delegations are set at 40 and 60, respectively. The partisan gap at equilibrium, however, is independent of the initial partisan gap.

Thus, equation A2.3 defines the post-election limit of the partisan gap at equilibrium, for any given value of W—that is, the gap to which the system will settle down after a sequence of elections. The post-election partisan gap at equilibrium is independent of the initial gap and is plotted in Figure A2.2A against the constraint W. Note that the equilibrium gap increases as W decreases from 50 down to 0; that is, party separation is greatest for tight party constraints.

136   APPENDIX TO CHAPTER 2

A2.1.4. Intraparty variance at equilibrium for a one-sided constraint

Letting X denote a random Republican member of the House, we first compute $E(X^2)$ using formulas analogous to those of equations A2.1, then employ the formula $Var(X) = E(X^2) - E(X)^2$ and evaluate when the system is at equilibrium. We obtain:

$$Var(X) = 10^4 \begin{cases} (1/48) + (1/8)(1 - 0.1\sqrt{200 - 4W})^2 - (1/16)(1 - \sqrt{200 - 4W})^4, & \bar{G} \le 2W \\ (1/48) + (0.5 - 0.1\sqrt{W})^2 \left[-0.5 + (4/3)(0.5 - 0.1\sqrt{W}) - (0.5 - 0.1\sqrt{W})^2 \right], & \bar{G} > 2W \end{cases}$$

By symmetry, the same formula holds for the Democrats. See Figure A2.2B for a plot of the intraparty standard deviation at equilibrium as a function of the party constraint W. Note that the intraparty standard deviation is smallest for tight constraints and largest for lax constraints.

Both the partisan means and their variance are depicted in Figure A2.3. For each part, this figure shows curves one standard deviation above the party mean and one standard deviation below that mean. Part A of that figure portrays these curves as a function of the party constraint as projected by the party-constraint model. Part B presents the same curves, based entirely on the empirical record 1856–2020, but here the X-axis is the year of the Congress.

A2.1.5. Gap at equilibrium for normally distributed district medians

So far, we have considered only a uniform distribution for the district medians. If instead the district medians are normally distributed, numerical calculation shows that, after successive elections, the post-election gap quickly approaches a limit whose plot against the constraint is similar in shape to that for the uniform distribution (as in Fig. A2.2A). The plots of gap versus constraint for the uniform and normal distributions of district medians are almost identical if the standard deviations of the two distributions are the same.

Empirically, the distributions of district medians have been very roughly normally distributed in each Congress over the past half century, and the standard deviation of the district medians has increased from about 11.8 for Congresses during the decade 1956–1964 to about 15.2 during the period 2006–2012 (using our 100-point scale). If, say, $W = 25$, it can be shown that the approximation above suggests partisan gaps at equilibrium in the House of about 20 points during 1956–1964 and about 26 points during 2006–2012. On a scale from −1 to +1, the latter translates to partisan gaps of 0.40 and 0.52, although this cannot be directly interpreted on the DW-NOMINATE scale. As indicated in the main text, we will see in Chapter 4 that heterogeneity of district medians is only one component of the partisan gap in the House.

APPENDIX TO CHAPTER 2 137

(a)
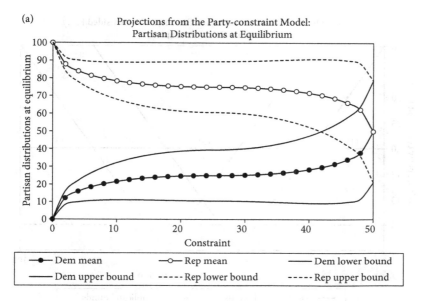

(b)
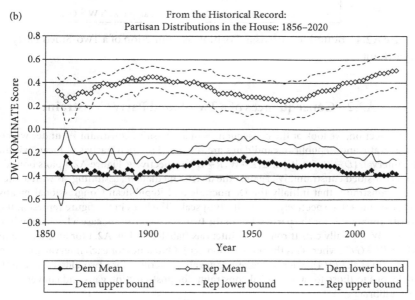

Figure A2.3. Theoretical and Empirical Partisan Distributions at Equilibrium

Note: In parts A and B, for each partisan mean, the curves on either side are one standard deviation above and below the mean. Equal, one-sided constraints are assumed in part A.

138 APPENDIX TO CHAPTER 2

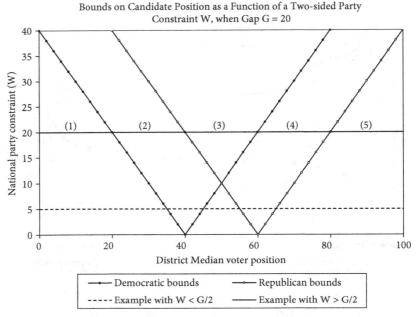

Figure A2.4. Bounds on Partisan Position as a Function of a Two-Sided Party Constraint

A2.2. Consequences of a Two-Sided Party Constraint

In this section, we look at the consequences of a *two-sided* constraint W under which Democratic and Republican candidates are restricted by their parties to locate within the intervals $[D-W, D+W]$ and $[R-W, R+W]$, respectively. Figure A2.4 plots bounds for a two-sided constraint, W, against the district median, m, assuming, as with a one-sided constraint, that initially the Democratic and Republican Congressional means fall at 40 and 60, respectively, on the [0, 100] scale. The lines in the figure represent the constraint bounds for the parties, but in the two-sided constraint case a horizontal line at level W typically cuts through five intervals (labeled in Fig. A2.4 for an example in which $W > G/2$, where G is the pre-election gap). Outcomes for each interval are given in Merrill et al. (2014), where calculations are also described for a two-sided constraint, analogous to those for a one-sided constraint, for post-election gaps and convergence to equilibria.

As is the case for one-sided constraints, the two-sided patterns of equilibria for other, symmetric district-median distributions are similar to one another. The gap between the partisan delegations, however, will vary with the degree of central concentration of the district median distribution.

A2.3. Effects of Asymmetry in the Strengths of the National Party Constraints

We consider the asymmetrical case in which one party's constraint may be tighter than that of the other party. Let us suppose that the Republican Party has a tighter constraint, and in particular that $W_R = q W_D$, where $0 < q < 1$. Figure 2.3 in the main text depicts the post-election partisan gap as a function of the Democratic Party's constraint W_D as the system approaches equilibrium, with q set equal to 0.5 (plots for other values of q show similar patterns).[2] The pattern of the plots are similar to those for equal constraints, except that—when constraints are unequal—the gap remains substantial for larger values of W_D because the other party still has a relatively tight constraint, W_R.

As noted in the main text, although the partisan gaps are not greatly different from the equal-constraint scenario, the partisan means are decidedly asymmetrical when constraints are unequal, as we saw in Figure 2.3. Replacing equal with unequal constraints transfers marginal seats from the party with the tighter constraint (in this example, the Republicans) to the party with the looser constraint (the Democrats). But this effect shifts the distributions of both partisan delegations in the direction of the party with the tighter constraint. For example, in Figure 2.3, when the Democratic constraint is of size 30 (on our 100-point scale) and the Republican constraint is 15, the Democratic mean is about 18 points from the center of the scale, whereas the Republican mean is about 33 points— that is, nearly twice as far—from that center. According to the model, in this example the Democratic delegation attains 60 percent of the seats by the second election.

---

[2] Because of the analytical complexity, we rely here on numerical calculations.

APPENDIX TO CHAPTER 3

Relation between Candidate and District Ideology: Statistical and Theoretical Analyses

A3.1. The Role of Dynamic versus Static DW-NOMINATE Scores

As indicated in the main text, the DW-NOMINATE scores used throughout the book are the *static* scores obtained from the website https://voteview.com/data. *Static* scores are used, because *dynamic* DW-NOMINATE scores (https://legacy.voteview.com/dwnomin. htm) are not available beyond the Congress elected in 2012. However, dynamic scores reflect ideological changes of individual legislators over time in successive Congresses (using a linear model), whereas static scores estimate a single fixed value for each legislator. The research described below suggests that both changes in individual legislators as well as replacement of legislators affect the partisan distribution of ideology.

Empirical analysis suggests that accounting for changes over time on the individual legislator level is important. Such changes have been noted by Bonica and Cox (2018, 208), who find empirically that a significant portion of ideological change for a party delegation is due to change over time by individual legislators. These authors state:

> Investigations by Theriault (2006, 2008) and Bonica (2014b) show that approximately 60% of the total increase in the ideological gap separating the parties has stemmed from the *replacement* of older and more moderate members by newer and more extreme legislators, with the remaining 40% due to *ideological migration*—that is, the movement of moderate members toward their respective parties' means over the course of their careers. Roberts and Smith (2003) find that increases in party voting can be parsed into similarly-sized effects due to replacement and behavioral change (emphases in the original).[1]

Bonica (2014b) further finds "that replacement drives polarization from the early 1970s through the mid-1990s, after which ideological migration drives the bulk of polarization." And it is during this more recent period (through the Congress elected in 2012) that Republican delegation means from dynamic scores have diverged from those from static scores.

Whether the dynamic or static scores are used to compute the means of party delegations can have a substantial effect on the results. Part A of Figure A3.1 demonstrates

---

[1] Reproduced with permission from Now Publishers.

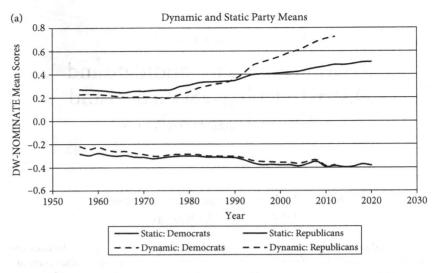

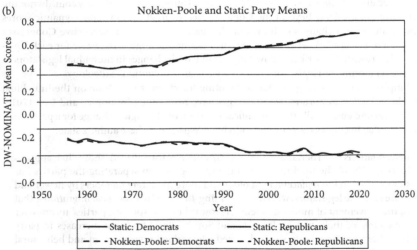

Figure A3.1. Comparison of Dynamic and Static Party Means of DW-NOMINATE Scores

that the party delegation means (and hence other statistics)—for Republican House members—are significantly different between the static and dynamic scores for the years through 2014 from which both types of scores are available. While the static and dynamic time series for Democrats are similar to one another, the dynamic time series for the Republican delegation have veered much more conservative than the static time series since the early 1990s. Thus, the dynamic time series provides strong evidence for asymmetric polarization, an inference we would argue is realistic.

APPENDIX TO CHAPTER 3   143

Alternative algorithms have been proposed in attempts to address shortcomings in constraints on legislator movement in the dynamic scores. One such method generates the Nokken-Poole scores (described in Nokken and Poole, 2004, and available through 2022 on the voteview.com website). These scores, however, yield delegation means almost identical to those of the static scores; see part B of Figure A3.1. Thus, use of Nokken-Poole scores would not significantly change the results of the analyses in this book, even though Nokken-Poole scores for individual legislators may vary over Congresses. In a more recent effort to incorporate a dynamic feature into the current algorithm for DW-NOMINATE scores, Lewis and Sonnet (2019) introduce a new alternative termed *penalized spline DW-NOMINATE scores* (PSDW-NOMINATE scores). This latter approach expands the constraints on long-serving legislators, permitting ideological movement, but still limits movement by constraining legislator positions to stay within the unit circle.

A3.2. Quadratic Analysis of the Relation of Candidate Ideology to District Ideology

We fit the following regression equation to the House data for 1956–2020:

$$\text{DW-NOMINATE score}_j = b_1 + b_2 \left[\text{District ideology}_j \right]$$
$$+ b_3 \left[\text{District ideology}_j \right]^2 + b_4 \left[South \right], \quad (A3.1)$$

where the DW-NOMINATE score$_j$ is representative j's DW-NOMINATE score.[2] The output from this quadratic regression analysis is presented in Table A3.1 (and reflected in the plots in Figure 3.1 in the main text).

The typical difference between the DW-NOMINATE scores of House members of the two major parties when the partisan composition of the district is 50–50 is indicated by the difference in *linear* regression intercepts (for this purpose, the horizontal scale is centered at a normalized presidential vote of 50–50). On the DW-NOMINATE scale of width 2.0 (with endpoints −1.0 and 1.0), this difference ranges from 0.49 to 0.56 units in the first four subperiods to 0.64 to 0.73 units in the three most recent subperiods, respectively, reflecting the increased polarization in the House. Clearly, party has a huge effect. Hence, in-district pressures from competitive races cannot be expected to dampen other incentives for polarization of members of Congress, such as pressures and constraints emanating from the national party or local activists.

As we have noted, given that districts with highly unequal partisanship are likely to be less competitive, conventional wisdom implies that we might observe the largest ideological gap between Republican and Democratic representatives in districts that feature lopsided presidential vote margins. Returning to the quadratic regression results in Table A3.1, the quadratic terms, which are fitted to the full 1956–2020 data and to its subperiods, do not conform to this conventional expectation. For both Democrats and Republicans, bowing *outward* is statistically significant at the 0.001 level for the full

---

[2] The South is defined as AL, AR, FL, GA, LA, MS, NC, SC, TN, TX, and VA. For simplicity, the party-specific regression curves and their confidence intervals in the figures are based on the full data set without the breakdown by region.

Table A3.1. Quadratic Regression of DW-NOMINATE Scores versus Ideology of the District

	Regression Coefficients							
Era	Democrats				Republicans			
	Intercept	South	Ideology	[Ideology]^2	Intercept	South	Ideology	[Ideology]^2
1956–2020 (full period)	−0.32*** (0.002)	0.12 *** (0.003)	−0.68 *** (0.01)	0.22 *** (0.05)	0.26*** (0.003)	0.07*** (0.004)	−1.23*** (0.04)	−1.45*** (0.18)
1956–1964	−0.36*** (0.005)	0.23 *** (0.01)	−0.32 *** (0.03)	0.15 (0.12)	0.22*** (0.006)	−0.01 (0.02)	−0.85*** (0.09)	−1.11** (0.42)
1966–1974	−0.34*** (0.005)	0.16 *** (0.01)	−0.57 *** (0.03)	0.05 (0.11)	0.21 *** (0.01)	0.00 (0.01)	−0.90*** (0.08)	−0.82 (0.49)
1976–1984	−0.33*** (0.005)	0.17 *** (0.01)	−0.82 *** (0.05)	0.58 (0.17)	0.21*** (0.01)	0.08*** (0.01)	−0.99*** (0.12)	0.81 (0.70)
1986–1994	−0.30*** (0.004)	0.07 *** (0.01)	−1.03 *** (0.04)	0.80 *** (0.15)	0.29*** (0.01)	0.03*** (0.01)	−1.03*** (0.10)	−0.80 (0.61)
1996–2004	−0.33*** (0.004)	0.04 *** (0.01)	−0.98 *** (0.04)	1.22 *** (0.13)	0.32*** (0.01)	0.03** (0.01)	−1.40*** (0.11)	−2.93*** (0.49)
2006–2014	−0.30*** (0.004)	0.02 *** (0.01)	−0.94 *** (0.04)	0.78*** (0.12)	0.34*** (0.01)	0.04*** (0.01)	−1.48*** (0.12)	−2.91*** (0.44)
2016–2020	−0.30*** (0.01)	0.00 (0.01)	−0.53 *** (0.07)	−0.15 (0.22)	0.38*** (0.01)	0.10*** (0.01)	−0.84*** (0.13)	−1.42 (0.43)

Notes. Significance levels are 2-sided. Significance at the 0.05 level is indicated by (*); that at the 0.01 level by (**); and that at the 0.001 level by (***). Ideology squared is indicated as significant only if the coefficient is significantly positive for Democrats and not positive for Republicans, or significantly negative for Republicans and not negative for Democrats, because curves satisfying these conditions indicate bowing out of the regression curves—that is, greater partisan divergence in more competitive districts. For neither the full period nor any of the subperiods did the evidence support bowing in. Ideology is proxied by the normalized Democratic proportion of the presidential vote in the district (the normalized Democratic vote was further rescaled to center at 0.5 to facilitate interpretation of the regression coefficients). For Democrats, $N = 7084$; for Republicans, $N = 5507$.

APPENDIX TO CHAPTER 3   145

period.[3] For four of the seven subperiods, both party coefficients are in the correct direction to imply bowing out and the coefficient for at least one of the parties is statistically significant at 0.01 or better. For no subperiod is the coefficient for either party significantly in the direction that would support bowing in.[4]

To summarize: For Republicans, curvature in the expected direction (i.e., bowing outward) is significant for the full period and for four of the seven eras; it never bows significantly in the opposite direction. Exactly the same holds for Democrats. Thus, we do not find evidence that the party curves bow toward each other. Overall, the analysis suggests that partisan candidates are about as ideologically separated, and in some cases more so, in competitive elections as/than in lopsided ones.

Overall, what is remarkable is that the curves do not consistently bow inward, as we would expect if the partisan gap narrowed in competitive districts, implying greater ideological proximity between partisan candidates in competitive elections. On the contrary, the evidence suggests that candidates are at least as widely separated in competitive districts as in lopsided ones. Further evidence for this tendency to bow outward is provided in Adams et al. (2013).

Analysis of Senate data by Adams et al. similarly demonstrates that DW-NOMINATE scores track district ideology while differing systematically between parties. Likewise, the Senate analysis supports the proposition that the differences between Democratic and Republican Senators' voting records are at least as great in states that are evenly divided, in partisan terms, as in states that are overwhelmingly Democratic or Republican. The regression curves bow out away from each other in the middle of the state ideology scale—that is, in states where the presidential vote mirrors the national vote—indicating that Republican and Democratic Senate winners are *as different* (and if anything, more different) in ideology in the most competitive states. The evidence for outward bowing was found to be significant at the 0.05 level for both parties for the full period and for the earliest and latest periods studied, whereas no curve for either party for either the full period or for any of the breakdown periods was found to bow significantly inward.

A3.3. The Competitive Polarization Proposition 3.1

The proportions of Democratic partisans, Republican partisans, and Independents are denoted by m_D, m_R, and m_I, respectively, where $m_D + m_R + m_I = 1$, and the means of these constituencies as μ_D, μ_R, and μ_I. We refer to the overall mean voter location $\mu_V = (m_D \mu_D + m_R \mu_R + m_I \mu_I)$ as the *center* of the voter distribution, and without loss of

---

[3] Outward bow for Republicans is represented by a negative sign for the quadratic regression coefficient; outward bow for Democrats is represented by a positive sign for the corresponding quadratic regression coefficient (see Table A3.1). Results are qualitatively similar if interaction terms between South and Ideology and between South and Ideology squared are included in the regression analysis.

[4] Figure 4 in Butler (2009) appears to suggest bowing out for both Republicans and Democrats. Erikson and Wright (2000, fig. 8.6) plot the mean perception of the ideology of incumbent House members during the 1980s against constituency ideology, obtaining (as we do) a sharp separation between Democrats and Republicans and trends reflecting party responsiveness. These authors' scatterplots for each party appear to show curvature that bows out between the parties, although this possible effect is not noted.

146 APPENDIX TO CHAPTER 3

generality, set the center to 0. Each voter i's utilities for voting for candidate $K, U_i(K)$, and i's alienation threshold $T_i(A)$ are given by:

$$U_i(D) = -a(x_i - D)^2 + bp_{iD} + \varepsilon_{iD},$$

$$U_i(R) = -a(x_i - R)^2 + bp_{iR} + \varepsilon_{iR} \tag{A3.2}$$

$$T_i = A + \varepsilon_{iA},$$

where a is an ideology-salience parameter, b is a partisan-salience parameter, and A is an alienation-threshold parameter; $p_{iD} = 1$ if the voter identifies with the Democratic party and 0 otherwise; similarly for p_{iR}; and the random variables $\varepsilon_{iD}, \varepsilon_{iR}$, and ε_{iA} represent unmeasured influences on the voter's utility and alienation threshold (see Adams, Merrill, and Grofman, 2005, 121). We use the conditional logit model, in which each random component is generated independently from a type I extreme value distribution.

Proposition 3.1 (Competitive Polarization). When the candidates select their positions from a finite set of platforms Z that include the platforms D_0 and R_0 whose positions are given by equations A3.3–A3.4 below, then, for a sufficiently small and positive values of the salience coefficient a, the equilibrium configuration in candidates' margin-maximizing strategies is (D_0, R_0), where

$$D_0 = c_D \mu_D,$$

$$\text{and } c_D = \frac{e^A(e^b - 1)m_D}{e^A(e^b - 1)m_D + \dfrac{(e^b - 1)^2 m_I}{(2 + e^A)} + (e^A + 2e^b)}, \tag{A3.3}$$

$$R_0 = c_R \mu_R,$$

$$\text{and } c_R = \frac{e^A(e^b - 1)m_R}{e^A(e^b - 1)m_R + \dfrac{(e^b - 1)^2 m_I}{(2 + e^A)} + (e^A + 2e^b)}. \tag{A3.4}$$

Proof. See Theorem 1 and its proof in Adams et al. (2010).[5]

We note several implications of Proposition 3.1 for margin-maximizing candidates:

When voters exhibit partisan loyalties (i.e., $b>0$), equations A3.3–A3.4 imply that $0 < c_D < 1$ and $0 < c_R < 1$ (to see this, note that in equations A3.3 and A3.4 the numerators are positive when $b>0$, while the denominators are equal to the numerator plus additional positive terms), and hence that as $a \to 0$ each candidate's equilibrium position diverges to a location between the center and the mean position of the candidate's partisan constituency. We

---

[5] Proposition 3.1 assumes that the policy-salience coefficient a is sufficiently small and positive. However, Adams et al. (2010, Table 1 and fig. 1) present computations that show that the substantive conclusions of Proposition 3.1 extend to significantly positive values of the policy salience parameter.

APPENDIX TO CHAPTER 3   147

therefore conclude that, when voters display partisan biases and abstention is from alienation, *each candidate's margin-maximizing position is shifted away from the center in the direction of the mean position of the candidate's partisan constituency.*[6]

More specifically, equations A3.3–A3.4 imply that when voters display partisan biases and $a{\to}0$, other things being equal, the following relationships hold:

1. The more extreme the position of the candidate's partisan constituency, the further the candidate diverges from the center in the direction of this constituency.
2. (a) The larger the candidate's partisan constituency, the further the candidate diverges from the center in the direction of this constituency; and (b) the larger the proportion of independent voters in the electorate, the less the candidate diverges from the center in the direction of her partisan constituency.

Conclusion (1) follows from the fact that the functions c_D and c_R are, by inspection, invariably positive when $b{>}0$.

To see conclusion (2a), note that the numerator and the first expression in the denominator of equations A3.3–A3.4 are each identical positive functions of the size of the candidate's partisan constituency (m_D or m_R), while the denominator contains additional positive terms. To see conclusion (2b), note that the proportion of independent voters m_I appears only in the denominators of equations A3.3–A3.4, and that in each case the denominator is a positive function of m_I. It follows that the values of c_D, c_R decline as m_I increases, which implies that the candidates converge toward the mean voter position as m_I increases.

As indicated above, Adams et al. (2010, Table 1 and Fig. 1) present computations that show that the substantive conclusions extend to significantly positive values of the policy salience parameter. In particular, for realistic values of the salience parameter, the candidates' equilibrium positions diverge from the mean voter position in the direction of their partisan constituencies. Candidate divergence, furthermore, is less when there is a significant proportion of Independent voters in the electorate. Plots of optimal positions for Democratic and Republican winners are provided in Figure 3.1 in the main text. For that figure, the ideology-salience parameter, a, is set at 0.25, the partisan parameter b is set to 2, and the alienation threshold is set at 2.

Margin-maximizing candidates are motivated to shift away from the center in the direction of their partisans. As indicated in the main text, this occurs because the marginal change in a candidate's probabilities of attracting her own partisans' votes via policy appeals is higher than is the marginal change in her probabilities of attracting votes from the rival candidate's partisans. To understand why this is true, note that the properties of the conditional logit (CL) probability function imply that the weight w_i that a candidate attaches to a voter i's policy preference increases as the probability that i votes for the candidate approaches 0.5 (from either direction). In a two-candidate election where voters have nonzero probabilities of abstaining, the higher of the voter's two vote probabilities

---

[6] Equations A3.3–A3.4 imply that, when partisanship does not influence the vote ($b = 0$), then $c_D = c_R = 0$ and hence that as $a{\to}0$ both candidates' equilibrium positions will converge to the mean voter position. This follows from the fact that when $b = 0$, then the expression $(e^b - 1)$ that appears in the numerator of both equations A3.3 and A3.4 equals zero. This result is consistent with previous spatial modeling work with probabilistic voting and variable voter turnout (Enelow and Hinich, 1989).

148   APPENDIX TO CHAPTER 3

must be the one nearest 0.5, and hence the voter is most marginal with respect to the candidate she is most likely to vote for. Because, when b>0 and a→0, partisan voters are guaranteed to be more likely to vote for their party's candidate than for the opposition party's candidate, it follows that under these conditions candidates attach greater weight to the policy preferences of the members of their own partisan constituency than to the preferences of the members of the rival candidate's constituency.

APPENDIX TO CHAPTER 4

Components of Legislative Polarization

A4.1. Derivation of the Three-Factor Decomposition

In the definitions that follow, we assume throughout that ideology is measured in a one-dimensional spatial model on a scale from 0 to 100, where 0 represents extremely liberal and 100 represents extremely conservative.

Definition 1: The *legislative gap* is the difference between the mean locations of the elected party delegations; that is,

$$legislative\ gap = \left[\left|\mu_R - \mu_D\right|\right],$$

where μ_D and μ_R are the Democratic and Republican mean ideological locations in the legislature, respectively.

Definition 2: We denote by $f(m)$ the density function over districts for the distribution of the district median voter, m. The *district heterogeneity* is the variance, σ_M^2, of this distribution.

Definition 3: The *district-specific partisan gap*, denoted by d, is the mean distance between winning Democratic and Republican candidates from ideologically comparable districts.[1]

Definition 4: For each party, *partisan proclivity* at the constituency level is the probability function $P_D(m)$ (for the Democrats) or $P_R(m)$ (for the Republicans) that that party wins in a district with median voter at m, if each party offers either identical policy platforms at the ideological location of the median voter or platforms at equal distance to the left and right of m—a likelihood that may differ across constituencies depending upon the ideological location of the median voter in the district.[2] Note that $P_D(m) = 1 - P_R(m)$.

Definition 5: As a measure of the level of partisan proclivity, we define the *mean partisan proclivity* as

$$mean\ partisan\ proclivity = \frac{2}{100} \int_0^{100} \left|P_R(m) - 0.5\right| dm. \qquad (A4.1)^3$$

---

[1] We compare winning Democratic and Republican candidates from ideologically comparable districts (rather than the winning and losing candidates from the same district), because assessments of voting records such as DW-NOMINATE scores are in general available only for winning candidates. As we will see empirically, the party-specific simple regression lines for DW-NOMINATE scores against m are roughly parallel.

[2] Again, as we will see empirically, $P_D(m)$ and $P_R(m)$ are primarily functions of m.

[3] In effect, the mean partisan proclivity is the aggregate deviation of the probability of partisan success from what that probability would be if success were unrelated to district ideology. The factor 2 is introduced so that mean partisan proclivity ranges from 0 to 1.0.

150 APPENDIX TO CHAPTER 4

We can readily see that $\mu_D(\mu_R)$ is the weighted average (over district medians m) of the expected ideological locations of Democratic (Republican) legislators for a given m, weighted by the density of the distribution of district medians and the propensity of districts with a given median to elect a Democrat (Republican). This relation is specified formally in Brunell, Grofman, and Merrill (2016b, equation 3).

Suppose, as a simple example, that f is uniform and that P_R is the step function for which $P_R(m) = 1$ for $m \geq 50$ and $P_R(m) = 0$ for $m < 50$ (i.e., districts with a median voter to the right of 50 always elect the Republican, while districts with median voter to the left always elect the Democrat). Assume further that the candidate locations straddle the district median symmetrically, 10 units on either side, so that $d = 20$. In this case,

$$\left| \mu_R - \mu_D \right| = \left| \frac{75/2}{1/2} - \frac{25/2}{1/2} \right| + 20 = 70,$$

resulting in a highly polarized legislature, with Democratic lawmakers centered around 15 and Republican legislators centered round 85 on a 0 to 100 scale. In practice, however, we will see that the candidate positions typically straddle what we call the *effective median*, m', which is intermediate between the district median m and the national median m_0, specifically, $m' = wm + (1-w)m_0$, where w is a weighting factor that can be estimated empirically (see subsection A4.3 below).

We next develop a proposition that relates our three factors explicitly to polarization in the legislature.

Proposition 4.1. If the distribution of district medians is symmetric, then the legislative gap is given by

$$Legislative\ gap = 0.08 \times (mean\ partisan\ proclivity) \times w\sigma_M^2 + d, \qquad (A4.2)$$

provided that the partisan proclivity function P_R is *linear* on the interval $[0, 100]$ (i.e., $P_R(m) = 0.5 + \gamma^*(m - 50)$ for some constant $\gamma, 0 \leq \gamma \leq 0.01$) and the partisan proclivity functions for the two parties are *complementary* (i.e., $P_D(50 - m) = P_R(50 + m), 0 \leq m \leq 50$). Recall that σ_M^2 is the variance of the distribution of district medians and w is the weighting factor of the effective median, specified by $m' = wm + (1-w)m_0$.

Proposition 4.1 is proved in the online Appendix http://static4.mathcs.wilkes.edu/ Gems/Merrill/BGMComponentsSupp.pdf to Brunell et al. (2016b).

A4.2. Determination of the Party Intercepts and the Common Slope for the Alternative 2-Factor Decomposition of Legislative Polarization

For the time periods we investigate, we model the DW-NOMINATE scores versus district medians as simple linear functions with a common slope in which DW-NOMINATE scores (y_D and y_R) and support (x) for the Democratic presidential candidate can be written as

$$y_D = \alpha_D + \beta x + \varepsilon \qquad (A4.3)$$

APPENDIX TO CHAPTER 4   151

for Democratic winners, and

$$y_R = \alpha_R + \beta x + \varepsilon \qquad (A4.4)$$

for Republican winners, where the intercepts α_D, α_R, and common slope β are coefficients and ε is normally distributed with mean 0.[4]

For the assumption of common slopes to be plausible, the party-specific regressions for the DW-NOMINATE scores should have at least approximately a common slope, so that their regression lines are roughly parallel. In other words, the gap between winning candidates of different parties in ideologically comparable districts should be roughly invariant as a function of the district-median m. Although the test for exact equality of slopes is rejected for the full period and for three of the seven subperiods (not surprising for large data sets), all we need is rough similarity between the partisan slopes, as suggested by the plots in Figure 2.1 in Chapter 2. Accordingly, we posit a common slope for both parties, shown by the parallel regression lines in Figure A4.1. In particular, the difference in intercepts represents a difference between elected Republicans and Democrats from ideologically similar districts—a difference that is roughly constant as a function of the district median.

For the full period 1956–2020 and for each of its subperiods (eras) by decades,[5] we obtain estimates a_D, a_R, and b (presented in Table A4.1) for the parameters α_D, α_R, and β of the two regression equations (A4.3–A4.4). These values will be used in our empirical calculations. To convert from the 2-point interval of DW-NOMINATE scores (which extends from -1 to $+1$) to our 100-point interval, we multiply the estimates by 50. Thus, $50(a_R - a_D)$ is our estimate of district-specific partisan gap—that is, the empirical estimate for the parameter d.[6] Parameter estimates of the model are provided in Table A4.1. (Estimates for the three components of legislative polarization for the full period 1956–2020 and for each of seven subperiods are given in Table 4.1 in the main text.)

A4.3. Weighting Factor

Empirical analysis (omitted for space reasons)[7] suggests that the Republican and Democratic candidates do not in fact, even on average, equally straddle the district median, but rather typically straddle a position intermediate between the district median and the national median of their party. This implies, *ceteris paribus*, that liberal districts will be much more likely to be won by Democrats and conservative districts much more likely to be won by Republicans than if both candidates located at the district median. Because

---

[4] We are simplifying here by ignoring the fact that many of the relationships are slightly quadratic (see section A3.2).

[5] The final subperiod, 2016–2020, includes three congresses, instead of the usual five.

[6] An alternative estimate of d can be obtained, without assuming that the partisan slopes are equal, by multiplying 50 times the difference between the two partisan regression lines that are centered (i.e., each evaluated at 0.5, representing a most competitive district). The results are almost identical to those obtained from $50(a_R - a_D)$, which uses the partisan intercepts and assumes equal slopes.

[7] See online Appendix of Brunell et al. (2016b), at http://static4.mathcs.wilkes.edu/Gems/Merrill/BGMComponentsSupp.pdf.

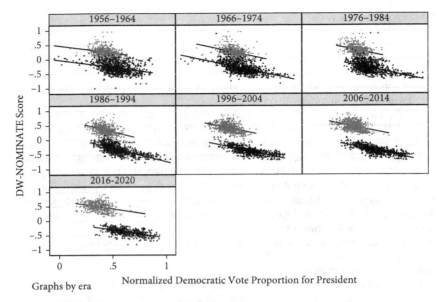

Figure A4.1. Linear Regression Lines for Democrats and Republicans Assuming Common Slopes in Each Decade

of this, we need to estimate a weighting factor, w, in equation A4.2, which can be done as follows. The value $|b|/2$, where b is the common-slope estimate from the regression above, represents the rate of change in policy position as district support increases and is thus an estimate of the weighting factor w. (We divide by 2 because the range of DW-NOMINATE scores is 2.) These estimates of w are provided in column 5 of Table A4.1.

A4.4. Alternative 2-Factor Decomposition of Legislative Polarization

We show that legislative polarization can empirically be decomposed into the district-specific partisan gap and a second factor called *district partisanship*, which reflects both district heterogeneity and partisan proclivity. We then assess the relative impact of each factor in this alternative, two-factor decomposition. Finally, we will compare the estimates of the legislative gap from the alternative decomposition with that implied by Proposition 4.1, a decomposition that in part employs different data.

Suppose that regressions of DW-NOMINATE scores versus presidential vote shares are performed separately for seats won by Democrats and seats won by Republicans and that they yield the same estimated slope, b, so that the estimated regression equations are of the form $\ddot{y}_D(x) = a_D + bx$ for the Democratic seats and $\ddot{y}_R(x) = a_R + bx$ for the Republican seats. Denote by $\bar{y}_D$ and $\bar{y}_R$ the respective mean locations of the Democratic and Republican delegations and by $\bar{x}_D$ and $\bar{x}_R$ the respective mean ideologies of the set of districts won by Democrats and the set of districts won by Republicans. Because, in

APPENDIX TO CHAPTER 4   153

Table A4.1. Empirical Estimates for Model Parameters for Alternative 2-Factor Decomposition of Legislative Polarization: 1956–2020

Era	Republican Intercept: a_R	Democratic Intercept: a_D	Common Slope: b	Estimate of w $(|b|/2)$
(1)	(2)	(3)	(4)	(5)
1956–2020	0.705	0.130	−0.813	0.406
1956–1964	0.478	−0.019	−0.499	0.249
1966–1974	0.612	0.117	−0.798	0.399
1976–1984	0.646	0.126	−0.789	0.395
1986–1994	0.755	0.189	−0.925	0.463
1996–2004	0.727	0.080	−0.767	0.384
2006–2014	0.769	0.100	−0.777	0.388
2016–2020	0.706	−0.020	−0.565	0.282

Note: The dependent variable is the DW-NOMINATE score. Eras are specified by the election dates of the composite Congresses. Columns 2–4 report estimates a_R, a_D, and b for the regression parameters α_D, α_R, and β for equations (A4.3) and (A4.4), over the full period under study and for each subperiod. To convert from the 2-point interval of DW-NOMINATE scores (which extends from −1 to +1) to our 100-point interval, we later multiply the estimates by 50.

general, the intercept a in a simple regression $\check{y} = a + bx$ is given by $a = \bar{y} - b\bar{x}$, it follows that, using the regression equation for Democratic seats,

$$\check{y}_D(\bar{x}_D) = a_D + b\bar{x}_D = (\bar{y}_D - b\bar{x}_D) + b\bar{x}_D = \bar{y}_D,$$

and similarly, using the regression equation for Republican seats,

$$\check{y}_R(\bar{x}_R) = \bar{y}_R.$$

Thus,

$$\bar{y}_R - \bar{y}_D = \check{y}_R(\bar{x}_R) - \check{y}_D(\bar{x}_D) = (a_R + b\bar{x}_R) - (a_D + b\bar{x}_D),$$

so that

$$\bar{y}_R - \bar{y}_D = (a_R - a_D) + b(\bar{x}_R - \bar{x}_D). \qquad (A4.5)$$

Hence we have shown that (on our 100-point scale) the legislative gap is the sum of two quantities: (1) $50(a_R - a_D)$ —that is, our estimate for d, the district-specific partisan

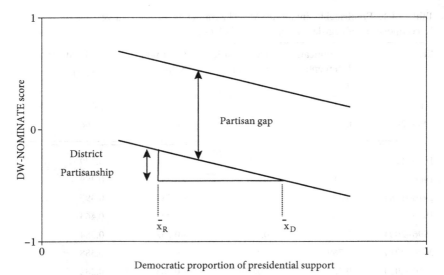

Figure A4.2. Decomposition of Legislative Polarization

gap—and (2) $50b(\bar{x}_R - \bar{x}_D)$—that is, district partisanship, which represents the combination of district heterogeneity and partisan proclivity. This decomposition is depicted schematically in Figure A4.2.[8] Accordingly, for the full period 1956–2020,

$$\text{Legislative gap} = 50(\bar{y}_R - \bar{y}_D) = 50(a_R - a_D) + 50b(\bar{x}_R - \bar{x}_D)$$
$$= 50(0.705 - 0.130) + 50(-0.813)(0.416 - 0.568) = 28.8 + 6.2 = 35.0.$$

Furthermore, not only is the district-specific partisan gap in the most recent subperiod nearly 50 percent higher than its value in the first two decades of the study (see Table 4.1); in addition, the other term in this formula (which we label district partisanship) tripled over the period of the study. Thus, legislative polarization has increased greatly.

We note that, generally, the values computed from the two methods (from Proposition 4.1 and from equation A4.5) are similar, although the values estimated from Proposition 4.1 run lower, in part because the linear form for the partisan-proclivity function likely underestimates its true deviation from 0.5, as we saw above, and because of possible asymmetry of the district-median distribution.

---

[8] Analytically, $(a_R - a_D)$ is the distance between the regression lines for the two parties, and $b(\bar{x}_R - \bar{x}_D)$ is the rise in the common slope of the DW-NOMINATE score between an MC representing an ideologically average Republican-won district and an MC of the same party representing an ideologically average Democrat-won district.

APPENDIX TO CHAPTER 5

Derivations for the
Appeal-to-the-Base Model

A5.1. Arguments in Support of Theoretical
Hypotheses 1 and 2

The arguments in this Appendix are taken from Merrill et al. (2022). To address Theoretical Hypothesis 1, note that when parties are equally polarized, we may take these two party positions to be x (> 0) and $-x$, respectively, on a $[-1, 1]$ scale (such as is used for DW-NOMINATE scores). If voter utility for a candidate is quadratic,[1] and $v \geq 0$, then, *ceteris paribus*, the utility difference between the two parties is $(v-x)^2 - (v-(-x))^2 = 4vx$. Similarly, if $v \leq 0$, the difference is $-4vx$, which is also non-negative since $v \leq 0$. Thus, *ceteris paribus*, for any non-zero location of the voter, v, that voter's utility difference increases as the candidates at x and $-x$ spread apart—that is, as polarization in Congress and hence among Congressional candidates increases. In other words, *ceteris paribus*, party loyalty should increase with increased Congressional polarization. Only purely centrist voters ($v = 0$) are not affected by this polarization, because then $4vx = 0$. Compare the more complex formulation of the voter utility function in Hinich and Munger (1997).[2]

To address Theoretical Hypothesis 2, note that holding the level of party polarization (i.e., the value of x) fixed, extremist voters are more affected by polarization than non-extremist voters (because as v moves away from 0, the expression for utility difference $|4vx|$ increases). Hence, voters with more extreme ideological positions are likely to show greater intensity about the election outcome than voters with more moderate views (because $|v|$ is larger), and this difference in intensity increases as polarization between parties (or their candidates) grows (because $|x|$ is larger).

A5.2. Derivation of Nash-Equilibrium Positions
under the Abstention Model

Let f_D and f_R denote the voter densities for voters who identify with the Democratic and Republican parties, respectively—that is, the two party bases (see, for example, Fig. 5.1). If, for the moment, we consider the Republican candidate as fixed at any location R that

---

[1] The quadratic utility of a voter located at position v for a candidate located at position x is given by $-(v - x)^2$—that is, utility declines with the square of the distance between voter and candidate.

[2] Note also that if utility is linear, then the utility difference is $|2v|$, which is not affected by the location of x—that is, is not affected by polarization. As indicated in the main text, we suggest that quadratic utility is more appropriate here, though, because it weights movement away from the voter by distant candidates more heavily than movement away by proximate candidates.

156 APPENDIX TO CHAPTER 5

is right of center (i.e., $R \geq 0$) but the Democratic candidate as movable, then the rate of change of D's vote margin vis-à-vis the Republican is the decreasing function

$$p_D[f_D(D+A) - f_D(D-A)] + p_I f_I[(D+R)/2],^3$$

so that a maximum vote share occurs for the Democratic candidate if

$$p_D[f_D(D-A) - f_D(D+A)] = p_I f_I[(D+R)/2]. \tag{A5.1a}$$

Similarly, for a fixed Democratic position left of 0, a maximum occurs for the Republican candidate when

$$p_R[f_R(R+A) - f_R(R-A)] = p_I f_I[(D+R)/2]. \tag{A5.1b}$$

It follows that the solutions of the two equations in (A5.1) for the respective parties constitute a Nash equilibrium.

If there are no Independents, then the Nash-equilibrium locations are simply the respective partisan voter medians.[4] This holds not only for normal party-base voter distributions but for any symmetric voter distribution. In general, if a party distribution—say, that for the Democratic Party—is symmetric, then the expression $p_D[-f_D(D-A) + f_D(D+A)]$ for the rate of change of D's vote margin is decreasing as D increases and equal to 0 when D is at the median of the party distribution, so the maximum vote share for D occurs at this median. If the Democratic Party distribution is not symmetric—say, skewed in the direction of moderation (so that there is a longer tail toward the center)—then the Democratic candidate will typically gain more votes near $D+A$ than he or she loses near $D-A$; thus, there is a motivation to moderate. If the skew is in the opposite direction, the motivation is to move even more toward the extreme. Mirror-image motivations follow if the Republican distribution is not symmetric.

A5.3. Further Robustness Checks on the Model

First, we vary the abstention threshold (and thus the proportion of the base voters who abstain due to alienation). As indicated above, an abstention threshold of 2.0 (as in Table 5.1 and Fig. 5.1) indicates that base members more than two standard deviations from the mean (median) abstain due to alienation. The values shown in Table A5.1 show that lowering the abstention threshold (thus, raising the proportion abstaining) increases candidate divergence at equilibrium, but by relatively small amounts. Likewise, if we assume (as does Butler, 2009) that base voters abstain only if the candidate is too moderate (not if the candidate is too extreme), then optima at equilibrium are a bit more extreme and closer to the median of the party base (e.g., for 10 percent Independents, equilibria

---

[3] Note that the fact that the midpoint moves only half as fast as D is exactly compensated by the fact that each Independent voter gained by the Democrat is a loss for the Republican candidate.

[4] If there are no Independents, equations A5.1 become $f_D(D-A) = f_D(D+A)$ and $f_R(R+A) = f_R(R-A)$.

APPENDIX TO CHAPTER 5 157

Table A5.1. Nash-Equilibrium Locations as a Function of the Abstention Threshold and Medians of Party Bases.

Abstention Threshold		1.0	1.5	2.0
Median of Democratic Base	Median of Republican Base	Nash-Equilibrium Locations		
−0.5	0.5	±0.32	±0.27	±0.10
−1.0	1.0	±0.82	±0.77	±0.60
−2.0	2.0	±1.82	±1.77	±1.60

Note: The proportion of Independents is set at 10 percent.

are shifted by 0.14 toward the extreme). Alternatively, if we assume that Independents abstain if they are further than A units from their preferred candidate's position, then equilibrium strategies move even less (by 0.06 for $A = 1$).

Second, suppose that the sizes of the bases are different. The effect of this change on the Nash equilibria of the parties is simple: The equilibrium strategies for both parties move in the direction of the party with the larger base, and do so in a way that varies approximately linearly with respect to difference between the sizes of the bases.[5] In this case, with $A = 2$ and base medians at ±2, the equilibrium strategies for the Democratic and Republican candidates move from −1.60 to −1.55 and from 1.60 to about 1.65, respectively. Thus, given symmetric polarization, the effect of base sizes alone on equilibrium strategies is quite small compared, say, with the effects of polarization between the bases. The case of unequal base sizes coupled with asymmetric polarization was covered in the main text.

Finally, we relax the assumption that all non-abstaining voters who identify with a party vote for that party's candidate. Insofar as the voter distributions for the two parties overlap as they would in a less polarized society, leakage of voters to the opposing candidate is to be expected from the moderate tail of a party's voter distribution (where voters may be more proximate to that opposing candidate). This leakage involves not only loss of votes (as under abstention) but also gain of votes by the opposition, so it is doubly damaging. Thus, in the presence of overlap of the party bases, the prospect of such leakage should motivate candidate movement toward the center. If, on the other hand, there is very little overlap of voter distributions—that is, if the electorate is highly polarized—then there is less opportunity for this loss to the opposing party, and the corresponding motivation for moderation is lessened. Overall, the leakage described in this paragraph is likely to augment the contrast between party divergence under high versus low polarization.

[5] In fact, the equilibrium strategies move (from their positions for equal-size bases) by a distance that is approximately half the difference between the base sizes. For example, if the Republican base exceeds the Democratic base by 0.10 (i.e., 10 percentage points), then both equilibrium strategies are about 0.05 units to the right of their equal-base-size strategies.

158   APPENDIX TO CHAPTER 5

A5.4. The Downsian Ceiling and Its Relation to Nash Equilibria

We prove that the conclusions for normal party-base densities about the Downsian ceiling, including the linear relationship (beyond the Downsian ceiling) between the equilibrium strategies and the partisan medians, as well as the positions of the equilibria relative to the partisan and overall medians, all extend to any symmetric, unimodal distributions.

Definition. Suppose that the party-base densities f_D and f_R are each symmetric and unimodal, with means (medians) $-\mu$ and μ, and otherwise identical. The *Downsian ceiling* is the maximum (supremum) value of μ such that the equilibrium strategies for both parties are at the overall median, 0.

Proposition 5.1. Suppose that g is a symmetric, unimodal distribution with mean (median) equal to 0, and for each $\mu > 0$, define $f_D(x) = g(x + \mu)$ and $f_R(x) = g(x - \mu)$. Let f_I also be symmetric and unimodal, with mean (median) equal to 0 and $p_I > 0$. Denote by R and $D (= -R)$ the equilibrium strategies. Then D and R are both 0 if and only if

$$f_R(R + A) - f_R(R - A) \le (p_I / p_R) f_I(0). \tag{A5.2a}$$

Hence, the Downsian ceiling is the solution R of the corresponding equation:

$$f_R(R + A) - f_R(R - A) = (p_I / p_R) f_I(0),$$

or, equivalently, the solution μ of

$$g(A - \mu) - g(A + \mu) = (p_I / p_R) f_I(0). \tag{A5.2b}$$

To compute the Downsian ceiling, this last equation can be solved recursively for (the first appearance of) the variable μ.[6]

Proof. The Downsian ceiling is that value of μ such that when D is 0 and the rate of change of party R's vote share, namely $f_R(R + A) - f_R(R - A) - (p_I / p_R) f_I(0)$, when evaluated at $R = 0$, is itself 0.[7] Hence, $f_R(A) - f_R(-A) = (p_I / p_R) f_I(0)$—that is, $g_R(A - \mu) - g_R(-A - \mu) = (p_I / p_R) f_I(0)$, which is in turn equivalent to equation A5.2b, using the symmetry of g. q.e.d.

When it is necessary to specify the dependence on μ of the equilibrium strategies and the partisan densities, we will denote the equilibria as $D(\mu)$ and $R(\mu)$, and the partisan densities as $f_{D(\mu)}$ and $f_{R(\mu)}$. We denote the Downsian ceiling by DC. We next show that,

---

[6] Roughly speaking, the Downsian ceiling increases as the density of Independents near the overall median increases—that is, as p_I/s.d.(I) increases, and as the standard deviation of the party base density increases (details omitted).

[7] Note that if μ is positive but sufficiently small, and $0 < R < \mu$, then $f_R(R + A) - f_R(R - A) < (p_I / p_R) f_I(0)$.

APPENDIX TO CHAPTER 5   159

beyond the Downsian ceiling, the equilibria are each linear functions of the partisan medians.

Corollary 1. Under the conditions of Proposition 5.1:

(a) $R(\mu) = \mu - DC$ for $\mu > DC$, and $R(\mu) = 0$ for $\mu \leq DC$.
(b) If μ is at least twice the Downsian ceiling, then the equilibrium strategy $R(\mu)$ is as close or closer to the party-base median than the overall median.

Proof.

Part (a): Note that $f_{R(\mu)}(x) = g(x - \mu)$, so that

$$f_{R(\mu)}(R(\mu) + A) - f_{R(\mu)}(R(\mu) - A)$$

$$= g(R(\mu) + A - \mu) - g(R(\mu) - A - \mu)$$

$$= f_{R(DC)}(R(\mu) + A - \mu + DC) - f_{R(DC)}(R(\mu) - A - \mu + DC)$$

$$= f_{R(DC)}(R(\mu) - (\mu - DC) + A) - f_{R(DC)}(R(\mu) - (\mu - DC) - A)$$

$$= (p_I / p_R) f_I(0).$$

It follows that $R(\mu) - (\mu - DC)$ is the (Republican) equilibrium strategy for $f_{R(DC)}$; but the latter is 0 by definition of DC, so $R(\mu) - (\mu - DC) = 0$, so $R(\mu) = \mu - DC$.

Part (b): We need to show that if $\mu \geq 2DC$, then $R(\mu) \geq \mu / 2$. But if $\mu \geq 2DC$, then

$$DC \leq \mu / 2, \text{ so } R(\mu) = \mu - DC \geq \mu - \mu / 2 = \mu / 2. \, q.e.d.$$

APPENDIX TO CHAPTER 6

Derivations Relating to Chamber and Party Medians

A6.1. Modeling the Linkage between Chamber Median and Party Medians

To gain insight into the relationships between chamber and party medians, we simplify by developing a theoretical model for the party distributions, with the goal of obtaining theoretical expectations about these relationships.[1] In this analysis, our basic assumption is that of a one-dimensional spatial model in which voters are assumed to choose the nearer of two candidates.

Given a two-party legislature, the mean position of the chamber members has a simple relationship to the respective party delegation means: the chamber mean is a weighted average of the two party delegation means, weighted by the respective proportions of the total membership of the parties. If both party caucuses follow a normal distribution, then the distribution of the chamber is said to have a mixed normal distribution, where the mixing parameters are the party proportions. Note that if the party delegations are normally distributed, for each party distribution the mean and median are identical.

But as we have seen, beginning with Downs (1957), most theories of two-party electoral competition emphasize the location of medians rather than means.[2] As indicated in Chapter 6, legislative-centric models of Congressional voting focus on the chamber median, while party-centric models emphasize the importance of the majority party median relative to the chamber median. The analytics of medians, however, is not so simple as that of means, and we turn to that subject in the next subsection. In particular, the behavior of chamber medians can be very different from that of chamber means, especially when the spatial distribution of legislators is highly polarized.

A6.1.1. A model approximation for the chamber median when party distributions overlap

Denote the overall chamber median by M and the party medians for Democrats and Republicans as M_1 and M_2, respectively, and assume that $M_1 < M_2$; furthermore, let σ_1 and σ_2 denote the standard deviations of the two party delegations. Recall that we define the *separation index* of the parties as the *ratio* between the difference in party *medians*

---

[1] Direct empirical calculation of medians for specific legislatures is not difficult, but numerical values for medians do not necessarily shed light on cause-and-effect relationships.

[2] Hinich (1977) is a noted exception. See also Schofield (2007).

162   APPENDIX TO CHAPTER 6

(divergence) and the sum of the party *standard deviations* (which varies inversely with party homogeneity). Hence, the separation index is given by

$$Separation\ index = \frac{M_2 - M_1}{\sigma_1 + \sigma_2}.^3$$ (A6.1)

To determine analytically the relationship between party medians and the overall chamber median, unlike the case of means, we need to take into account the standard deviations of each party's ideological distribution in addition to the relative sizes of the party delegations in the legislature. Merrill et al. (1999, Proposition 1 and Corollary 1) show that, under specified conditions, the chamber median, M, satisfies an approximation result, stated below in Proposition A6.1. Denote the proportions of legislative seats in party 1 and party 2, respectively, by p_1 and p_2.

Proposition A6.1. If the ideological distributions of the party delegations are each symmetric, are greater than zero at their respective medians, have bounded derivatives, and sufficiently overlap so that the separation index does not exceed 1; that is,

$$\frac{M_2 - M_1}{\sigma_1 + \sigma_2} \leq 1,$$ (A6.2)

then the chamber median is (approximately) a weighted average of the party medians, namely:

$$M \cong \frac{\alpha_2 M_1 + \alpha_1 M_2}{(\alpha_1 + \alpha_2)},^4$$ (A6.3)

where $\alpha_i = \sigma_i / p_i, i = 1, 2$.

Corollary 1. Under the assumptions of Proposition A6.1,

$$distance\ from\ M\ to\ M_1 = \frac{\alpha_1}{\alpha_1 + \alpha_2}(M_2 - M_1)$$ (A6.4a)

and, similarly,

---

[3] The separation index could, alternatively, be defined as $(M_2 - M_1)/\sqrt{\sigma_1^2 + \sigma_2^2}$. We prefer the form in equation A6.1, because of its simplicity and because of its relation to condition (A6.2) in Proposition A6.1.

[4] Bounds for the approximation are given in Merrill et al. (1999), Table A1. For normally distributed party distributions, these errors are found to be less than $0.04(M_2 - M_1)$ (and typically much less) as long as the proportions for the two parties remain between 0.4 and 0.6 and $1/2 \leq \sigma_1/\sigma_2 \leq 2$.

APPENDIX TO CHAPTER 6   163

$$distance\ from\ M\ to\ M_2 = \frac{\alpha_2}{\alpha_1 + \alpha_2}(M_2 - M_1), \qquad (A6.4b)$$

so that M_1 is closer to M than is M_2 if and only if

$$\alpha_1 < \alpha_2, \text{i.e., if.} \sigma_1 / p_1 < \sigma_2 / p_2. \qquad (A6.5)$$

Proof of Proposition A6.1 and Corollary 1. Under the assumption of condition (A6.2), the approximation formula for the chamber median given by (A6.3) is obtained by multiplying both numerator and denominator of the expression for M, derived in Proposition 1 of Merrill et al. (1999), by σ_1 / p_2.[5]

Statements (A6.4) and (A6.5) follow from the observation that, given the approximation in equation (A6.3), $M - M_1 \cong \dfrac{\alpha_2 M_1 + \alpha_1 M_2}{\alpha_1 + \alpha_2} - \dfrac{\alpha_1 M_1 + \alpha_2 M_1}{\alpha_1 + \alpha_2} = \dfrac{\alpha_1 (M_2 - M_1)}{\alpha_1 + \alpha_2}$, and a similar formula holds for $M - M_2$. q.e.d.

Note that normal distributions that satisfy the overlap condition (A6.2) also satisfy the other conditions of Proposition A6.1, so the Proposition and its Corollary apply to normal distributions for the party delegations. In any event, from inequality (A6.5) in Corollary 1, given sufficient overlap between the party distributions, and unequal variances, if the minority party, say party 1, is sufficiently concentrated (specifically, if $\sigma_1 / p_1 < \sigma_2 / p_2$), then the chamber median is closer to the *minority* party delegation's median than the majority delegation's median.[6] If each party proposes legislation at the location of its respective median voter, then, *ceteris paribus*, under our spatial model assumptions, the chamber median legislator can be expected to choose the minority-party proposal; thus, the minority-party proposal would defeat that of the majority party.

For example, suppose that M_1 and M_2 are normalized to 0 and 1, and that the Democrats have 40 percent of the seats, but the standard deviation of their delegation is 0.5 while the standard deviation for the Republicans is 1.0. Then $\alpha_1 = \sigma_1 / p_1 = 0.5/0.4 = 1.25$, while $\alpha_2 = \sigma_2 / p_2 = 1/0.6 = 1.67$, so that, using equation (A6.4a), $M \cong \dfrac{\alpha_1}{\alpha_1 + \alpha_2} = \dfrac{1.25}{1.25 + 1.67} = 0.429$, which is closer to the minority median, which is at 0.

The formulation in (A6.5) indicates that the quantity $\alpha_i = \sigma_i / p_i$ can be used as a measure of closeness of the party median to the chamber median. In fact, the distance from M_i to M is proportional to α_i, and as we have seen, the median of that party i for which the quantity σ_i / p_i is smaller is closer to the chamber median.

---

[5] See also Al-Hussaini and Osman, 1997; Mood, Graybill, and Boes, 1974; Patel and Read, 1996.

[6] As indicated above, the relative locations of medians can be calculated empirically in a specific legislature. But the insight that a party that constitutes a concentrated minority may propose legislation that is more attractive to the median legislator than that of the majority party arises from a theoretical viewpoint. Note that if both party delegations have the same variance (i.e., $\sigma_1 = \sigma_2$), the median location of the majority party (i.e., the party with the larger value of p_i) will be closer to the chamber median.

164 APPENDIX TO CHAPTER 6

A6.1.2. Recursive calculation of the model approximation for the chamber median

In general, the chamber median can be calculated as the limit of a recursive algorithm (involving iterative formulas) derived by solving for each occurrence of M in terms of the other occurrence of M in the definition of the median:

$$p_1 F_1(M) + p_2 F_2(M) = 0.5, \tag{A6.6a}$$

where F_i is the cumulative distribution function for party i. If, furthermore, the party distributions are normally distributed, with means M_i and standard deviations σ_i, equation (A6.6a) becomes:

$$p_1 \Phi\left[(M - M_1)/\sigma_1\right] + p_2 \Phi\left[(M - M_2)/\sigma_2\right] = 0.5, \tag{A6.6b}$$

where Φ denotes the standard normal cumulative distribution function.

A6.1.3. The relative eccentricity of the chamber median

In order to track the degree to which the chamber median tracks the median of the majority caucus, we define the *relative eccentricity of the chamber median* as the ratio of the distance between the chamber median and the minority-party median to the distance between the two party medians.[7] The arguments above show that if the assumptions of Proposition A6.1 hold, then the relative eccentricity of the chamber median is (approximately) $\alpha_1 / (\alpha_1 + \alpha_2)$.[8]

Suppose now that the party distributions are normally distributed, with medians (means) M_i and standard deviations σ_i, $i = 1, 2$. (We will refer to these assumptions as specifying the *normal party-distribution model*.) Then the relative eccentricity of the chamber median increases as a majority party augments its seat share and as its party distribution becomes more concentrated (i.e., when its intraparty standard deviation decreases). This result is stated more precisely as Proposition A6.2.

Proposition A6.2. In our normal party-distribution model, suppose $p_2 > p_1$ (the statement and argument for $p_1 > p_2$ are similar). Then, for any fixed value of the

---

[7] Analytically, if, say, the minority delegation is the Democrats (party 1), then the *relative eccentricity of the chamber median* $= |M - M_1| / |M_2 - M_1|$, and similarly if the Republicans are the minority.

[8] This follows because, by equation (A6.3),

$$|M - M_1| = M - M_1 \cong \frac{\alpha_2 M_1 + \alpha_1 M_2}{\alpha_1 + \alpha_2} - \frac{\alpha_1 M_1 + \alpha_2 M_1}{\alpha_1 + \alpha_2} = \frac{\alpha_1(M_2 - M_1)}{\alpha_1 + \alpha_2}, \text{ so that relative eccentricity of}$$

the chamber median is given by $|M - M_1| / |M_2 - M_1| \cong \dfrac{\alpha_1(M_2 - M_1)}{\alpha_1 + \alpha_2} \Big/ |M_2 - M_1| = \dfrac{\alpha_1}{\alpha_1 + \alpha_2}.$

APPENDIX TO CHAPTER 6   165

distance between the party medians, the relative eccentricity of M in the normal party-distribution model

(a) increases as σ_2 decreases (for fixed σ_1 and p_2), and

(b) increases as p_2 increases (for fixed σ_1 and σ_2).

Proof: To prove part (a), perform implicit differentiation with respect to σ_2 on equation (A6.6b)—that is, on $p_1 \Phi[(M - M_1)/\sigma_1] + p_2 \Phi[(M - M_2)/\sigma_2] = 0.5$, with fixed σ_1 and p_2. Solving for $\partial M / \partial \sigma_2$ yields an expression that is clearly negative, which establishes part (a).

To prove part (b), note that the cumulative distribution function for the mixed normal distribution is given by $F(x) = p_1 \Phi[(x - M_1)/\sigma_1] + p_2 \Phi[(x - M_2)/\sigma_2]$ and $F(M) = 0.5$, where M denotes the chamber median in the normal party-distribution model. Now if σ_1 and σ_2 are fixed, and p_2 is replaced by $p_2 + \Delta p_2$, then the integral defining F from $-\infty$ to M increases by the quantity $-\Delta p_2 \Phi[(M - M_1)/\sigma_1] + \Delta p_2 \Phi[(M - M_2)/\sigma_2]$—that is, by a negative quantity, because $\Phi[(M - M_1)/\sigma_1] \geq 0.5 \geq \Phi[(M - M_2)/\sigma_2]$. Thus, an increase in p_2 to $p_2 + \Delta p_2$ leads to decrease in the integral defining F from $-\infty$ to M, so that the new median must be at least as large as M. q.e.d.

A6.2. Condition for Chamber Median to Be a Member of the Minority Party

Without loss of generality, suppose that the minority party is party 2, and assume that the scale has been normalized so that $M_1 = 0$ and $M_2 = 1$. In general, the probability that the chamber median M is a member of the minority party is equal to the ratio of the weighted probability density of party 2 at M to the sum of this weighted density for both parties—that is,

$$\Pr[M \ is \ a \ member \ of \ party \ 2] = \frac{p_2 f_2(M)}{p_1 f_1(M) + p_2 f_2(M)}$$

so that

$$Odds[M \ is \ a \ member \ of \ party \ 2] = \frac{p_2 f_2(M)}{p_1 f_1(M)},$$

which is more convenient to compute. For a mixed normal distribution,

$$Odds = \frac{p_2}{P_1} \frac{\sigma_1}{\sigma_2} \exp\left[\frac{M^2}{2\sigma_1^2} - \frac{(M-1)^2}{2\sigma_2^2}\right]$$

166   APPENDIX TO CHAPTER 6

$$\cong \frac{p_2}{p_1}\frac{\sigma_1}{\sigma_2}\exp\left[\frac{p_2-p_1}{2(p_1\sigma_2+p_2\sigma_1)^2}\right],$$

where we have used the approximation in Eq. (A6.3). The probability that the chamber median is in party 2 is then given by

$$\Pr\left[M\ is\ a\ member\ of\ party\ 2\right]=\frac{Odds}{1+Odds}.q.e.d.$$

To get some sense of this result, note that for $\sigma_1 = \sigma_2 = \sigma$, the condition derived above simplifies to

$$Odds = \frac{p_2}{p_1}\exp\left[\frac{p_2-0.5}{\sigma^2}\right],$$

or equivalently,

$$\Pr\left[M\ is\ a\ member\ of\ party\ 2\right]=1/\left[1+(p_1\ /\ p_2)\exp\left\{(0.5-p_2)/\sigma^2\right\}\right].$$

In this case, the probability that M is a member of the minority party is approximately equal to p_2 for very large values of σ; for values of σ below 1, this probability can drop considerably below p_2. For example, if $p_2 = 0.4$, then the probabilities that M is a member of the minority party for $\sigma = 1.5, 1.0$, and 0.5 are $0.389, 0.376$, and 0.309, respectively.

On the other hand, if $\sigma_2 < \sigma_1$, then the probability that M is a member of the minority party can exceed 0.5. For example, if $\sigma_2 = 0.3$ and $\sigma_1 = 0.6$ and $p_2 = 0.45$ then the probability is 0.557 that M is a member of the minority party. Note that, in this case, $M = 0.621$, substantially closer to M_2 than to M_1.

Bibliography

Abramowitz, Alan. 2010. *The Disappearing Center: Engaged Citizens, Polarization, and American Democracy*. New Haven, CT: Yale University Press.

Abramowitz, Alan. 2015. "The New American Electorate: Partisan, Sorted, and Polarized." In *American Gridlock: The Sources, Character, and Impact of Political Polarization*, edited by James Thurber and Antoine Yoshinaka, 19–44. New York: Cambridge University Press.

Abramowitz, Alan, and Kyle Saunders. 2008. "Is Polarization a Myth?" *Journal of Politics* 70(2): 542–555.

Acharya, Avidit, Matthew Blackwell, and Maya Sen. 2016. "The Political Legacy of American Slavery." *Journal of Politics* 78(3): 621–641.

Acharya, Avidit, Matthew Blackwell, and Maya Sen. 2018. *Deep Roots: How Slavery Still Shapes Southern Politics*. Princeton, NJ: Princeton University Press.

Adams, James, Thomas Brunell, Bernard Grofman, and Samuel Merrill III. 2010. "Why Candidate Divergence Should Be Expected to Be Just as Great (or Even Greater) in Competitive Seats as in Non-Competitive Ones." *Public Choice* 145(3–4): 417–433.

Adams, James, Thomas Brunell, Bernard Grofman, and Samuel Merrill III. 2013. "Do Competitive Districts Necessarily Produce Centrist Politicians?" In *Advances in Political Economy: Institutions, Modelling and Empirical Analysis*, edited by Norman Schofield, Gonzalo Caballero, and Daniel Kselman, 331–350. Berlin: Springer.

Adams, James, Erik Engstrom, Danielle Joeston, Jon Rogowski, Boris Shor, and Walt Stone. 2017. "Do Moderate Voters Weigh Candidates' Ideologies? Voters' Decision Rules in the 2010 Congressional Elections." *Political Behavior* 39(1): 205–227.

Adams, James, and Samuel Merrill III. 2006. "Why Small, Centrist Third Parties Motivate Policy Divergence by Major Parties." *American Political Science Review* 100(3): 403–417.

Adams, James and Samuel Merrill III. 2008. "Candidate and Party Strategies and Two-Stage Elections Beginning with a Primary." *American Journal of Political Science* 52(2), 344–359.

Adams, James and Samuel Merrill III. 2014. "Candidates' Policy Strategies in Primary Elections: Does Strategic Voting by the Primary Electorate Matter?" *Public Choice* 160(1–2): 7–24.

Adams, James, Samuel Merrill III, and Bernard Grofman. 2005. *A Unified Theory of Party Competition: A Cross-National Analysis Integrating Spatial and Behavioral Factors*. Cambridge: Cambridge University Press.

Al-Hussaini, Essam K., and Magued I. Osman. 1997. "On the Median of a Finite Mixture." *Journal of Statistical Computation and Simulation* 58: 121–144.

Albertson, Bethany, Lindsay Dun, and Shana Kushner Gadarian. 2020. "The Emotional Aspects of Political Persuasion." In *Oxford Handbook of Electoral Persuasion*, edited by Elizabeth Suhay, Bernard Grofman, and Alex Trechsel, 169–183. New York: Oxford University Press.

168 BIBLIOGRAPHY

Aldrich, John H. 1983. "A Downsian Spatial Model with Party Activism." *American Political Science Review* 77: 974–990.

Aldrich, John H., and M. D. McGinnis. 1989. A Model of Party Constraints on Optimal Candidate Positions. *Mathematical and Computer Modeling* 12: 437–450.

Aldrich, John H. 1995. *Why Parties? The Origin and Transformation of Political Parties in America.* Chicago: University of Chicago Press.

Aldrich, John H., and David W. Rohde. 2000. "The Consequences of Party Organization in the House: The Role of the Majority and Minority Parties in Conditional Party Government." In *Polarized Politics: Congress and the President in a Partisan Era*, edited by Jon R. Bond and Richard Fleisher, 31–72. Washington, DC: Congressional Quarterly Press.

Aldrich, John H., David W. Rohde, and Michael W. Tofias. 2007. "One D is Not Enough: Measuring Conditional Party Government, 1887–2002." In *Party, Process, and Political Change in Congress, Vol 2: Further New Perspectives on the History of Congress*, edited by David W. Brady and Mathew D. McCubbins, 102–112. Stanford, CA: Stanford University Press.

Alexander, Dan, and Asya Magazinnik. 2022. "Income Inequality and Electoral Theories of Polarization." *Journal of Political Institutions and Political Economy* 3(3–4): 317–342.

American Political Science Association. 1950. *Toward a More Responsible Two-Party System: A Report of the Committee on Political Parties.* Washington, D.C.: APSA (Printed as Supplement to *American Political Science Review*, September 1951).

Amitai, Yair. 2023. "The Activists Who Divide Us: A Cross-Country Analysis of Party Activists' Influence on Polarization and Representation." *Comparative Political Studies* 0: 1–33.

Ansolabehere, Stephen, David Brady, and Morris Fiorina. 1992. "The Vanishing Marginals and Electoral Responsiveness." *British Journal of Political Science* 22(1): 21–38.

Ansolabehere, Stephen, James M. Snyder, Jr., and Charles Stewart III. 2001. "Candidate Positioning in U.S. House Elections." *American Journal of Political Science* 45(1): 136–159.

Aranson, Peter H., and Peter C. Ordeshook. 1972. "Spatial Strategies for Sequential Elections." In *Probability Models of Collective Decision Making*, edited by Richard G. Niemi and Herbert F. Weisberg, 298–331. Columbus, OH: Charles E. Merrill.

Austen-Smith, David. 1984. Two-Party Competition with Many Constituencies. *Mathematical Social Sciences* 7(2): 177–198.

Austen-Smith, David. 1986. "Legislative Coalitions and Electoral Equilibrium." *Public Choice* 50: 185–210.

Bafumi, Joseph, and Michael C. Herron. 2010. "Leapfrog Representation and Extremism: A Study of American Voters and Their Members in Congress." *American Political Science Review* 104(3): 519–542.

Barker, David C., and Morgan Marietta. 2020. "Misinformation, Fake News, and Dueling Fact Perceptions in Public Opinion and Elections." In *Oxford Handbook of Electoral Persuasion*, edited by Elizabeth Suhay, Bernard Grofman, and Alex Trechsel, New York: Oxford University Press.

Bartels, Larry. 2000. "Partisanship and Voting Behavior, 1952–1996." *American Journal of Political Science* 44: 35–50.

Bartels, Larry. 2016. "Failure to Converge: Presidential Candidates, Core Partisans, and the Missing Middle in American Electoral Politics." *ANNALS of the American Academy of Political and Social Science* 667(1): 143–165.

BIBLIOGRAPHY 169

Bartels, Larry. 2020. "Under Trump, Democrats and Republicans Are More Divided—on Nearly Everything." *Washington Post*. May 2.

Bennett, Brian. 2019. "'My Whole Life Is a Bet.' Inside President Trump's Gamble on an Untested Re-Election Strategy." *Time Magazine*. June 20. https://time.com/longform/donald-trump-2020.

Berman, Russell, and Molly K. Hooper. 2010. "Waxman Sees Bright Side to November: 'Difficult' Democrats Won't Be Back." *The Hill* (blog). August 5. http://theh ill.com/homenews/house/112767-waxman-sees-bright-side-to-nov-losses (accessed March 22, 2020).

Boatright, Robert G. 2013. *Getting Primaried: The Changing Politics of Congressional Primary Challenges*. Ann Arbor: University of Michigan Press.

Bonica, Adam. 2014a. "Mapping the Ideological Marketplace." *American Journal of Political Science* 58(2): 367–387.

Bonica, Adam. 2014b. "The Punctuated Origins of Senate Polarization." *Legislative Studies Quarterly* 39: 5–26.

Bonica, Adam, and Gary W. Cox. 2018. "Ideological Extremists in the U.S. Congress: Out of Step but Still in Office." *Quarterly Journal of Political Science* 13: 207–236.

Brady, David W. 2015. "Sure, Congress Is Polarized. But Other Legislatures Are More So." In *Political Polarization in American Politics*, edited by Daniel J. Hopkins and John Sides, 115–119. New York: Bloomsbury.

Brady, David W., and Hahrie Han. 2015. "Our Politics May Be Polarized, but That Is Nothing New." In *Political Polarization in American Politics*, edited by Daniel J. Hopkins and John Sides, 137–143. New York: Bloomsbury.

Brazill, Timothy J., and Bernard Grofman. 2002. "Factor Analysis Versus Multidimensional Scaling: Binary Choice Roll-Call Voting and the U.S. Supreme Court." *Social Networks* 24: 201–229.

Broockman, David, et al. 2021. "Why Local Party Leaders Don't Support Nominating Centrists." *British Journal of Political Science* 51(2): 724–749.

Brunell, Thomas L. 2008. *Redistricting and Representation: Why Competitive Elections Are Bad for America*. New York: Routledge.

Brunell, Thomas L., and Bernard Grofman. 2008. "Evaluating the Impact of Redistricting on District Homogeneity, Political Competition, and Political Extremism in the U.S. House of Representatives, 1962–2006." In *Designing Democratic Governments*, edited by Margaret Levi et al., 117–140. New York: Russell Sage.

Brunell, Thomas L., and Bernard Grofman. 2009. "Testing Sincere Versus Strategic Split-Ticket Voting: Evidence from Split House–President Outcomes, 1900–2004." *Electoral Studies* 28(1): 62–69.

Brunell, Thomas and Bernard Grofman. 2018. "Using U.S. Senate Delegations from the Same State as Paired Comparisons: Evidence for a Reagan Realignment." *PS: Political Science and Politics* 51(3): 512–516.

Brunell, Thomas L., Bernard Grofman, and Samuel Merrill III. 2012. "Magnitude and Durability of Electoral Change: Identifying Critical Elections in the U.S. Congress 1854–2010." *Electoral Studies* 31(4): 816–828.

Brunell, Thomas, Bernard Grofman, and Samuel Merrill III. 2016a. "Replacement in the U.S. House: An Outlier-Chasing Model." *Party Politics* 22(4): 440–451.

Brunell, Thomas, Bernard Grofman, and Samuel Merrill III. 2016b. "Components of Party Polarization in the U.S. House of Representatives." *Journal of Theoretical Politics* 28(4): 598–624.

170 BIBLIOGRAPHY

Brunell, Thomas, Bernard Grofman, and Samuel Merrill III. 2016c. "The Volatility of Median and Supermajoritarian Pivots in the U.S. Congress and the Effects of Party Polarization." *Public Choice* 166(1–2): 183–204.

Buchler, Justin. 2018. *Incremental Polarization: A Unified Spatial Theory of Legislative Elections, Parties, and Roll Call Voting*. New York: Oxford University Press.

Buisseret, Peter, and Richard Van Weelden. 2020. "Crashing the Party? Elites, Outsiders, and Elections." *American Journal of Political Science* 64(2): 356–370.

Bullock, John G. 2020. "Party Cues." In *Oxford Handbook of Electoral Persuasion*, edited by Elizabeth Suhay, Bernard Grofman, and Alex Trechsel, 129–150. New York: Oxford University Press.

Burden, Barry C. 2001. "The Polarizing Effects of Congressional Elections." In *Congressional Primaries and the Politics of Representation*, edited by Peter F. Galderisi, Marni Ezra, and Michael Lyons, 95–115. Lanham, MD: Rowman and Littlefield.

Burden, Barry C. 2004. "Candidate Positioning in U.S. Congressional Elections." *British Journal of Political Science* 34(2): 211–227.

Butler, Daniel. 2009. "The Effect of the Size of Voting Blocs on Incumbents' Roll-Call Voting and the Asymmetric Polarization of Congress." *Legislative Studies Quarterly* 36(3): 297–318.

Cain, Bruce. 2015. "Two Approaches to Lessening the Effects of Partisanship." In *Solutions to Political Polarization in America*, edited by Nathaniel Persily, 157–164. New York: Cambridge University Press.

Callander, Steven, and Catherine H. Wilson. 2007. "Turnout, Polarization and Duverger's Law." *Journal of Politics* 69(4): 1047–1056.

Canes-Wrone, Brandice, David W. Brady, and John F. Cogan. 2002. "Out of Step, Out of Office: Electoral Accountability and House Members' Voting." *American Political Science Review* 96(1): 127–140.

Carmines, Edward G., Michael J. Ensley, and Michael W. Wagner. 2012. "Who Fits the Left-Right Divide? Partisan Polarization in the American Electorate." *American Behavioral Scientist* 56(12): 1631–1653.

Carmines, Edward G., and J. A. Stimson. 1989. *Issue Evolution: Race and the Transformation of American Politics*. Princeton, NJ: Princeton University Press.

Carroll, Royce, Jeff Lewis, James Lo, Nolan McCarty, Keith Poole, and Howard Rosenthal. 2015. "DW-NOMINATE Scores with Bootstrapped Standard Errors." Voteview.com, September 17. https://legacy.voteview.com/dwnomin.htm.

Chatfield, Sara, Jeffery A. Jenkins, and Charles Stewart III. 2021. "Polarization Lost: Exploring the Decline of Ideological Voting in Congress After the Gilded Age." *Journal of Historical Political Economy* 1: 183–214.

Clinton, Joshua D. 2006. "Representation in Congress: Constituents and Roll Calls in the 106th House." *Journal of Politics* 68(2): 397–409.

Coleman, James S. 1971. "Internal Processes Governing Party Positions in Elections." *Public Choice* 11(1): 35–60.

Cotter, Ryan G., Milton Lodge, and Robert Vidigal. 2020. "When, How, and Why Persuasion Fails: A Motivated Reasoning Account." In *Oxford Handbook of Electoral Persuasion*, edited by Elizabeth Suhay, Bernard Grofman, and Alex Trechsel, 51–65. New York: Oxford University Press.

Cox, Gary W. 1990. "Centripetal and Centrifugal Incentives in Electoral Systems." *American Journal of Political Science* 31: 82–108.

BIBLIOGRAPHY 171

Cox, Gary W. 1997. *Making Votes Count: Strategic Coordination in the World's Electoral Systems*. New York: Cambridge University Press.

Cox, Gary W., and Mathew D. McCubbins. 2005. *Setting the Agenda: Responsible Party Government in the U.S. House of Representatives*. Cambridge: Cambridge University Press.

Cox, Gary W., and Mathew D. McCubbins. 2007. *Legislative Leviathan: Party Government in the House*. 2nd ed. Cambridge: Cambridge University Press.

De Angelis, Andrea. 2020. "How Voters Distort Their Perceptions and Why This Matters." In *Oxford Handbook of Electoral Persuasion*, edited by Elizabeth Suhay, Bernard Grofman, and Alex Trechsel, 946–976. New York: Oxford University Press.

Downs, Anthony. 1957. *An Economic Theory of Democracy*. New York: Harper and Row.

Edmonson, Catie. 2020. "G.O.P. Congressman Is Ousted from Right After Officiating at Same-Sex Wedding." *New York Times*. June 14..

Enelow, James M., and Melvin J. Hinich. 1989. "A General Probabilistic Spatial Theory of Elections." *Public Choice* 61(2): 101–113.

Erikson, Robert. 1976. "Is There Such a Thing as a Safe Seat?" *Polity* 8: 623–632.

Erikson, Robert, and David Romero. 1990. "Candidate Equilibrium and the Behavioral Model of the Vote." *American Political Science Review* 84: 1103–1126.

Erikson, Robert, and Gerald Wright. 1997. "Voters, Candidates, and Issues in Congressional Elections." In *Congress Reconsidered*, edited by Lawrence Dodd and Bruce Oppenheimer, 6th ed, 91–106. Washington, DC: Congressional Quarterly Press.

Erikson, Robert and Gerald Wright. 2000. "Representation of Constituency Ideology in Congress." In *Continuity and Change in House Elections*, edited by David Brady, John Cogan, and Morris Fiorina, 149–177. Stanford, CA: Stanford University Press.

Fagan, E. J. 2022. "Elite Polarization and Partisan Think Tanks." *Journal of Political Institutions and Political Economy* 3(3–4): 395–411.

Feigenbaum, James J., Alexander Fouirnaies, and Andrew B. Hall. 2017. "The Majority-Party Disadvantage: Revising Theories of Legislative Organization." *Quarterly Journal of Political Science* 12(3): 269–300.

Feld, Scott L., and Bernard Grofman. 1988. "Ideological Consistency as a Collective Phenomenon." *American Political Science Review* 82(3): 64–75.

Fiorina, Morris P. 2017. *Unstable Majorities: Polarization, Party Sorting, and Political Stalemate*. Stanford, CA: Hoover Institution Press.

Fiorina, Morris, with Samuel J. Abrams and Jeremy C. Pope. 2005. *Culture War: The Myth of a Polarized America*. New York: Longman.

Fiorina, Morris, with Samuel J. Abrams. 2009. *Disconnect: The Breakdown of Representation in American Politics*. Norman: University of Oklahoma Press.

Fowler, Anthony, and Andrew B. Hall. 2017. "Long-Term Consequences of Election Results." *British Journal of Political Science* 47(2): 351–372.

Fraenkel, Jon, and Bernard Grofman. 2020. "Ethnicity and the Classification of Party Systems." Unpublished manuscript.

Gerber, Elizabeth R., and Rebecca B. Morton. 1998. "Primary Election Systems and Representation." *Journal of Law Economics and Organization* 14: 304–324.

Gidron, Noam, James Adams, and Will Horne. 2021. "Who Dislikes Whom? Affective Polarization between Pairs of Parties in Western Democracies." *British Journal of Political Science* 51: 1–19.

172 BIBLIOGRAPHY

Gimpel, James G., Frances E. Lee, and Shanna Pearson-Merkowitz. 2008. "The Check Is in the Mail: Interdistrict Funding Flows in Congressional Elections." *American Journal of Political Science* 52(2): 373–394.

Glazer, Amihai, and Bernard Grofman. 1989. "Why Representatives Are Ideologists Though Voters Are Not." *Public Choice* 61: 29–39.

Glazer, Amihai, Bernard Grofman, and Guillermo Owen. 1989. "A Model of Candidate Convergence Under Uncertainty About Voter Preferences." In *Formal Theories of Politics: Mathematical Modelling in Political Science*, edited by P. E. Johnson, 471–478. Oxford: Pergamon.

Glazer, Amihai, Bernard Grofman, and Guillermo Owen. 1998. "A Neo-Downsian Model of Group-Oriented Voting and Racial Backlash." *Public Choice* 97: 23–34.

Goedert, Nicholas. 2017. "The Pseudoparadox of Partisan Mapmaking and Congressional Competition." *State Politics & Policy Quarterly* 17(1): 47–75.

Golder, Matthew. 2006. "Presidential Coattails and Legislative Fragmentation." *American Journal of Political Science* 50(1): 34–48.

Graham, Matthew H., and Milan W. Svolik. 2020. "Democracy in America? Partisanship, Polarization, and the Robustness of Support for Democracy in the United States." *American Political Science Review* 114(2): 392–409.

Greenberg, Stanley. 2005. *The Two Americas: Our Current Political Deadlock and How to Break It*. New York: Macmillan.

Grofman, Bernard. 1987. "Models of Voting." In *Micropolitics Annual*, edited by Samuel Long, 31–61. Greenwich, CT: JAI Press.

Grofman, Bernard. 1998. "Rebuttal to Wuffle and Collet's Supposedly Irrefutable Evidence That Higher Turnout Benefits Republicans." *Journal of Theoretical Politics* 10(2): 251–255.

Grofman, Bernard. 2004. "Downs and Two-Party Convergence." In *Annual Review of Political Science*, edited by Nelson W. Polsby, 7:25–46.

Grofman, Bernard. 2020a. "Reasoned Persuasion." In *Oxford Handbook of Electoral Persuasion*, edited by Elizabeth Suhay, Bernard Grofman, and Alex Trechsel, 88–104. New York: Oxford University Press.

Grofman, Bernard. 2020b. "Persuasion and Issue Voting." In *Oxford Handbook of Electoral Persuasion*, edited by Elizabeth Suhay, Bernard Grofman, and Alex Trechsel, 105–128. New York: Oxford University Press.

Grofman, Bernard, and Timothy J. Brazill. 2002. "Identifying the Median Justice on the Supreme Court Through Multidimensional Scaling: Analysis of 'Natural Courts' 1953–1991." *Public Choice* 112: 55–79.

Grofman, Bernard, and Thomas Brunell. 2001. "Explaining the Ideological Differences Between the Two U.S. Senators Elected from the Same State: An Institutional Effects Model." In *Congressional Primaries in the Politics of Representation*, edited by Peter Galderisi, 132–142. New York: Rowman and Littlefield.

Grofman, Bernard, Robert Griffin, and Amihai Glazer. 1990. "Identical Geography, Different Party: A Natural Experiment on the Magnitude of Party Differences in the U.S. Senate, 1960–84." In *Developments in Electoral Geography*, edited by Ron Johnston, Fred M. Shelley, and Peter J. Taylor, 207–217. London: Routledge.

Grofman, Bernard, William Koetzle, Michael McDonald, and Thomas Brunell. 2000. "A New Look at Split Ticket Voting for House and President: The Comparative Midpoints Model." *Journal of Politics* 62(1): 34–35.

BIBLIOGRAPHY 173

Grofman, Bernard, William Koetzle, Samuel Merrill III, and Thomas Brunell. 2001. "Changes in the Location of the Median Voter in the U.S. House of Representatives, 1963–1996." *Public Choice* 106(3–4): 221–232.

Grofman, Bernard, Samuel Merrill, III, Thomas L. Brunell, and William Koetzle. 1999. "The Potential Electoral Disadvantages of a Catch-All Party: Ideological Variance Among Republicans and Democrats in the 50 U.S. States." *Party Politics* 5(2): 199–210.

Grofman, Bernard, Guillermo Owen, and Christian Collet. 1999. "Rethinking the Partisan Effects of Higher Turnout: So What's the Question?" *Public Choice* 99: 357–376.

Grofman, Bernard, Guillermo Owen, Nicholas Noviello and Amihai Glazer. 1987. "Stability and Centrality of Legislative Choice in the Spatial Context." *American Political Science Review* 81(2): 539–553.

Groseclose, Timothy. 2001. "A Model of Candidate Location When One Candidate Has a Valence Advantage." *American Journal of Political Science* 45(4): 862–886.

Grynaviski, Jeffrey D. 2006. "A Bayesian Learning Model with Implications for Party Identification." *Journal of Theoretical Politics* 18(3): 323–346.

Grynaviski, Jeffrey D. 2009. *Partisan Bonds: Political Reputations and Legislative Accountability*. New York: Cambridge University Press.

Hacker, Jacob. S., and Paul Pierson. 2006. *Off Center: The Republican Revolution and the Erosion of American Democracy*. New Haven, CT: Yale University Press.

Hall, Andrew, and Daniel Thompson. 2018. "Who Punishes Extremist Nominees? Candidate Ideology and Turning Out the Base in US Elections." *American Political Science Review* 112(3): 509–524.

Halperin, Mort, and Soren Dayton. 2020. "Can Congress Reclaim Authority It Has Handed Over to the President? It's Trying." *Washington Post*. August 20.

Hare, Christopher, Keith T. Poole, and Howard Rosenthal. 2015. "Polarization in Congress Has Risen Sharply. Where Is It Going Next?" In *Political Polarization in American Politics*, edited by Daniel Hopkins and John Sides, 144–150. New York: Bloomsbury Academic.

Henrici, Peter. 1964. *Elements of Numerical Analysis*. New York: Wiley.

Hill, Seth. 2017. "Changing Votes or Changing Voters? How Candidates and Election Context Swing Voters and Mobilize the Base." *Electoral Studies* 48: 131–148.

Hill, Seth, Daniel Hopkins, and Gregory Huber. 2021. "Not by Turnout Alone: Measuring the Sources of Electoral Change, 2012 to 2016." *Science Advances* 7(17). https://www.science.org/doi/10.1126/sciadv.abe3272.

Hill, Seth, and Chris Tausanovitch. 2015. "A Disconnect in Representation? Comparison of Trends in Congressional and Public Polarization." *Journal of Politics* 77(4): 1058–1075.

Hillygus, D. Sunshine, and Todd G. Shields. 2008. *The Persuadable Voter: Wedge Issues in Presidential Campaigns*. Princeton, NJ: Princeton University Press.

Hinich, Melvin J. 1977. "The Median Voter Is an Artifact." *Journal of Economic Theory* 16: 208–219.

Hinich, Melvin, and Michael Munger. 1994. *Ideology and the Theory of Political Choice*. Ann Arbor: University of Michigan Press.

Hinich, Melvin and Michael Munger. 1997. *Analytical Politics*. Cambridge: Cambridge University Press.

Hinich, Melvin, and Peter Ordeshook. 1970. "Plurality Maximization Versus Vote Maximization." *American Political Science Review* 64: 772–791.

Hogg, Robert, and Allen Craig. 1995. *Introduction to Mathematical Statistics*. Englewood Cliffs, NJ: Prentice Hall.

174 BIBLIOGRAPHY

Holstege, Sean. 2016. "Do Voter Purges Discriminate Against the Poor and Minorities?" *NBC News.* https://www.nbcnews.com/news/us-news/do-voter-purges-discriminate-against-poor-minorities-n636586.

Homans, Charles, Jazmine Ulloa, and Blake Hounshell. 2022. "How the Worst Fears for Democracy Were Averted in 2022." *New York Times.* December 24.

Hopkins, Daniel J. 2020. "Should Biden and Trump Focus More on Persuading Swing Voters or on Mobilizing the Base." *Washington Post.* October 30.

Hopkins, Daniel, and John Sides. 2015. *Political Polarization in American Politics.* New York: Bloomsbury Academic.

Hussey, Wesley, and John Zaller. 2011. "Who Do Parties Represent?" In *Who Gets Represented?*, edited by Peter K. Enns and Christopher Wlezien, 311–344. New York: Russell Sage.

Iyengar, Shanto, Yphtach Lelkes, Matthew Levendusky, Neil Malhotra, and Sean Westwood. 2019. "The Origins and Consequences of Affective Polarization in the United States." *Annual Reviews of Political Science* 22: 129–146.

Iyengar, Shanto, Gaurav Sood, and Yphtach Lelkes. 2012. "Affect, Not Ideology: A Social Identity Perspective on Polarization." *Public Opinion Quarterly* 76(3): 405–431.

Iyengar, Shanto, and Sean Westwood. 2015. "Fear and Loathing Across Party Lines: New Evidence on Group Polarization." *American Journal of Political Science* 59(3): 690–707.

Jacobson, Gary. 1987. "The Marginals Never Vanished: Incumbency and Competition in Elections to the U.S. House of Representatives, 1952–82." *American Journal of Political Science* 31(1): 126–141.

Jacobson, Gary. 2006. *The Politics of Congressional Elections.* 7th ed. New York: Longman.

Jacobson, Gary. 2015. "Eroding the Electoral Foundations of Partisan Polarization." In Solutions to Political Polarization in America, edited by Nathaniel Persily, 83–95. New York: Cambridge University Press.

Jessee, Stephen. 2009. "Spatial Voting in the 2004 Presidential Election." *American Political Science Review* 103(1): 59–81.

Kam, Dara. 2020. "Florida Gov. DeSantis, Still Trying to Stop Felons from Voting, Takes 'Poll Tax' to Federal Appeals Court." *Orlando Weekly.* June 19. https://www.orlandowee kly.com/news/florida-gov-desantis-still-trying-to-stop-felons-from-voting-takes-poll-tax-to-federal-appeals-court-27485371.

Kamarck, Elaine C. 2015. "Geography and Gridlock in the United States." In Solutions to Political Polarization in America, edited by Nathaniel Persily, 96–103. New York: Cambridge University Press.

Karol, David. 2009. *Party Position Change in American Politics: Coalition Management.* New York: Cambridge University Press.

Key, V. O., Jr. 1949. *Southern Politics.* New York: Knopf.

Kiewiet, D. Roderick, and Mathew D. McCubbins. 1991. *The Logic of Delegation: Congressional Parties and the Appropriations Process.* Chicago: University of Chicago Press.

Klar, Samara. 2014. "A Multidimensional Study of Ideological Preferences and Priorities Among the American Public." *Public Opinion Quarterly* 78: 344–359.

Klein, Ezra. 2020. *Why We're Polarized.* New York: Avid Reader Press.

Klein, Ezra, and Alvin Chang. 2015. "Political Identity Is Fair Game for Hatred: How Republicans and Democrats Discriminate." *Vox,* December 7. https://www.vox.com/2015/12/7/9790764/partisan-discrimination.

BIBLIOGRAPHY 175

Koger, Gregory, and Matthew J. Lebo. 2012. "Strategic Party Government and the 2010 Elections." *American Politics Research* 40(5): 927–945.

Krasa, Stefan, and Mattias Polborn. 2014. "Policy Divergence and Voter Polarization in a Structural Model of Elections." *Journal of Law and Economics* 57(1): 31–76.

Krasa, Stefan, and Mattias Polborn. 2018. "Political Competition in Legislative Elections." *American Political Science Review* 112(4): 809–825.

Krehbiel, Keith. 1990. "Are Congressional Committees Composed of Preference Outliers?" *American Political Science Review* 84(1): 149–163.

Krehbiel, Keith. 1992. *Information and Legislative Organization*. Ann Arbor: University of Michigan Press.

Krehbiel, Keith. 1998. *Pivotal Politics: A Theory of U.S. Lawmaking*. Chicago: University of Chicago Press.

Ladewig, Jeffrey W. 2005. "Conditional Party Government and the Homogeneity of Constituent Interests." *Journal of Politics* 67(4): 1006–1029.

Lebo, M. J., A. J. McGlynn, and G. Koger. 2007. "Strategic Party Government: Party Influence in Congress, 1789–2000." *American Journal of Political Science* 51: 464–481.

Lee, David. S., Enrico Moretti, and Matthew J. Butler. 2004. "Do Voters Affect or Elect Policies? Evidence from the U.S. House." *Quarterly Journal of Economics* 119(3) 807–859.

Lee, Frances. 2016. *Insecure Majorities: Congress and the Perpetual Campaign*. Chicago: University of Chicago Press.

Leeper, Thomas J., and Rune Slothuus. 2020. "How the News Media Persuades: Framing Effects and Beyond." In *Oxford Handbook of Electoral Persuasion*, edited by Elizabeth Suhay, Bernard Grofman, and Alex Trechsel, 151–168. New York: Oxford University Press.

Levendusky, Matthew. 2009. *The Partisan Sort: How Liberals Became Democrats and Conservatives Became Republicans*. Chicago: University of Chicago Press.

Levendusky, Matthew, Jeremy C. Pope, and Simon D. Jackman. 2008. "Measuring District-Level Partisanship with Implications for the Analysis of U.S. Elections." *Journal of Politics* 70(3): 736–753.

Lewis, Jeffrey, and Luke Sonnet. 2019. "Estimating NOMINATE Scores over Time Using Penalized Splines." Unpublished manuscript. Department of Political Science, University of California Los Angeles.

Lijphart, Arend. 2015. "Polarization and Democratization." In *Solutions to Political Polarization in America*, edited by Nathaniel Persily, 73–82. New York: Cambridge University Press.

Lubell, Samuel. 1952. *The Future of American Politics*. New York: Greenwood-Heinemann.

Mann, Thomas E., and Norman Ornstein. 2012. *It's Even Worse Than It Looks: How the American Constitutional System Collided with the New Politics of Extremism*. New York: Basic Books.

Marshall, William. 1998. "American Political Culture and the Failures of Process Federalism." *Harvard Journal of Law and Public Policy* 22: 139.

Masket, Seth. 2009. *No Middle Ground: How Informal Party Organizations Control Nominations and Polarize Legislatures*. Ann Arbor: University of Michigan Press.

Masket, Seth. 2015. "Our Political Parties Are Networked, Not Fragmented." In *Political Polarization in American Politics*, edited by Daniel Hopkins and John Sides, New York: Bloomsbury Academic.

176 BIBLIOGRAPHY

Matthews, Donald R. 1960. *United States Senators and Their World*. Chapel Hill: University of North Carolina Press.

Mayer, Jane. 2016. *Dark Money: The Hidden History of the Billionaires Behind the Rise of the Radical Right*. New York: Doubleday.

Mayhew, David. 1974. *Congress: The Electoral Connection*. New Haven, CT: Yale University Press.

Mayhew, David. 1974. "The Marginals Never Vanished: Incumbency and Competition in Elections to the U.S. House of Representatives." *Polity* 6(3): 295–317.

McCarty, Nolan. 2015. "What We Know and Do Not Know About Our Polarized Politics." In *Political Polarization in American Politics*, edited by Daniel J. Hopkins and John Sides, 1–8. New York: Bloomsbury Academic.

McCarty, Nolan. 2019. *Polarization: What Everyone Needs to Know*. New York: Oxford University Press.

McCarty, Nolan, Keith Poole, and Howard Rosenthal. 2001. "The Hunt for Party Discipline in Congress." *American Political Science Review* 95(3): 673–687.

McCarty, Nolan, Keith Poole, and Howard Rosenthal. 2006. *Polarized America*. Cambridge, MA: MIT Press.

McCarty, Nolan, Keith Poole and Howard Rosenthal. 2009. "Does Gerrymandering Cause Polarization?" *American Journal of Political Science* 53(3): 666–680.

McGann, Anthony, Bernard Grofman, and William Koetzle. 2002. "Why Party Leaders Are More Extreme Than Their Members: Modeling Sequential Elimination Elections in the U.S. House of Representatives." *Public Choice* 113: 337–356.

McGann, Anthony J., William Koetzle, and Bernard Grofman. 2002. "How an Ideologically Concentrated Minority Can Trump a Dispersed Majority: Nonmedian Voter Results in Plurality, Run-off and Sequential Elimination Elections." *American Journal of Political Science* 46(1): 134–147.

Merrill, Samuel III. 1988. *Making Multicandidate Elections More Democratic*. Princeton, NJ: Princeton University Press.

Merrill, Samuel III, and James Adams. 2002. "Centrifugal Incentives in Multicandidate Elections." *Journal of Theoretical Politics* 14: 273–300.

Merrill, Samuel III, and Bernard Grofman. 1999. *A Unified Theory of Voting: Directional and Proximity Spatial Models*. New York: Cambridge University Press.

Merrill, Samuel III, Bernard Grofman, and Thomas Brunell. 2008. "Cycles in American National Electoral Politics, 1854–2004." *American Political Science Review* 102(1): 1–17.

Merrill, Samuel III, Bernard Grofman, and Thomas Brunell. 2014. "Modeling the Electoral Dynamics of Party Polarization in Two-Party Legislatures." *Journal of Theoretical Politics* 26(4): 548–572.

Merrill, Samuel III, Bernard Grofman, and Thomas Brunell. 2022. "Identifying the 'Downsian Ceiling': When Does Polarization Make Appealing to One's Base More Attractive Than Moderating to the Center." *Journal of Political Institutions and Political Economy* 3(3–4): 273–293. http://dx.doi.org/10.1561/113.00000060.

Merrill, Samuel III, Bernard Grofman, Thomas Brunell, and William Koetzle. 1999. "The Power of Ideologically Concentrated Minorities." *Journal of Theoretical Politics* 11(1): 57–74.

Miller, Gary, and Norman Schofield. 2003. "Activists and Partisan Realignment in the United States." *American Political Science Review* 97: 245–260.

Milbank, Dana, and Mike Allen. 2004. "Bush Fortifies Conservative Base: Campaign Seeks Solid Support Before Wooing Swing Voters." *Washington Post*. July 15.

BIBLIOGRAPHY 177

Miniter, Brendan. 2005. "The McCain Myth: The Moderation That Makes Him a Senate Powerhouse Will Keep Him Out of the White House." *Wall Street Journal*. May 31.

Mood, Alexander M., Franklin A. Graybill, and Duane C. Boes. 1974. *Introduction to the Theory of Statistics*. 3rd ed. New York: McGraw-Hill.

Muñoz, Maria Murias, and Bonnie Meguid. 2021. "Does Party Polarization Mobilize or De-mobilize Voters? The Answer Depends on Where Voters Stand." *Electoral Studies* 70: 1–9.

Nagel, Jack H., and Christopher Wlezien. 2010. "Centre-Party Strength and Major-Party Divergence in Britain, 1945–2005." *British Journal of Political Science* 40: 279–304.

Nagourney, Adam. 2003. "Political Parties Shift Emphases to Core Voters." *New York Times*, August 30.

Neal, Zachary P. 2020. "A Sign of the Times? Weak and Strong Polarization in the U.S. Congress, 1973–2016." *Social Networks* 60: 103–112.

Nokken, Timothy P., and Keith T. Poole. 2004. "Congressional Party Defection in American History." *Legislative Studies Quarterly* 29: 545–568.

Owen, Guillermo, and Bernard Grofman. 2006. "Two-Stage Electoral Competition in Two-Party Contests: Persistent Divergence of Party Positions." *Social Choice and Welfare* 26: 547–569.

Park, Hong Min. 2022. "Partisan Manipulation of Dimensionality and Party Polarization in the U.S. Congress." *Journal of Political Institutions and Political Economy* 3(3–4): 371–393.

Patel, J. K., and C. B. Read. 1996. *Handbook of the Normal Distribution*. 2nd ed. New York: Marcel Dekker.

Pearson, Kathryn. 2015. *Party Discipline in the U.S. House of Representatives*. Ann Arbor: University of Michigan Press.

Peress, Michael. 2008. "Selecting the Condorcet Winner: Single-Stage Versus Multi-Stage Voting Rules." *Public Choice* 137: 207–220.

Persily, Nathaniel. 2015a. *Solutions to Political Polarization in America*. New York: Cambridge University Press.

Persily, Nathaniel. 2015b. "Introduction." In *Solutions to Political Polarization in America*, edited by Nathaniel Persily, 3–14. New York: Cambridge University Press.

Pildes, Richard. 2015. "How to Fix Our Polarized Politics? Strengthen Political Parties." In *Political Polarization in American Politics*, edited by Daniel Hopkins and John Sides, 155–160. New York: Bloomsbury Academic.

Polsby, Nelson. 1968. "The Institutionalization of the U.S. House of Representatives." *American Political Science Review* 62(1): 144–168.

Poole, Keith T., and Howard Rosenthal. 1984. "The Polarization of American Politics." *Journal of Politics* 46: 1061–1079.

Poole, Keith T., and Howard Rosenthal. 1997. *Congress: A Political-Economic History of Roll Call Voting*. New York: Oxford University Press.

Poole, Keith T., and Howard Rosenthal. 2007. *Ideology and Congress*. New York: Routledge.

Putnam, Robert D., with Shaylyn Romney Garrett. 2020. *The Upswing: How America Came Together a Century Ago and How We Can Do It Again*. New York: Simon and Schuster.

Riker, William. 1982. *Liberalism Against Populism*. San Francisco: W. H. Freeman.

Ripley, Randall. 1975. *Congress: Process and Policy*. New York: Norton.

Roberts, J. M., and S. S. Smith. 2003. "Procedural Contexts, Party Strategy, and Conditional Party Voting in the U.S. House of Representative, 1971–2000." *American Journal of Political Science* 47: 305–317.

178   BIBLIOGRAPHY

Rodden, Jonathan. 2015. "Geography and Gridlock in the United States." In *Solutions to Political Polarization in America*, edited by Nathaniel Persily, 104–120. New York: Cambridge University Press.

Rohde, David W. 2010. *Parties and Leaders in the Post-Reform House*. Chicago: University of Chicago Press.

Rosenfeld, Sam. 2017. *The Polarizers: Postwar Architects of Our Partisan Era*. Chicago: University of Chicago Press.

Runciman, David. 2018. *How Democracy Ends*. London: Profile Books.

Schlesinger, Arthur, Jr. 1951. "Toward a More Responsible Two-Party System. A Report of the Committee on Political Parties." *ANNALS of the American Academy of Political and Social Science* 274(1): 222–222.

Schofield, Norman. 2007. "The Mean Voter Theorem: Necessary and Sufficient Conditions for Convergent Equilibrium." *Review of Economic Studies* 74(3): 965–980.

Seo, Jungkun, and Sean M. Theriault. 2012. "Moderate Caucuses in a Polarized U.S. Congress." *Journal of Legislative Studies* 18(2): 203–221.

Serra, Giles. 2011. "Why Primaries? The Party's Trade-Off Between Policy and Valence." *Journal of Theoretical Politics* 23(1): 21–51.

Shapiro, Catherine R., David W. Brady, Richard A. Brody, and John A. Ferejohn. 1990. "Linking Constituency Opinion and Senate Voting Scores: A Hybrid Explanation." *Legislative Studies Quarterly* 15: 599–623.

Shapiro, Robert Y. 2015. "Can Young Voters Break the Cycle of Polarization?" 2015. In *Political Polarization in American Politics*, edited by Daniel Hopkins and John Sides, 151–154. New York: Bloomsbury Academic.

Shaw, Daron, and John Petrocik. 2020. *The Turnout Myth: Voting Rates and Partisan Outcomes in American National Elections*. Oxford: Oxford University Press.

Shor, Boris, and Nolan McCarty. 2022. "Two Decades of Polarization in American State Legislatures." *Journal of Political Institutions and Political Economy* 3(3–4): 343–370.

Sides, John, Chris Tausanovitch, Lynn Vavreck, and Christopher Warshaw. 2020. "On the Representativeness of Primary Electorates." *British Journal of Political Science* 50(2): 677–685.

Simas, Elizabeth. 2021. "Extremely High Quality?" *Public Opinion Quarterly* 84(3): 699–724.

Skocpol, Theda, and Alexander Hertel-Fernandez. 2016. "The Koch Network and Republican Party Extremism." *Perspectives on Politics* 14(3): 681–699.

Smith, Steven, Jason Roberts, and Ryan Vander Wielen. 2013. *The American Congress*. 8th ed. Cambridge: Cambridge University Press.

Snyder, James M., Jr. 1994. "Safe Seats, Marginal Seats, and Party Platforms: The Logic of Platform Differentiation." *Economics and Politics* 6: 201–213.

Snyder, James M., Jr., and Timothy Groseclose. 2000. "Estimating Party Influence in Congressional Roll-Call Voting." *American Journal of Political Science* 44(2): 193–211.

Snyder, James M., Jr., and Timothy Groseclose. 2001. "Estimating Party Influence on Roll Call Voting: Regression Coefficients Versus Classification Success." *American Political Science Review* 95(3): 689–698.

Sorauf, Frank J. 1992. *Inside Campaign Finance: Myths and Realities*. New Haven, CT: Yale University Press.

Stimson, James A. 1999. *Public Opinion in America: Moods, Cycles, and Swings*. 2nd ed. Boulder, CO: Westview Press.

BIBLIOGRAPHY

Suhay, Elizabeth, Bernard Grofman, and Alex Trechsel (eds.). 2020. *Oxford Handbook of Electoral Persuasion*. New York: Oxford University Press.

Sulkin, Tracy, Paul Testa, and Kaye Usry. 2015. "What Gets Rewarded? Legislative Activity and Constituency Approval." *Political Research Quarterly* 68(4): 690–702.

Svolik, Milan W. 2020. "When Polarization Trumps Civic Virtue: Partisan Conflict and the Subversion of Democracy by Incumbents." *Quarterly Journal of Political Science* 15(1): 3–31.

Theriault, Sean M. 2006. "Party Polarization in the U.S. Congress: Member Replacement and Member Adaptation." *Party Politics* 12(4): 483–503.

Theriault, Sean M. 2008. *Party Polarization in Congress*. Cambridge: Cambridge University Press.

Theriault, Sean M., and David Rohde. 2011. "The Gingrich Senators and Party Polarization in the U.S. Senate." *Journal of Politics* 73(4): 1011–1024.

Thomsen, Danielle. 2017. *Opting Out of Congress: Partisan Polarization and the Decline of Moderate Candidates*. Cambridge: Cambridge University Press.

Trechsel, Alex, and Diego Garcia. 2020. "Voting Advice Applications: The Power of Self-Persuasion." In *Oxford Handbook of Electoral Persuasion*, edited by Elizabeth Suhay, Bernard Grofman, and Alex Trechsel, 925–945. New York: Oxford University Press.

Utych, Stephen M. 2020. "Man Bites Blue Dog: Are Moderates Really More Electable than Ideologues?" *Journal of Politics* 82(1): 392–396.

Van Houweling, Robert P. and Paul M. Sniderman. 2005. "The Political Logic of a Downsian Space." Working Paper.

Wawro, Gregory J., and Eric Schickler. 2018. "Reid's Rules: Filibusters, the Nuclear Option, and Path Dependence in the US Senate." *Legislative Studies Quarterly* 43(4): 619–647.

Westwood, Sean, Shanto Iyengar, Stefaan Walgrave, Rafael Leonisio, Luis Miller, and Oliver Strijbis. 2018. "The Tie That Divides: Cross-National Evidence of the Primacy of Partyism." *European Journal of Political Research* 57: 333–354.

Wildavsky, Aaron. 1965. "The Goldwater Phenomenon: Purists, Politicians, and the Two-Party System." *Review of Politics* 27(3): 386–413.

Winer, Stanley, Larry Kenny, and Bernard Grofman. 2014. "Explaining Variation in the Degree of Electoral Competition in a Mature Democracy: U.S. Senate Elections 1922–2004." *Public Choice* 161(3–4): 471–497.

Wiseman, Alan E., and John R. Wright. 2008. "The Legislative Median and Partisan Policy." *Journal of Theoretical Politics* 20(1): 5–29.

Wittman, Donald. 1973. "Parties as Utility Maximizers." *American Political Science Review* 18: 490–498.

Wittman, Donald. 1977. "Candidates with Policy Preferences: A Dynamic Model." *Journal of Economic Theory* 14: 180–189.

Wittman, Donald. 1983. "Candidate Motivation: A Synthesis of Alternatives." *American Political Science Review* 77: 142–157.

Wuffle, A., et al. 1989. "Finagle's Law and the Finagle Point, a New Solution Concept for Two-Candidate Competition in Spatial Voting Games Without a Core." *American Journal of Political Science* 33(2): 348–375.

Zingher, Joshua N. 2018. "Polarization, Demographic Change, and White Flight from the Democratic Party." *Journal of Politics* 80(3): 860–872.

Zingher, Joshua N. 2022. *Political Choice in a Polarized America: How Elite Polarization Shapes Mass Behavior*. New York: Oxford University Press.

Index

For the benefit of digital users, indexed terms that span two pages (e.g., 52–53) may, on occasion, appear on only one of those pages.

Tables and figures are indicated by *t* and *f* following the page number

abstention threat. *See* threat of abstention
activist influence. *See* partisan loyalty and activist influence
Affordable Health Care (Obamacare), 36
African-American electorate, 18, 42, 128
alienation, 9, 14, 16, 49–52, 59–60, 77, 82, 105, 123, 146–47, 156–57
American Political Science Association, 3, 18, 21, 120
ANNALS of the American Academy of Political and Social Science, 3
appeal-to-the-base model
  arguments in support, 155
  Downsian ceiling and, 158–59
  Nash-equilibrium positions under abstention model, 155–56
  robustness checks, 156–57, 157*t*
asymmetry constraints, 33–36, 122–23, 139

Biden, Joe, 14, 24
bipartisan support, 17, 103–4
Boehner, John, 25–26
Build Back Better bill, 105
Bush, George W., 57

cable news, 7
campaign resources, 25, 76, 79
candidate ideology, 99, 143–45, 144*t*
candidate polarization, 11–13, 51
candidate position differences
  bounds on, 133*f*
  in competitive districts, 46–48
  data analysis on US House, 44–46
  district competitiveness and, 41–48
  maximum divergence, 48–52

  motivations for, 48–49
  quadratic analysis on candidate ideology, 46, 143–45
  spatial model with partisan loyalty and abstention, 49–52
  vote-maximizing candidates, 48–49, 51
ceteris paribus, 62, 78–79, 90–93, 99–100, 117, 151–52, 155, 163
chamber medians
  concentrated minority and, 109–10
  Congressional decision making and, 103–9, 107*f*
  introduction to, 17–18
  legislative-centric *vs.* party centric government, 104–9, 107*f*, 119
  majority-party medians and, 115–16
  minority party membership conditions, 165–66
  party distributions overlap, 161–63
  party medians *vs.,* 161–65
  Polsby Paradox and, 52–53
  recursive calculations, 164
  relative eccentricity of, 164–65
Cheney, Liz, 11, 21, 33
civil rights, 39
Civil Rights Act (1964), 128–29
Clean Air Act, 111
cloture. *See* gridlock
collective-action problem, 61, 98–99
concentrated minority, 17–18, 95–96, 109–10
conditional logit, 146, 147
conditional party government (CPG) model, 17, 37, 104–6, 123
Congressional decision making, 16–17, 95–96, 103–15
Congressional delegations, 12, 29, 76, 124

182 INDEX

constraint. *See* party constraint model, and
party discipline constraints
COVID-19 pandemic, 120, 129
crosscutting cleavages, 9–10, 79–80, 124–25
cyclical time trends polarization and, 120,
127–28

district competitiveness, 41–48
district heterogeneity. *See* heterogeneity
across districts
district ideology, 26–27, 43, 45–46, 67, 70,
118, 143–45, 144*t*
district medians, 30–31, 62–66, 68, 132,
136, 150
district partisanship, 68, 152, 154*f*, 154
district-specific partisan gap, 59, 62–63,
65–66, 67, 68–69, 149, 151, 154
divergence and convergence. *See* median
voter
Dowd, Matthew, 57, 58
Downs, Anthony, 13–15
Downsian ceiling, 58, 86–88, 105,
158–59
Downsian convergence, 13, 86–87, 119
Downsian model of party competition, 8,
13–15, 23, 49, 75–76, 97
Downsian pressures, 13, 41
DW-NOMINATE scores
alternating patterns of, 121–22
in competitive districts, 47*f*
crosscutting cleavages, 124
data analysis on US House, 44–46
dynamic *vs.* static, 141–43, 142*f*
gridlock, 111–14
ideological polarization, 43
party delegations, 4–5, 111
party discipline, 20–23, 27–29, 28*f*
regional realignment, 101–3, 102*f*
2-factor decomposition of
polarization, 68–69, 150–51,
152–54, 153*t*, 154*f*

Electoral College, 14–15
electoral competition, 11, 16–17, 22–23,
46, 95–103, 161
equal-constraint scenario, 34–35, 139
ethnic divisions, 7, 10–11, 129
extreme ideological positions, 12–13, 76,
79, 155

extreme policy stance, 24–25, 75
extreme voters, 76–77, 79–80, 81, 89–90, 94

gerrymandering, partisan. *See* redistricting
Gingrich, Newt, 22
Goldwater, Barry, 128–29
Greenberg, Stanley, 57–58
gridlock, 3–4, 16–17, 33, 95–96, 103,
110–14, 113*f*, 114*f*, 119

Hastert, Dennis (Hastert rule), 17, 104–5
heterogeneity across districts, 16, 18–19,
43–44, 58, 59, 62–65, 66–67, 68–70,
136, 149, 152, 153–54
homogeneity. *See* intraparty variance
hyperpartisanship, 3–4
hyper-polarization, 8–9, 103–4, 120, 125

ideological convergence, 3–4, 123
ideologically responsible parties, 7–8
ideological polarization, 12, 29, 43, 46, 60,
123
immigration impact on polarization, 7
income inequality, 7, 60–61, 121–22, 127
Inflation Reduction Act, 115
intraparty variance, 4, 5, 6*f*, 12, 33, 61–62,
136

Johnson, Lyndon, 39

Kerry, John, 26
Klein, Ezra, 8–9

leapfrog politics, 15–16, 36, 97
Lee, Frances, 14–15
legislative-centric government, 95–96,
103, 104–9, 116, 161
legislative gap
defined, 62
district-specific partisan gap, 59, 62–63,
65–66, 67, 68–69, 149, 151, 154
heterogeneity across districts, 16, 18–19,
43–44, 58, 59, 62–65, 64*t*, 66–67,
68–70, 136, 149, 152, 153–54
measuring changes in, 69–71
partisan proclivity, 16, 59, 62–63, 66–69,
70, 149, 150, 152, 154
3-factor decomposition of, 63–67
2-factor decomposition of, 68–69

legislative polarization. *See* polarization
legislator-centric government, 17, 103,
104–9, 116, 119

majority-party medians, 103–4, 106, 107*f*,
109–10, 115–16, 119
McCarthy, Kevin, 24
McGovern-Fraser Commission, 9
median voter
candidate platform preferences, 23,
75–76
Downsian theory and, 13, 96, 105
heterogeneity across districts, 59–60, 62
ideological location, 68, 70–71
ideologically divergence, 53
introduction to, 13, 15–19
maximum divergence in competitive
races, 48–52
national party constraints, 41–43
partisan proclivity, 59–60, 62, 66–67
polarization consequences and, 91, 98,
99–101, 131–32, 133*f*, 138*f*
redistricting and, 124
regional realignment, 96
3-factor decomposition of polarization,
61–63, 149–50
winning candidates and, 118
minority party membership conditions,
165–66
moderate voters, 13, 36, 58, 76–77, 78–80,
94
moneyed interests, 8

Nash equilibrium, 82–88, 83*f*, 85*t*, 87*f*
nationalization of Congressional
elections, 43
national party constraints. *See also* party-
constraint model; party discipline
constraints
asymmetry constraints, 33–36, 122–23,
139
district competitiveness and, 41–42
one-sided constraints, 24, 29–33, 32*f*,
34*f*, 36, 131, 133–36, 135*f*, 138
party discipline, 5–7, 12, 15, 26–29, 30,
31, 33–36, 41–42, 48–49, 131, 138*f*,
139
two-sided constraints, 29–33, 36, 131,
138*f*, 138

national party discipline, 10, 22–23, 60,
76, 117
negative affective polarization, 16
negative partisanship, 8–9
neo-Downsian model, 75–76, 97
New York Times, 26

Obama, Barack, 111
office-seeking, 12–13, 23–25, 49, 56–57,
105, 118
one-sided constraints, 24, 29–33, 32*f*, 34*f*,
36, 131, 133–36, 135*f*, 138

partisan identification strength, 78–79
partisan loyalty
candidate divergence and, 49–52,
57, 58
divergent party positions and, 14–15
ideological heterogeneity and, 18–19
legislative polarization and, 16
negative partisanship and, 9
non-convergent candidate behavior
without, 15
party discipline and, 8–9
polarization consequences and, 95, 117,
118, 119, 129, 155
partisan loyalty and activist influence
effects of polarization on, 78–89,
90–93
extreme voters, 76–77, 79–80, 81,
89–90, 94
introduction to, 75–77
Nash equilibria, 82–88, 83*f*, 85*t*, 87*f*
partisan identification
strength, 78–79
persuasion *vs.* focus on support
bases, 80–81
response to abstention threat, 82–84
summary of findings, 88–89
theoretical analysis findings, 89–90, 91*f*,
92*f*, 93*f*
turnout *vs.* persuasion, 82–84
partisan media outlets, 8
partisan overlap, 103, 104, 109, 115–16,
119
partisan proclivity, 16, 59, 62–63, 66–69,
70, 149, 150, 152, 154
party-centric government, 95–96, 103,
104–9, 116, 161

184 INDEX

party-constraint model, 15–16, 98,
131–32, 135*f*, 137*f*, 138–39.
See also national party constraints
basic model, 131–32
changes in polarization, 131–36
equal-constraint scenario, 34–35, 139
one-sided constraints, 24, 29–33, 32*f*,
34*f*, 36, 131, 133–36, 135*f*, 138
two-sided constraints, 29–33, 36, 131,
138*f*, 138
unequal constraints, 34*f*, 34–35, 139
party delegations
components of polarization, 149
extreme voting, 22
homogeneity of, 15, 21–22
ideologies of, 11–12, 20–21, 36, 117–18,
123
mean positions of, 4–5, 6*f*, 10, 31–32,
32*f*
median positions of, 71, 114, 161–62,
163
partisan gap, 37–38, 105–6, 109–10, 111
party differentiation, 37, 60, 95, 101–3
party discipline constraints. *See also*
national party constraints
constituency level, 23–26
constraint of, 20–23
defined, 21
median voter convergence *vs.*, 26–29
national party constraints, 5–7, 12, 15,
26–29, 30, 31, 33–36, 41–42, 48–49,
131, 138*f*, 139
post-election gap, 31–32, 133–36, 135*f*,
138
Party Discipline in the U.S. House of
Representatives (Pearson), 21–22
party distributions overlap, 161–63
party leadership, 7, 11, 26, 35, 42–43, 61
party loyalty. *See* partisan loyalty
party medians
chamber medians *vs.*, 161–65
concentrated minority and, 109–10
Congressional decision making and,
103–8, 107*f*
majority-party medians, 103–4, 106,
107*f*, 109–10, 115–16, 119
Polsby Paradox and, 52–56
shifts in, 15–16, 57

party responsibility, 9
Pearson, Kathryn, 21–22
Persily, Nathaniel, 3
polarization
candidate polarization, 11–13, 51
cyclical time trends and, 120, 127–28
defined, 4–7
district partisanship, 68, 152, 154*f*,
154
effects on partisan loyalty and activist
influence, 78–89, 90–93
explaining growth of, 7–11
growth since WWII, 128–29
hyper-polarization, 8–9, 103–4, 120,
125
immigration impact on, 7
introduction to, 3–4
measuring in US Congress, 4–7, 6*f*
overview of, 15–19
party loyalty and, 16
policy disagreements and, 13
reversal of, 120–25
slight polarization, 83*f*, 85–86
3-factor decomposition of, 61–63,
149–50
triggering events for, 7, 13, 18, 20, 120,
128
2-factor decomposition of, 68–69,
150–51, 152–54, 153*t*, 154*f*
polarization begets polarization, 12,
18–19, 98–99, 119
polarization consequences
chamber medians, 106–9, 107*f*, 116,
161–64
Congressional decision making, 16–17,
95–96, 103–15
electoral competition, 11, 16–17, 22–23,
46, 95–103, 161
gridlock, 3–4, 16–17, 33, 95–96, 103,
110–14, 113*f*, 114*f*, 119
increases within Congress, 95–103,
100*f*, 101*f*, 102*f*
in legislative-centric government, 95–96,
103, 104–9, 116, 161
majority-party medians, 103–4, 106,
107*f*, 109–10, 115–16, 119
partisan overlap and, 103, 104, 109,
115–16, 119

in party-centric government, 95–96, 103, 104–9, 116, 161
party-constraint model, 15–16, 98, 131–32, 135*f*, 137*f*, 138–39
party loyalty and, 95
regional realignment, 95–96, 101–3, 102*f*
relating to concentrated minority, 17–18, 95–96, 109–10
supermajoritarian pivots, 110–12, 114, 115
volatility, 108–9, 111–14
voter choice and, 16–17, 95–103
policy-seeking, 5–7, 23–25
Polsby, Nelson, 15–16
Polsby Paradox, 15–16, 35, 52–56
post-election gap, 31–32, 133–36, 135*f*, 138
Proposition 3.1 (competitive polarization), 50–51, 145–48

quadratic analysis on candidate ideology, 46, 143–45

racial divisions, 7, 10–11, 18, 42, 124–25, 128–29
redistricting, 18, 46–48, 99, 124, 128–29
reelection campaigns, 23, 24, 25–26, 57, 61
regional realignment, 95–96, 101–3, 102*f*
Reid, Harry, 115
roll-call voting, 4, 37–38, 61, 95, 104
Rules Committee, 22

Schlesinger, Arthur, Jr., 3, 121
separation index, 105–6, 107*f*, 161–62
siloization of political communication, 7
slight polarization, 83*f*, 85–86
Snyder-Groseclose measure of party pressure, 37–39, 38*f*
Solutions to Political Polarization in America (Persily), 3

spatial model, 4, 13, 14, 49, 57, 118, 163
split-ticket voting, 9–10, 16–17, 94, 95–96, 99–100, 119
supermajoritarian pivots, 110–12, 114, 115
swing voters. *See* moderate voters

talk radio, 7
think tanks, 8
threat of abstention, 15, 16, 57, 59–60, 77, 82–84, 94, 105, 117, 118, 119
3-factor decomposition of polarization, 61–63, 149–50
triggering events for polarization, 7, 13, 18, 20, 120, 128
Trump, Donald, 8–9, 24–25, 33, 57, 75, 77, 111
turnout. *See* threat of abstention
2-factor decomposition of polarization, 68–69, 150–51, 152–54, 153*t*, 154*f*
two-party system, 3, 13, 20, 23, 26, 27–29, 41, 63–65, 120, 131, 161
two-sided constraints, 29–33, 36, 131, 138*f*, 138

unequal constraints, 34*f*, 34–35, 139

volatility, 108–9, 111–14
vote-maximizing candidates, 48–49, 51
voter choice, 16–17, 95–103
voting rights, 39, 120, 128–29
Voting Rights Act (1965), 120, 128–29

Wallace, George, 128–29
weighting factor, 69, 150, 151–52, 152*f*
Why We're Polarized (Klein), 8–9
winning candidates, 15, 43–44, 46, 69, 118, 151
within-Congress policy divergence, 95–103, 100*f*, 101*f*, 102*f*
within-district partisan gap, 39, 95–96
Wright, Jim, 22

The manufacturer's authorised representative in the EU for product safety is Oxford
University Press España S.A. of El Parque Empresarial San Fernando de Henares,
Avenida de Castilla, 2 – 28830 Madrid (www.oup.es/en or product.safety@oup.com).
OUP España S.A. also acts as importer into Spain of products made by the manufacturer.

Printed in the USA/Agawam, MA
May 16, 2025

887590.004